P9-CBM-460

FIGHTING WITHOUT FIGHTING

FIGHTING WITHOUT FIGHTING

KUNG FU CINEMA'S JOURNEY TO THE WEST

LUKE WHITE

REAKTION BOOKS

Published by
REAKTION BOOKS LTD
Unit 32, Waterside
44–48 Wharf Road
London N1 7UX, UK
www.reaktionbooks.co.uk

First published 2022

Printed and bound in Great Britain by TJ Books Ltd, Padstow, Cornwall

A catalogue record for this book is available from the British Library

ISBN 978 1 78914 533 5

CONTENTS

David Carradine in the pilot of the television show *Kung Fu*, which introduced Western audiences to the novel and exotic ideas, images and mythologies of the Chinese martial arts.

INTRODUCTION

On 16 May 1973, something unprecedented – and since unrepeated – in the history of American cinema happened. The entertainment-industry magazine *Variety* reported that three foreign-language films were sitting at the top of the week's national box-office charts. Making the event even more extraordinary, these films were all made on what in Hollywood would be considered a shoestring budget. Furthermore, all came from one tiny colony within the last vestiges of the British Empire, Hong Kong. At the time, this was an enclave with some 4 million inhabitants, many of whom lived in third-world conditions, tucked against the side of the People's Republic of China (PRC), then still in the grip of Mao's Cultural Revolution.

What this curious box-office fact signals is that what became known as 'the kung fu craze' was under way. At number one was *The Big Boss* (1971), released in the USA as *Fists of Fury* and starring the charismatic Bruce Lee. At number two was *Lady Whirlwind* (1972), released under the title *Deep Thrust* and starring hapkido-trained Angela Mao Ying. At number three, Lo Lieh starred in *King Boxer* (1972), known in the USA under the lurid and melodramatic title *Five Fingers of Death*.[1] *King Boxer*, the film that first sparked America's enthusiasm for Hong Kong's martial arts cinema, had in fact been in *Variety*'s charts since 28 March and would remain there until 13 June. In the chart for the week following *King Boxer*'s exit, there were still no fewer than five kung fu films in the American top fifty, and as the film scholar David Desser has noted, even before the release in late August of the real smash hit of the year, Bruce Lee's *Enter the Dragon* (1973), 'almost a dozen Hong Kong films had already made their mark.'[2] By mid-October, in fact, some fifteen pictures from the colony had taken a place in the top fifty, with six of these hitting the top spot in the charts. Overall, films from Hong Kong occupied this position for around a fifth of the peak season for cinema attendance. These figures are even more startling when you take into consideration the fact that they do not include *Enter the Dragon*, the first Hong Kong–Hollywood kung fu co-production, which remained in the top twenty for eleven weeks, and for nine of these was in the top ten.[3]

Though their impact was slowly declining, Hong Kong martial arts films remained a significant presence in the charts for the rest of the year. It would actually be February 1974, nearly a year after the kung fu craze was launched, before there was a week with no kung fu film listed within them. When Bruce Lee's *The Way of the Dragon* was released in August that year, it still took a million dollars in New York alone in its first five days.[4] Lee's enduring stardom, however, was the exception to a rule of diminishing returns, and although kung fu films would continue to be released in America and the West throughout the 1970s, this would increasingly be done by minor distributors in restricted runs in grindhouse inner-city cinemas, drive-ins and double bills in small-town theatres.[5] Though it certainly remained an abiding passion for some, kung fu cinema would increasingly become a marginal niche. In terms of the box office at least, it seemed that the kung fu craze had already subsided by the spring of 1974, causing the commercial machine of the movie business to move on to exploit fresh fashions.

However, the kung fu craze was much more than a short-lived and quickly forgotten cinematic fad fuelled by the culture industry's eternal quest for novelty. Kung fu's 'journey to the West' has a significance that extends beyond its brief life and, moreover, beyond the realm of film history alone. The fascination with Chinese kung fu in particular and the Asian martial arts more broadly that exploded in the early 1970s in America, in the broader West and even across the globe is not only to be found in movies, but has become an enduring presence within a wide range of media – from music videos and computer games to comic books and children's cartoons – that continues unabated today.

KUNG FU BEYOND THE MOVIES

Foreshadowing and paving the way for the success of the Hong Kong films was the American-made television series *Kung Fu*, which starred David Carradine and ran from 1972 to 1975. This told the story of a Buddhist monk from the Shaolin Temple in China who wanders the American West, righting wrongs with a winning mixture of pacifist philosophy and kung fu fisticuffs. It was this series, above all else, that first introduced Western audiences to the mythology around the Chinese martial arts. For the broad public, it even introduced the new and exotic term 'kung fu' itself, which was not commonly understood by English speakers before this time.[6] (See the graph on p. 71, which shows the sudden appearance and subsequent commonness of the term.) The martial arts would, of course, continue to find their place in television schedules. Hanna-Barbera, for example, launched the popular children's cartoon *Hong Kong Phooey* in 1974. This featured the animated exploits of a police-station janitor who lives a double life as a bungling superhero, fighting crime with the help of his martial arts manual, 'The Hong Kong Book of Kung Fu'. In the UK, even the comedy series *The*

Goodies devoted an episode, 'Kung Fu Kapers' (24 March 1975), to parodying the craze, inventing the fictional Lancashire martial art of 'Ecky-Thump', which primarily involved walloping an opponent over the head with a black pudding. From 1976 until 1978, the BBC screened an English dub of *The Water Margin*, a series shot in China in 1973–4 by the Japanese company Nippon Television, which adapted a classic Chinese novel of the same name telling the tale of a band of Song-dynasty outlaws. Nippon and the BBC repeated its success with *Monkey*, adapted from another classic Chinese novel, *Journey to the West.* This was shown in Japan from 1978 and in the UK, Australia and New Zealand from 1979, and went on to gather a cult following in the countries where it aired.

Pulp adventure novels such as Warren Murphy and Richard Sapir's *Destroyer* series (starting in 1971) or Dennis O'Neil and Jim Berry's *Dragon's Fists* (1974) focused on martial arts within their narratives. Writing in 1974, B. P. Flanigan claimed that over a hundred of these novels had been published since the start of the kung fu boom.[7] In the realm of comic books, Marvel introduced kung fu-enhanced protagonists such as Iron Fist, Shang-Chi and Colleen Wing into its pantheon of heroes. To service the growing fan base for martial arts actors, a series of magazines such as *Fighting Stars* or *Inside Kung Fu* in the USA and *Kung Fu Monthly* in the UK appeared on newsagents' shelves. Bruce Lee posters hung in bedrooms – mainly of young men – across the world. According to the American journalist (and co-founder of the New York Asian Film Festival) Grady Hendrix, 'A 24″ × 36″ shot of a bare-chested Bruce became the second-best-selling poster of the decade, right after that iconic shot of Farrah Fawcett in her red swimsuit.'[8] In the realm of popular music, Blondie hymned 'Kung Fu Girls' in a track on their eponymous 1976 new-wave album, while Carl Douglas rose to the very top of the British, American, Canadian and Australian pop charts alike with his iconic 1974 disco hit 'Kung Fu Fighting', which sold 11 million copies worldwide. By the mid-1980s, martial arts were also to find their place within the growing industry of video games, with influential franchises such as *Street Fighter* (1987), *Mortal Kombat* (1992) and *Tekken* (1994).[9] Indeed, as Paul Bowman's book *The Invention of Martial Arts* has charted in the case of British visual culture, this broad wave of media representations of martial arts – seen everywhere from kung fu manuals and magazines, through the phenomenon of mixed martial arts spectacles on television, to video games, music videos, advertisements and even children's cartoons – has only swelled into a tsunami in the intervening decades, becoming today more ubiquitous than ever before.[10]

Beyond the entertainment industries, the kung fu craze also sparked an explosion in real-world martial arts instruction, with the movies birthing the desire in audiences across the West to emulate on-screen images of power, grace and freedom.[11] One scholar, Michael Molasky, has traced the evidence of advertisements in phone books in the USA for local martial arts instruction across the second half of the twentieth century.[12] He remarks on the early 1970s as involving a 'nationwide explosion in the number and type of martial arts classes being offered, with Chinese martial arts entering the public consciousness for the first time'.[13] The best-selling author and Bruce Lee fan Davis Miller makes the point even more dramatically:

> Before Lee's death, there were fewer than 500 martial arts schools in the world; by the late 1990s, owing a lot to his influence, there were more than 20 million martial arts students in the United States alone.[14]

All this suggests that the kung fu craze was not just a matter of films but a much broader cultural phenomenon. It also suggests that in order to understand it, we need to step away from looking solely at film history and towards a wider study of visual and even physical culture. This book thus takes as its object of study a corpus of films and their development, but it also considers how, from the material of Hong Kong's martial arts cinema, a global cultural phenomenon arose. It considers the kinds of meaning and pleasure that the images and iconographies of kung fu took on within American, European and Australasian culture and across the world. How are we to make sense of not only the films, but the 'craze' itself?

KUNG FU'S LEGACY

In attempting to answer this, I do not treat the kung fu craze as an ephemeral fad whose significance ended as the tide of box-office receipts for Hong Kong films ebbed. Rather, kung fu has left a lasting legacy on Western – and global – culture. This is certainly evident in the narrow domain of film itself. As the kung fu craze waned, Hollywood began to offer a series of home-grown American martial artists as action stars. Blaxploitation films increasingly included karate or kung fu elements, as can be traced clearly in the subsequent career of Lee's *Enter the Dragon* co-star Jim Kelly. The 1980s saw the rise of Chuck Norris, Steven Seagal and Jean-Claude Van Damme. Furthermore, Lee's iconic muscular torso was very different from the 'barrel-chested' exemplars of movie masculinity before him and its influence is to be seen far beyond the existence of other martial arts stars in the rise of bodybuilder actors such as Sylvester Stallone and Arnold Schwarzenegger.[15] The physical vocabulary of kung fu cinema caused an even more fundamental shift in how films could imagine hand-to-hand combat scenes. Gone was the ponderous to-and-fro slugging of John Wayne and

Bruce Lee flexes his muscles in *The Way of the Dragon*, demonstrating his impressive physique.

the cowboy film. Where kicking had once stood as a sign of villainy or lack of masculine honour, after the kung fu craze it became a marker of virtuoso physical skill, and 'martial arts are now employed in nearly every fight in almost every action movie.'[16] From Buffy to Batman to Bourne, contemporary cinema would look very different without kung fu.

Many of these observations already draw us beyond the realm of cinema as such. The influence of Lee's physique on bodybuilder stars points us to more fundamental changes in ideals and images of masculinity.[17] Similarly, the introduction of the kung fu kick points us to a broader change in how our culture imagines physical combat. As the martial arts scholar Paul Bowman has pointed out, you have only to walk past a school playground and hear the emulated kung fu shouts that form an integral part of play-fighting – made by children surely far too young to have ever actually seen a martial arts film – to get a glimpse of how ingrained in our cultural imagination this is.[18]

The 1990s saw a further influx of Hong Kong influence on American – and global – cinema. The gangster films of John Woo, such as *A Better Tomorrow* (1986) or *Hard Boiled* (1992), for example, became cult classics in the West. Woo had cut his teeth in the film industry as assistant director to Chang Cheh, one of the first and foremost auteurs to pioneer the kung fu film. He drew from these works not just an ultra-violent sensibility but also modes of filming action and a thematic concern with blood-brotherhood and warrior masculinity. He transposed such narratives into the present-day realm of Hong Kong's underworld to create a genre of 'balletic gunplay' and 'heroic bloodshed'.[19] Woo was prominent in the first generation of Hong Kong talent to break into Hollywood, with films such as *Hard Target* (1993), *Face/Off* (1997) and *Mission: Impossible 2* (2000), and it is in part through him that styles not only of physical performance but of shooting and editing action from Hong Kong entered the Hollywood mainstream. Soon after Woo, veteran martial arts choreographer Yuen Woo-ping came to Hollywood. Yuen had directed, among many other films, *Drunken Master* (1978), the movie that made Jackie Chan's name. In Hollywood, he provided action sequences for the Wachowskis on *The Matrix* (1999) and its sequels, as well as Quentin Tarantino's two-part homage to 'extreme' Asian cinema, *Kill Bill* (2003–4). French director Luc Besson was also fascinated with Hong Kong cinema and drew on this for his own brand of stylish and spectacular action, for example employing Jackie Chan's opera-school classmate Corey Yuen to choreograph sequences on a number of his productions, such as *Kiss of the Dragon* (2001) and *The Transporter* (2002). As the 1990s were drawing to a close, Chan himself finally made his Hollywood breakthrough with *Rush Hour* (1998), and by the time of the *Forbes* 2015 rich list he had become the second-highest-paid actor in the world, with superstardom spanning both Asia and the West.

With this resurgence of interest in Hong Kong action cinema came Ang Lee's *Crouching Tiger, Hidden Dragon* (2000).

Combining martial arts themes and action sequences with an art-house sensibility, and bringing Western audiences unfamiliar and exotic images of gracefully and weightlessly leaping swordsmen and swordswomen, *Crouching Tiger* managed to break from the 'world cinema' circuit onto mainstream screens. It smashed box-office records for a foreign-language film, bringing in $128 million in American theatres and over $200 million worldwide.[20] *Crouching Tiger*'s runaway success – a repeat in many respects of *Enter the Dragon*, which had also been an international co-production – stimulated a boom in twenty-first-century Chinese martial-art-house movies made for (and successful within) the global market. These included Zhang Yimou's *Hero* (2002) and *House of Flying Daggers* (2004), Feng Xiaogang's *The Banquet* (2006) and more recently Wong Kar-wai's *The Grandmaster* (2013) and Hou Hsiao-hsien's *The Assassin* (2015). Along with fist-fighting films such as the comedy *Kung Fu Hustle* (2004) or the more straightforwardly epic-heroic *Ip Man* (2008), this may in itself amount to something of a resurgent 'kung fu craze'. To emulate it, new martial arts films emerged from other East and Southeast Asian countries, such as, for example, Thailand's *Ong Bak* (2003), starring Tony Jaa, and South Korea's *The Man from Nowhere* (2010).

All this suggests that, at the very least in the realm of cinema, the significance of the kung fu craze can hardly be contained within its narrow moment. The Hong Kong cinematic style of action that it introduced has now become an integral part of the international visual language of action cinema. As the twenty-first century has progressed into its third decade, it is perhaps the superhero film, now surely the dominant blockbuster action genre, which best demonstrates this fact. In these films, alongside the wizardry of computer-generated effects and *Matrix*-style 'bullet-time', it is martial arts choreography (along with its associated cinematic techniques) that has made it possible to portray the superhuman abilities of the genre's heroes and villains in a convincing and compelling manner. As well as taking their place within the visual language of the superhero film, the martial arts have also increasingly found themselves thematized there. In *Batman Begins* (2005), for example, the young Bruce Wayne travels to the Himalayas and undergoes training as a ninja assassin before coming back to use the skills he gains to combat crime. In the Netflix television series *Daredevil* (2015–18), which draws on comic-book storylines from the 1980s, the eponymous hero is also trained in the martial arts and pitted against ninja enemies. In addition, we are now seeing the cinematic appearance of the martial artist comic-book heroes first introduced in the wake of the kung fu craze, such as Iron Fist and the Daughters of the Dragon (in the series *Iron Fist*, 2017–18, and *The Defenders*, 2017, both premiering on Netflix) or Shang-Chi (in the film *Shang-Chi and the Legend of the Ten Rings*, 2021).

Again, this lasting legacy is not merely to be felt within film history. Bruce Lee once more serves as an example here. Lee is remembered not only as a film star but as a martial arts teacher, and he has inspired an avalanche of publications that treat him less as a performer and more as a guru through whose influence students seek to transform their lives and selves.[21] It is in this role of a teacher – and as an icon or an image for identification, a poster on the wall as much as an actor – that Lee contributed to the changing ideals of the male body described above. Davis Miller, in a book that recounts his personal transformation through Lee's image and philosophy, argues that his 'streamlined, functional, no-scrap muscularity' paved the way for the 'hyperfitness body culture of the later part of this century'.[22] The importance of the martial arts as an influence within this culture is underlined by the success in the 1990s of Billy Blanks's Tae Bo exercise system, which combined aerobic movement with kung fu and taekwondo moves. Blanks has claimed that his practise-at-home video, selling 150 million copies worldwide, outperformed *Titanic* (1997), becoming 'the most popular video in the world'.[23] For Miller, this is a fitness and body culture that is not just about masculinity but now defines ideals for men and women alike. If Lee and the kung fu craze influenced the ways we feel about, imagine and shape our very bodies, this is no small thing.

Miller, furthermore, proposes that Lee attained a level of fame that only a handful of others in the century can compete with.[24] Certainly, in my own experience teaching in a London university, it is rare to find a young person who does not instantly recognize Lee's image, even if relatively few have now actually watched any of his films, some fifty years after his death. Miller, however, also notes the sheer global scale of his fame, which is 'known in almost every city, town, and village on the planet'. In 1973, *Esquire* magazine claimed there were tribes in Malaysia that worshipped him as a god, and when taekwondo practitioner Jhoon Rhee visited Moscow in 1992, he found Bruce Lee posters everywhere.[25] Lee, considered the 'first truly international film luminary', was popular 'not only in the United States, Great Britain and Europe, but in Asia, the Soviet Union, the Middle East and on the Indian subcontinent – in those pre-Spielberg days people in most nations were not particularly worshipful of the Hollywood hegemony'.[26]

Exploring this significance beyond both greater China and the West, May Joseph has analysed how kung fu cinema, and Lee as its primary icon, were enthusiastically adopted in the youth culture of newly independent East African nations such as Tanzania in the 1970s, and Ivo Ritzer has further explored the longer and broader response to Hong Kong action across Africa, which has included not only the consumption but the production of martial arts pictures.[27] The cultural theorist Vijay Prashad remembers how as a young activist in Mumbai in 1974 he had on his wall an image of Bruce Lee as a figure of inspiration, liberation and Asian pride.[28] In fact, it was neither Lee's native Hong Kong, nor America (where he lived much of his adult life), nor even any rich Western country that first erected a statue to him. Instead, it was Mostar, a town in Bosnia–Herzegovina. When, in the wake of civil war and genocide, the city sought to put up a peace memorial, citizens chose Lee over a shortlist of figures including Gandhi and the Pope. For them, Lee stood as a clear symbol for 'solidarity, justice and racial harmony'. In the face of religious, ethnic or political differences, a love of Lee and his films (which of course had been banned during the years of Communist rule) was one of the few things that they could agree on.[29] In 2019, pro-democracy protesters in Hong Kong, fearing the region's increasing subsumption into the mainland and the erosion of civil liberties, drew inspiration from Lee as both a local hero and

An inspirational figure. Cao Chong-en's statue of Bruce Lee on the Avenue of Stars, Hong Kong.

a philosopher, basing their tactics in running battles with the police on Lee's admonition to 'be like water.'[30]

These examples testify that the legacies of Lee and of the kung fu craze are far from trivial. They dig deep into the social, political and cultural fabric of global culture, involving questions about how we live together, racial and gender identities, the desire for peace and freedom, histories of decolonization and political struggle, and even how we experience our bodies and selves.

KUNG FU AND THE 'ENCOUNTER WITH ASIA'

The deeper cultural significance of the kung fu film revolves above all around how, at a very particular historical moment, it staged an 'encounter' between 'the East' and 'the West' – an encounter which Rudyard Kipling's famous pronouncement that 'never the twain shall meet' claimed was impossible.[31] Of course, in many ways, 'East and West' (or, in the particular case of this book, 'China and the West') have been meeting in partial, complicated and ultimately political ways for centuries. The colonial or imperial history to which Kipling's poetry belongs has been a primary mode of such contact. The kung fu film, arriving in the wake of the post-war era's dismantlement of much of the colonial and imperial apparatus – or perhaps its reorganization in terms of a neocolonial and globalized world order – seems to mark a new stage in the history of East–West encounters. Even if kung fu does not form an efficient cause for them, it preceded and foreshadowed the appearance of a range of phenomena from Ken Hom's cookery shows through to the popularity of acupuncture, Japanese cartoons and Korean pop music that constitutes a much broader and growing Western fascination with East Asian culture. All this amounts to a wider geographical transmission that reverses the direction of that told in the original novel, *Journey to the West*, to which this book's title refers. *Journey to the West* gave a highly fictionalized account of the real-life priest Xuanzang's seventh-century pilgrimage from China to India to bring Buddhist scriptures home along the Silk Road, that first superhighway of goods, people and ideas connecting the furthest reaches of Europe, Asia and Africa. But where Xuanzang brought scriptures eastwards to China, kung fu cinema brought Chinese images and ideas to the West.

Risking a slip from the sublime to the ridiculous – from the Lotus Sutra to *Five Fingers of Death* – this comparison may entail rather untenable claims for the cultural significance of kung fu movies, but there is nonetheless something epochal in the event of so many Hong Kong films arriving at the top of the American – and European and Australasian – charts. Certainly, nothing of its like had been seen before with regard to the Western popular acceptance of East Asia on a truly mass scale. Bruce Lee's stardom is also extraordinary in these terms, and once more allows us to understand some of what is at stake in the novelty of kung fu. Up until this point, prominent male Chinese characters in English-language cinema, whether heroes or villains, had largely been played in 'yellowface' by white actors. Even in 1971, the producers of the *Kung Fu* television series were unwilling to cast an Asian actor in the role of Kwai Chang Caine, feeling that the American public would not accept this, so decided instead to cast David Carradine.[32] For *Enter the Dragon* – the first Hollywood-produced film starring a Chinese male lead – the studio still hedged its bets, casting Lee alongside American actors John Saxon and Jim Kelly.

Lee's role offered a significant rewriting of the kinds of image Hollywood offered of Chinese men. Two long-running franchises over the previous decades had defined the two archetypes through which Chinese masculinity was imagined. On the one hand was Fu Manchu, a sadistic, perverse, cold-hearted and calculating 'yellow peril' villain, with the single goal of annihilating the West and dominating the globe. On the other was Charlie Chan, a humble, polite and ultimately – in the terms of the day – feminized 'model minority' stereotype, happy to remain subservient. These archetypes were two sides of a single coin and allowed a white audience to imagine their supposed superiority in relation to Asians. Moreover, it defined the moral position of these Asians in terms of their refusal or acceptance of a Caucasian racial destiny to rule. Owing to the international military, economic and cultural power of America and Europe, these representations and the racial hierarchies they implied took on a dominant force within global circuits of representation. The arrival from East Asian popular culture of kung fu stars such as Lo Lieh, Jimmy Wang Yu and Bruce Lee – tough, glamorous, macho, dynamic, heroic and, above all, sexually magnetic – redefined and scrambled this field of representation. Furthermore, in these films East Asian actors and directors represented *themselves*, rather than merely being the object of another's representations. All this, of course, is not to say that there were only positive things about the new images – kung fu also quickly became another kind of East Asian stereotype, and it remained an Orientalizing one, connected to a mystical and exotic Far East and, further, one which was imagined as a place of obscene violence. But as the cultural theorist Meaghan Morris has argued in relation to the working-class Australian contexts she was intimately familiar with, even with its perpetuation of such stereotypes the kung fu craze was significant in producing an interest and connection – a 'gaze' towards Asia – where often none existed before.[33] The chapters of this book will take up the task of understanding in a more nuanced manner the nature of these changing stereotypes and how they were negotiated by different groups.

What we must note for now is that this moment occurred when old relations between 'the West' and its 'Asian Others' were being more generally challenged and even dismantled. A decolonization movement had swept the world, and images of the power and superiority of the West had taken a heavy blow in conflicts such as the Korean and Vietnam wars. At home, the civil rights movement had struck against racial and ethnic hierarchies and the hippy counterculture had launched a biting and wholesale critique of the values through which Western culture had come to define itself and its relations to those from outside its boundaries. Furthermore, international trade and, in particular, a globalizing media were increasingly linking the world up in new ways. On the one hand, this made insular attitudes less and less sustainable as the previously unfamiliar cultures became increasingly present within the texture of daily life. On the other, it raised new anxieties about disintegrating cultural barriers. If the kung fu craze cannot take credit for these larger shifts, it was nonetheless an important instance through which they were played out. In fact, as Morris has argued, many of the martial arts action films that appeared in the wake of the kung fu craze – perhaps precisely because they were created through cross-cultural collaborations and addressing cross-cultural audiences – offer plots that revolve precisely around '"contact" between rival ways of life', dramatizing just these forms of encounter.[34] Analysing this will be another part of this book's task.

However, the very notions of East and West are themselves hugely problematic. They pitch us into the territory of what Edward Said has famously analysed as 'Orientalism'. The pair of terms carves the world into two halves, set in opposition to each other. Each is imagined as a giant and homogeneous geopolitical or civilizational entity, where in fact these generalizations are largely lacking coherence. In particular, the 'East' or the 'Orient' is expected to unify and offer an essential identity to places as different as the Middle East, Russia, India and China.

The Orient/Occident binary pair, in Said's account, developed as a means for the growing European empires to assert power and control over their colonies. The notion of the Orient, he argues, was taken up across realms of literature, art, academic analysis and colonial administration alike. The East was a landscape to be at once fantasized, known and controlled. Moreover, Said argues that the Orient wasn't something 'out there' waiting to be discovered but rather was actively produced through these circuits of Western knowledge, representation and practice. Orientalism's vision of the world positioned the Western subject in a place of control and validated its subjection of the Oriental Other.[35] As well as a realm of adventure and erotic promise, the Orient was imagined as 'feminine', backwards, superstitious and decadent. It was a space beyond history, into which progressive Western actors could enter with the civilizing mission of modernization that the colonial mindset suggested 'Orientals' themselves were not capable of.

Further, to the degree that the East names an Other, it also serves to define a self. The notion of the Orient names that which 'we' ('the West') are not, and it implicitly defines 'us' in terms of this opposition, projecting outwards onto others that which is opposite to our ideal self-image.[36] Representing the Eastern Other as backwards and superstitious is to define the West as progressive and rational. Seeing the East as passive and placing it in the position of an object of 'our' knowledge defines the West as an active, thinking subject who comes to know that object. Imagining the East as feminine allows the construction of the West in terms of patriarchal masculinity. Our senses of East and West – whenever we use either of these problematic terms – remain profoundly formed by these histories and attitudes, even if underlying geopolitical relationships have shifted, with the USA increasingly taking over from Europe the role of the central referent of 'the West' and globalized networks replacing the systems of power that structured the age of empire. Problematic as the notions of East and West are, however, they seem unavoidable in this book. As the historian Derek Massarella put it, '"Asia" and "Europe" are easy to deconstruct but difficult to replace.'[37] The terms, after all, have had a concrete role in shaping political and cultural boundaries, and when looking at the kung fu craze we are in many ways examining the changing nature and function of these notions of East and West.

Given the ways that such representations of others are profoundly bound up with notions of the self, a core context for the kung fu craze may well be the ways in which identities and social relations were being transformed in America and the broader West at the time in terms of race and ethnicity, gender, sexuality and class alike. The civil rights movement of the 1960s had in many ways uprooted a white Western subject from the centre of its universe. Feminism and changes in the family, too, had challenged attitudes to masculinity. Youth countercultures increasingly opposed the values, ways of life and identities that a materialistic mainstream culture expected them to accept. One way in which we can understand the new interest in the images of the East that the kung fu film offered is to recognize that they provided an uncanny mirror of fantasy within which identity could be renegotiated, reimagined and reformulated at a moment of crisis and doubt. This use of the East had already become an established countercultural strategy, with the Beatles, among many others, going to India to 'find themselves', and others at home flocking to the philosophy of Zen, as popularized by West Coast gurus such as Alan Watts. By the mid-1970s, of course, some of the attitudes of the previous decade were starting to change, and the renewed conservatism of the Thatcher–Reagan years was already visible on the horizon. Starting from this understanding, a key part of my broader approach to the task of tracing the significance of the kung fu film will be to explore the ways in which – between the liberalism and radicalism of the hippies and the return to order of the conservatism that grew up in their wake – martial arts cinema provided images through which race, class, gender and nationality were negotiated.

With this task in mind, it is worth noting some particularities of my use of the term 'West'. The West discussed here is primarily an English-speaking one, and though I do discuss Britain, and to some extent Australasia, my account focuses on the United States. This is in part because this is where the mass of existing sources are available, but it is also because America has been the leading cultural power within the realm of anglophone popular culture since at least the mid-twentieth century. Where America has led, others have followed, so it is the pivotal location around which kung fu's journey westward turns.

In spite of America's de facto importance, placing it centrally in an account of the kung fu craze or even setting it up as one pole with 'Asia' as its opposite risks losing sight of another startling aspect, which is the craze's spread across a global landscape that cannot be reduced to the East/West or China/America binaries. Though the global nature of the enthusiasm for kung fu and its arrival in the West are intimately bound together – with influences, we shall see, going both ways – they are not exactly the same thing, and to treat them as such is to fail to displace America and Europe from their privileged position, mistaking the West for the world.

THE PROBLEM OF VIOLENCE

This book will also set out to make sense of another significant aspect of the nature of the kung fu craze and its reception: the striking fact of its highly aestheticized and stylized depiction of violence and the controversies that this stirred up within the media. Audiences were to various degrees startled, horrified and thrilled by a level of explicit gore still not usual within Hollywood cinema. Much press attention was given to the scene in *King Boxer*, the first kung fu film to become a mainstream hit, where one character's eyes are plucked out and seen rolling across a floor. Scenes with particularly graphic violence or 'cult' kung fu weapons were soon heavily cut from international releases, and several American states banned possession of Bruce Lee's iconic *nunchaku*, concerned about an explosion of copycat crime. (This ban was only recently lifted in New York, in 2018.[38])

From the very outset, critics were alarmed. They could barely suppress their scorn for the genre and for what they interpreted as a crude brutality that made the films morally dubious to a high degree. Drawing a parallel between kung fu films and pornography, *Variety*, in an early piece on the genre, complained that 'sheer violence remains as potent at the b.o. [box office] as . . . sheer sex.'[39] The studios, too, obviously imagined the genre in these kinds of terms: when *Lady Whirlwind* was released in America, it was under the title *Deep Thrust*, clearly attempting to make an associative link with the previous year's controversial hit *Deep Throat* (1972), which had notoriously brought porn to mainstream cinemas.

The close equation between pornography and kung fu also signals that we are back within the realm of the 1970s 'culture wars' between radicals and conservatives. If the flip side of the 'craze' for kung fu was an equally hysterical moral panic, these both drew their energy from larger debates around the degree to which permissive liberalization was desirable and the extent to which new images of what had previously been censored were corrosive to the social order. Similar debates had already been ignited around the violent content of the films, for example, of Sam Peckinpah, or Stanley Kubrick's *A Clockwork Orange* (1971), which was ultimately withdrawn from release in many countries. Just as new images of sex could be connected to women's liberation and the 'sexual revolution', images of violence also raised the spectre of unruly lower classes or ethnic others who had also appeared as newly militant and assertive in the wake of the 1960s. It was around these others that much of the fear about real-world violence expressed in discussions of its cinematic counterpart revolved. Here, again, the fact that the kung fu film's origins were in East Asia was hardly coincidental to their fascination in terms of violent content: one way of understanding this has been to see it as a matter of the projection of an 'obscene' violence into an imaginary Orient marked by recent history as a site of bloody and traumatic war (Japan, Korea, Vietnam, the Cultural Revolution). The kung fu film – so argues Sylvia Shin Huey Chong – was, like the Vietnam movie, a means by which a bruised America sought to restore and reimagine itself.[40]

TAKING A POSITION

The moral danger in producing an account of Hong Kong cinema that concentrates on responses to it in the West, and which explores Western rather than East Asian identities, is that it fails to acknowledge the profound dislocation of the Western subject from the centre of its universe. Such a failure would be particularly ironic considering that the kung fu film itself contributed to this dislocation. Could such an account end up somewhat like the equivalent of the recent Bruce Lee biopic *Birth of the Dragon* (2016)? This film provoked outrage among some sectors of the Asian American community for 'whitewashing', as it placed at its centre a fictional white character, Steve McKee, in the process sidelining its portrayal of Lee himself. As one reviewer on imdb.com complained, 'Asian males can never take the lead role. Only the sidekick even in their own movie . . . White people, would it kill you to stop inserting yourselves into everything?'[41] Does an account of Western responses to kung fu films also end up relegating East Asian artists to the equivalent of sidekicks in what ought to be their own story?

I seek to avoid this through a critical awareness towards my own position, writing as I do as a white, male university lecturer based in London, and by examining the kung fu craze as a moment of exchange in which Westerners are implicated, and in which differences are made problematic precisely because it is a moment of exchange. In doing so, I draw succour from arguments put forward by the Taiwanese critical theorist Kuan-Hsing Chen in his book *Asia as Method*. This proposes that global justice and democracy can only come about if there is a symmetrical coming to account with the colonial and imperial past: a 'decolonization' in the former colonies and a 'deimperialization' in the former imperialist centres. In both cases, these processes involve developing a critical understanding of the ways in which imperial/colonial histories have left their mark on subjectivity.[42] Following Chen's argument, the urgent task for a work by a white Westerner such as me would seem to be to further understand the ways that the kung fu craze functioned as an episode in the West's ongoing encounter with the East rather than to produce further knowledge for the consumption of Western scholars or connoisseurs so they might better know East Asian cinema. I very much hope that the benefits of this reflexivity outweigh the inevitable result that the West (and America) may remain a more central presence in this book than the richness of global interchange around the martial arts might otherwise call for.[43]

Another, more practical reason for focusing on the West is simply that this seems a contribution I can make to a burgeoning body of English-language literature on Hong Kong's martial arts cinema. This literature has been steadily growing since the late 1990s, and it has made the history and analysis of the kung fu film, especially considered in the light of Hong Kong social history, relatively accessible. The most significant works in this field are listed in this book's bibliography.

STRUCTURE OF THE BOOK

The task of this book, then, is twofold. First, in a 'historical' mode, it sets out to tell the story of kung fu's journey to the West. Second, it also sets out to offer an analysis of these events and to think through their implications. It does so in particular in terms of questions of global encounter, changing experiences of identity and the meaning of violence. Of course, the two tasks of history and analysis are deeply entwined, and I seek to keep them in relationship to each other throughout. However, broadly speaking the first three chapters are primarily historical, examining the conditions and unfolding of the kung fu craze, while the next three are more analytical and thematic in organization. They each examine different aspects of the impact of the kung fu craze, but in doing so they nonetheless each edge us further towards the present in their investigation of the craze and its legacy.

Chapter One starts off by looking at the background of the kung fu craze in the development of Hong Kong's film industry. It culminates in the appearance, at the start of the 1970s, of the new kung fu genre and the creation of the films that initially sparked the fever for martial arts cinema, first in Hong Kong and then across the world. I place these in the context of the social histories of China and Hong Kong, the developing movie industries there and the international dimensions of cultural exchange already in place early in the history of Chinese martial arts cinema. Chapter Two turns to examine the developing conditions in America that paved the way for the explosion of the kung fu craze there. Central in this are the changing attitudes to and ideas about East Asia fostered within a rapidly changing social landscape. Through this lens, I trace the growing awareness of martial arts and the ways their meanings mutated. By the early 1970s, this changing awareness made the English-speaking world ripe for the appearance of kung fu – catalysed in particular by the appearance of the film *Billy Jack* (1971), the TV series *Kung Fu* (1972–5) and the visit of Richard Nixon to China. This last reopened relations between the two countries and sparked a wave of curiosity about the world behind the Bamboo Curtain. The third chapter traces the rise and fall of the kung fu craze itself, examining the response to it and the ways in which we might understand both the popular enthusiasm and the critical dismay it brought. The chapter pays special attention to the film that sparked the craze, *King Boxer*, and the Hollywood–Hong Kong co-production *Enter the Dragon*, which marked its zenith.

In the chapters that follow I examine the significance and the legacies of the craze in terms of identity. Chapter Four focuses on kung fu's lasting connection with Black American popular culture, from its inclusion in blaxploitation films through to continued references in hip-hop and rap music today. To contextualize this, I discuss the ways 'Asia' (kung fu, the Vietcong, Maoism) became imagined by the radical Black Power movement and the interconnections between this and the global decolonization struggles within which kung fu also took on significance. Chapter Five turns to look at how kung fu was then appropriated within 1980s American culture to offer new, home-grown martial arts stars as a means to renegotiate white masculinities. Chapter Six examines the flip side of these questions of gender. Though kung fu fandom has often been considered the preserve of (usually adolescent) men, it also offered a surprising number of startling images of women warriors. These, I argue, have played a part in challenging assumed gender roles and characteristics for women, as 'kung fu' performance has become in recent years a common means to visualize empowered women within action cinema and television, as well as to create new images of fetishized 'action babes'.

The final chapter takes stock of the themes discussed throughout the book and brings us to examine their relevance in the present. It traces the accelerating interest in 'kung fu' imagery and Hong Kong culture in American cinema in the 1990s and the subsequent appearance, in the early 2000s, of a new wave of Chinese martial arts pictures. These were produced through the accelerated internationalization of cinema's production and distribution and garnered both box-office dividends and critical acclaim in the West. I make detailed analyses of three of these films – *Crouching Tiger, Hidden Dragon* (2000), *Hero* (2002) and *The Grandmaster* (2013) – and examine their differing approaches to the landscape of production and consumption linking the East Asian and Euro-American spheres. The picture they offer of this transnational landscape – a result of processes of globalization started in the era of the kung fu film – illuminates both continuities and discontinuities with the 1970s and helps to explain the enduring meaning of the kung fu craze.

1
HONG KONG'S MARTIAL ARTS CINEMA

Commenting on his own experience of the kung fu craze, the film scholar David Desser has used the vivid metaphor of being 'always left with the feeling that it came and went like a brief, but to me welcome, summer storm'.[1] The metaphor not only encapsulates the seemingly short-lived nature of the craze but highlights its abruptness and unexpectedness, just as a downpour might catch us unprepared. Western audiences in 1973 may well have experienced the arrival of Hong Kong martial arts films as a violently sudden phenomenon that came from nowhere – strange, surprising and, for some like Desser at least, refreshing, even if for others it seemed more of a cause for alarm, sending them running for cover. But as Desser goes on to point out, kung fu cinema did not come from nowhere: it had a history, and the ground was laid for it in numerous ways, although its new audiences in London or New York would perhaps have had little sense of the movies they watched belonging to a history of Chinese martial arts cinema that stretches back into the early twentieth century. To start to make sense of the films that sparked the kung fu craze, and to understand how a film industry from the tiny island of Hong Kong became a competitor for the Hollywood behemoth – and to move beyond the bafflement we often feel in front of seemingly sudden or novel events – we need to reach back into this history.

CHINA'S FIRST KUNG FU CRAZE

The first boom in Chinese martial arts cinema occurred in the late 1920s, during the era of the silent screen and the flowering of Shanghai as the nation's centre of film production. As the film and media scholar Man-Fung Yip has noted, in many ways these first martial arts films were a far cry from the kung fu movies we came to know in the 1970s or enjoy today. To a contemporary sensibility they 'look rather tame' and 'lack the kind of dazzling action choreography' of more recent films.[2] Nonetheless, audiences were enthralled by tales of heroism set in ancient China and by the spectacle of the seemingly superhuman feats of warriors, facilitated both by the physical skills of actors and their stunt doubles but also by new technologies of cinematic special effects: wires and trampolines helped them take flight; reverse filming allowed impossible vertical leaps; and animated visuals drawn onto the negatives created magical 'flying swords' and beams or bolts of energy with which the characters duelled each other. The new genre gained a name, *wuxia*, which literally means 'martial chivalry', but is often translated into English (rather loosely) as 'swordplay'. It is to this swordplay genre that, for example, more recent films such as *Crouching Tiger, Hidden Dragon* (2000) or *Hero* (2002) belong, rather than to the kung fu genre more properly and narrowly defined. When *Crouching Tiger* and its ilk were first seen in the West, they seemed novel developments from kung fu conventions, but in fact they marked a return to the roots of a much older and longer film-making tradition. Full of elements of the fantastical, driven by special effects and set in the near-mythical past, the *wuxia* genre in many ways seems a diametric opposite to the ethos of gritty corporeal 'realism' and physical 'authenticity' through which the kung fu film would later promote itself. Their cinematic and special effects – as well as their martial artistry – may pale in comparison to more recent *wuxia*, but in the 1920s the new genre was nonetheless an enormous hit at the box office, to the degree that between 1928 and 1931, some 250 *wuxia* pictures were made, amounting to 60 per cent of Shanghai cinema's total output.[3] One might say that China's first 'kung fu craze' came half a century before the American one.

The reliance on the sheer technological wonder of special effects on the one hand and on elements of more traditional physical performance skill on the other points us towards a paradoxically double orientation of the new genre: it was suspended between impulses towards both tradition and modernity and towards both national myth and globalizing competition.[4] *Wuxia* films competed with and drew on the conventions of imported American swashbucklers such as those starring Douglas Fairbanks Sr, which had already found a popular market in China. In competing in this new international and technological medium of cinema, they implicitly set out China's stall as a modern, industrial nation. They asserted the status of Shanghai as not only the largest city in Asia at this time, but arguably also its most progressive and fashionable. But even in making this bid for cinematic modernity, the *wuxia* film also played on the traditional and the culturally specific, conjuring images of ancient China through its performances of the martial arts and its evocations of their traditional lore.

These tensions might be seen at work even in the origins of Chinese cinema itself. These are exemplified by what is usually accepted as the very first Chinese film, *Mount Dingjun*. This was made in 1905, while China was still under imperial rule, by Ren Qingtai, the owner of a Beijing photography studio. Around half an hour long, it depicted three scenes from a Beijing opera production played by Tan Xinpei, probably the most famous performer of his era.[5] Produced in a silent medium, it was clearly not Tan's voice

China's first martial arts film? Tan Xinpei performing in Ren Qingtai's *Mount Dingjun*, 1905.

which was the focus of interest for viewers, famous as it was, and *Mount Dingjun* has also in fact been regarded as the first Chinese martial arts film.[6] Beijing opera, far more than its European counterpart, is a physical as well as a musical art form, and acrobatic martial display is as central to its spectacle and craft as singing. Tan, moreover, was renowned for his 'complete mastery' not only of the vocal but of gesture and combat. The original footage of Tan's performance is now lost. What does remain to us of the film is a still from the production showing Tan in his warrior garb, striking a heroic posture, stroking his beard and brandishing a polearm. Testimony from the time represents the audience as entranced by his performance with it.[7]

The precedent of *Mount Dingjun* helps point us towards the extent that *wuxia* cinema, too, was rooted in longer operatic, literary and folk-cultural traditions. The term 'opera' in the West perhaps conjures an elite pastime: polite company, adorned in formal eveningwear, enjoying a high-cultural outing in opulent surroundings. However, what is usually translated as 'Chinese opera' refers to a theatrical tradition that for centuries has been the primary form of popular entertainment. This was engrained in the very texture of everyday life, and opera remained a pre-eminent popular art well into the twentieth century. As noted above, virtuoso displays of acrobatics and martial artistry are a key pleasure within it. A significant part of the repertoire, including the opera that *Mount Dingjun* was excerpted from, involves heroic stories – and performances – of martial valour. It is, to a large extent, to this tradition of performance and storytelling that early *wuxia* cinema looked for its models (alongside, of course, Western imports). As well as a pool of expert performers, opera offered Chinese film-makers a ready-made language for action choreography that was understood and appreciated by popular audiences. Its enduring importance in Chinese martial arts cinema is further underlined if we remember that it was in Beijing opera that Jackie Chan (among a host of his contemporaries) received his primary training. Bruce Lee, too, was the son of a renowned opera performer, and it was through his father's film contacts that he got his first taste of acting as a child star.[8]

Opera in its turn was also bound up with a broader tradition of martial arts literature and folklore, from which it drew its stories. A literary canon based around the fantastical deeds of martial artists stretches back at least to short stories of the Tang era (690–907 CE). Many of China's great 'classical' epics emerged from much older cycles of stories and dramas that placed martial artists and martial artistry at their heart: for example, the sixteenth-century *Journey to the West* (also known as *Monkey*); the fourteenth-century *Outlaws of the Marsh* (also known as *The Water Margin*); and *Romance of the Three Kingdoms*, from which *Mount Dingjun* draws its plot. Aside from the written word and the stage, popular stories were promulgated to the illiterate by professional storytellers in markets and teahouses, helped by prompt books. As the nineteenth century progressed, something more like modern martial arts novels appeared. By the early twentieth century, *wuxia* had emerged as a highly popular literary genre, integrated into the circuits of the new mass-media technologies. Tales of wandering swordsmen were serialized in newspapers and also adapted for radio. The novel that above all lit the fuse for the *wuxia* craze was Xiang Kairan's *Marvellous Gallants of the Rivers and Lakes*, which began serialization in 1923.[9] This was adapted in its turn to create the definitive martial arts movie of the 1920s, *Burning of the Red Lotus Temple* (1928). In this, the young swordsman Lu Xiaoqing, returning from his martial arts apprenticeship, stays the night at a Buddhist monastery, only to discover that an evil gang have substituted themselves for the real monks there and are using the temple as a headquarters for their operations kidnapping and trafficking women. Along with a group of other young heroes, and under the mentorship of the mysterious and powerful Red Maiden, he fights his way through the monastery's hidden mechanical traps, defeats the bandit gang and puts the temple to the torch. Reputedly, some four hundred martial artists were recruited to provide the stunts. The film was so popular that the studio immediately decided to extend it into a ten-film series, and by the time it eventually finished in 1931 this had ballooned to eighteen instalments and some 27 hours of screen time.[10] Its success defined the swordplay cinema of the era.

The nature of the enormous enthusiasm for the *Red Lotus Temple* films, and for their many imitators, can be better understood when we further place their images of the martial arts in historical context. Just a century and a half beforehand, in the late eighteenth century, China had been probably the world's largest, most prosperous and most powerful nation. Silver flooded out of Europe to pay for luxury goods such as tea, porcelain, lacquerware, silk and spices, which symbolized the height of luxury and sophistication in the West.[11] The Qing dynasty, which had come to power in 1644, was very much at its height. However, as the nineteenth century developed, things changed dramatically for China. European economies had been bolstered by colonial expansion and the Industrial Revolution, and China was increasingly faced with confident, assertive and technologically advanced competitors. At home, growing political corruption was combined with monetary crises and a population whose growth had significantly outstripped that of agricultural production to create social unrest, and this was amplified by ineffective government.[12] The confrontation between the rising West and a stagnating China was precipitated in the 1840s by the first of the Opium Wars. In this, Britain asserted the right to export opium grown in India into southern Chinese ports, something that local officials strenuously resisted. China was badly beaten in the ensuing conflict and was forced to pay out vast war reparations. It was also compelled to cede the island of Hong Kong to British control and open its previously closed ports to European and American trade. The ongoing Opium Wars and the 'unequal treaties' that came in their wake dealt a powerful blow to both the economic basis of the Qing government and its image as holding a 'mandate of heaven' to rule the country. In the wake of these conflicts, the late nineteenth century saw a whole spate of uprisings, including the Taiping Rebellion (1850–64). With a death toll of more than 20 million people, this was 'not only the most destructive war of the nineteenth century, but likely the bloodiest civil war of all time'.[13]

With China subject to chaos, socio-economic collapse and reduction to semicolonial status, there grew at the end of the nineteenth century an increasingly intense debate about the modernization, Westernization and national self-strengthening needed to rebuild the state so that it might survive in the world of modern international politics. The inability of the Qing rulers to introduce viable reforms ultimately led, in 1911, to a republican revolution, which put an end to the imperial system that had lasted for thousands of years.

Alongside the new nationalist government, the New Culture Movement also emerged. This called for a parallel revolution in literature and the arts to expunge from the nation the 'feudal' ideas that, according to the movement's ideologues, held China back from necessary technological, economic, military and social progress. Much of the history of twentieth-century China and its culture has been dominated by this struggle to rebuild a stable and effective modern government and social order, recover from impoverishment and re-establish a strong position within the regional and global scene.

The martial arts became an important part of this nation-building. Though rooted in what might be understood as 'feudal' practices, they nonetheless offered an image of a strength that was not borrowed from the West but asserted a native identity. In doing so, they allowed a refutation of 'sick man of East Asia' stereotypes, which had increasingly circulated. These presented China as a weak and 'effeminate' power, lacking the properly 'masculine' virtues necessary for a modern state. Martial arts reformers looked to Japan as a model, where images of samurai culture had been leveraged to promote the militaristic ethos that had supported increasing national confidence and power on the world stage. Reformers sought to promote 'modernized' and scientifically justifiable martial arts – cleansed of reference to superstition – and to spread their practice through the ranks of China's new urban classes. In doing so, they looked to strengthen the body politic through the engineering of fit, healthy and martially prepared individual physiques.[14]

The boom in martial arts cinema in this period can be understood as a part of this phenomenon. Through the images of the martial arts, film-makers presented spectacles that carried implicit messages regarding national identity, strength and modernity.[15] Perhaps it would not be going too far to see these as essentially anti-imperialist films, articulating pride at a moment of weakness. Certainly, this is what many intellectuals of the time valued in the genre. The figure of the warrior and their fight for justice in a chaotic world, usually against the wealthy, powerful and corrupt, seemed to suggest a medium capable of raising consciousness and encouraging militancy.[16] I shall argue in upcoming chapters that the residue of such messages within the genre – its militant DNA, if you like – will hardly be incidental to some of the ways in which kung fu cinema was taken up in new situations across the globe in the decades to come.

However, for many intellectuals the popularity of the *wuxia* genre was more a cause for concern than celebration, in large part because of ambivalence towards the martial arts themselves, inasmuch as these were connected to the pre-modern past. For these intellectuals, the Boxer Rebellion of 1899–1901 was still a very recent memory. In this, a mass peasant movement had swept into Beijing to lay siege to the foreign legations there, hoping to eject the Western powers and their influence from Chinese soil. The 'Boxers' were so named because they practised martial-arts-like spirit possession, which they believed would give them invulnerability to enemy weapons in battle. Needless to say, the Boxers were quickly cut down by the firearms of the eight-nation army sent to relieve the siege.[17] For many, this epitomized the ways that backwardness and superstition had plunged the nation into the humiliating position in which they found themselves, and the martial arts were tarred by association with this shame.[18] In this regard, they appeared as a vehicle not of national strength but of weakness and folly.

The new martial arts cinema, in particular, seemed deeply suspicious in these terms. Its stories harked back to the mythical past rather than to the reality of present-day politics in a period of ongoing civil war and international threat.[19] It also frequently mixed martial display with the fantastical and magical in ways that seemed tinged with aspects of folk religion. The powers of the depicted heroes and heroines, enhanced by cinematic technology, entered the realm of the supernatural. With some degree of condescension, critics worried that the response of popular audiences was too like the irrational, cultic mania of the Boxers. Film historian Stephen Teo has recounted how critics of the time bemoaned the fact that

> audiences reputedly put up incense altars before the cinema to pray to the gods before watching the film, and young people were reported to be so affected that they 'left their homes and took to the hills, heading to Mount Emei in Sichuan Province in search of immortals to teach them the supernatural arts'.[20]

The critic Mao Dun – a prominent figure in the New Culture Movement – went as far as to describe the responses of *The Burning of the Red Lotus Temple*'s fans in terms of hysteria. In this, he argued, the rational and dispassionate enjoyment proper to art descended into an emotionally charged compulsion where the very distinction between reality and imagination had disintegrated:

> You only have to enter the cinema showing this particular series to see its magic power at work on the petty urbanites . . . From start to finish, a fanatical audience surrounds you and whenever the knights-errant engage in a combat scene and start projecting their flying swords, the audience screams hysterically as if they are themselves right in the midst of battle. When the character Hong Gu [Red Maiden] enters the scene from flying through the sky, they break out in applause, not because Butterfly Wu plays her, but because she is a swordswoman, the central protagonist of *The Burning of the Red Lotus Temple*. When they criticize the film, they don't say this or that actor has given a good performance. Instead they criticize the merits or demerits of the Kunlun school or the Emei school. To them, the film is real, not a play of shadows on the screen.[21]

Mao certainly seems to be describing a 'kung fu craze', in the most literal sense of the phrase, viewing cinema spectation as a form of madness. In doing so he anticipates something of the anxiety of American critics nearly half a century later, faced with the enthusiasm of a different generation of fans. However, we might well wonder whether Mao's moral panic isn't just as hysterical as the pleasure of the film audiences he describes.

Intellectuals on both the left and right of politics shared this condemnation of *wuxia*. For leftists, its evocation of old-fashioned, traditionalist ideas and values made it inherently conservative. Furthermore, as an escapist form it seemed to project what ought to be the struggle for justice in the present into the long-gone past, substituting real revolt with compensatory fantasy.[22] For those on the right, *wuxia* films – especially as they increasingly tended to include salacious sexual elements – threatened moral degeneration and corruption. Furthermore, the anarchic ethos of their individualistic heroes threatened order and authority. As Christine Harris has put it, 'For a Nationalist Government concerned with stability and control, the problem was not that these films were insufficiently revolutionary, but rather that they were *too rebellious*.'[23] As a popular genre, the literature that *wuxia* cinema drew on in fact had a long history of rebellion. For example, the classic novel *Outlaws of the Marsh* (a Robin Hood-like story of bandits' struggle against tyrannical officials) has been banned repeatedly since it was written in the fourteenth century.[24]

It was ultimately the right-wingers who took control of the nation in the late 1920s, under Chiang Kai-shek's leadership. He set in motion a programme of conservative and neo-Confucian moral reform, and under this the government banned *wuxia* films in 1931, bringing the first explosion of Chinese martial arts cinema to an end. Sadly, of the hundreds of swordplay films made at the time, only one complete example remains, *Red Heroine* (1929); the others having fallen prey to the ravages first of censorship and then war.

HONG KONG AND THE NEW ACTION ERA

The Japanese occupation of 1937–45 marked the end of Shanghai's dominance as China's film capital. Even after the occupation ended, China remained in the throes of civil war, and when the Communists emerged victorious from this in 1949, they rapidly repurposed the film industry as a propaganda tool with little tolerance for a genre as ideologically dubious – or as rebellious – as *wuxia*. Both the filmmakers and the financiers who had supported them had in any case largely deserted the mainland, fleeing first the Japanese and then the Communists. The primary beneficiary of this flight was Hong Kong. This remained a colonial and capitalist enclave under British rule, offering a favourable business environment within which to continue film production. With no access to the strictly censored screens of the PRC, and with Hong Kong itself providing only a relatively small audience, film-makers operating there oriented their production to a regional rather than merely local market. Their products targeted not only Hong Kong and Taiwan, but a Chinese diaspora with significant populations across Southeast Asia, and beyond that in Pacific Rim Chinatowns.

One novelty in the martial arts cinema of this period that is often presented as paving the way for the kung fu film proper was the emergence of the hugely popular Wong Fei-hung film series. Wong, a southern Chinese martial artist who lived during the late nineteenth and early twentieth centuries, was something of a local folk hero in Hong Kong culture and has since been played both by Jackie Chan, in the *Drunken Master* films (1978/94), and Jet Li, in the *Once Upon a Time in China* series (1991–7). Though Wong had already been the subject of novels and radio serials, his cinematic depiction began in 1949, when a series of films was launched depicting his life and exploits. These starred the opera-trained performer Kwan Tak-hing and ran throughout the 1950s and '60s. By the end of this period, Wong had already been represented in some 83 movies.[25]

Where the usual *wuxia* films tended to be set in the deep or mythological past, Wong was presented in a concrete, historical time not so distant to our own. In line with the nearness and realness of the historical setting, the Wong Fei-hung fight sequences rejected the fantastical wirework, trampolines and other special effects of the *wuxia* films. Instead, they employed local martial artists, often trained in the same martial arts style (hung gar) that had been practised by Wong himself, to represent the kung fu movements of southern China with a much greater degree of what film theorist Leon Hunt has called 'archival authenticity'. This term refers to the attempt to represent particular, historical martial arts styles, rather than concoctions of stunts created for the screen itself.[26] Indeed, the early Wong Fei-hung films often seem to stray into the stylistic territory of documentary. In them, the narrative will stop for a performer to display a particular martial arts routine for the camera, as if being observed by an ethnographer.[27] Watching them, one gets the sense that the films were made in part to preserve a vanishing cultural tradition in the face of the onset of modernity, and this nostalgic appeal to the past and to local as well as national identity may have been an important pleasure of these films for their first audiences. This appeal to tradition would certainly have been congruent with the character of Wong himself, who was played by Kwan Tak-hing as an icon of old-fashioned Confucian morality and upright patrician virtue.

Also of particular significance in the new Hong Kong industry was the film company Tianyi. Tianyi had been one of the major players in the production of swordplays in Shanghai and had moved production to Hong Kong in 1933–4, escaping the ban on these films on the mainland.[28] The four brothers who ran it – Runje, Runde, Runme and Run Run Shaw – set about establishing an international entertainment empire with a reach and fluidity of capital that transgressed territorial boundaries. In 1957, reorganized under the helm of Run Run, this would become the famous Shaw Brothers studio, probably the most significant player in the development of the kung fu film. As well as owning theme parks and dancehalls, the Shaws established a network of cinema venues across Southeast Asia. Here, their Chinese-language productions ran alongside films they made in their Malaysian studios and films imported from Japan, America, Europe and India. This guaranteed an outlet for their pictures and so enabled more and more lavish standards of production. Other studios increasingly struggled to compete with them, and Shaw Brothers became the single dominant player in the

Hong Kong industry. Thriving in this manner, the Shaws established a vast, technologically cutting-edge studio complex in Hong Kong's Clearwater Bay, which began operation in 1961 and was dubbed the 'dream factory'.[29] Here, stars trained in the Shaws' acting school and housed in their dormitories worked under exclusive contract to churn out films on something like a production-line basis.[30] The international nature of the Shaws' business also led easily to ambitions to make theirs a truly global Chinese-language cinema. Run Run Shaw was already proclaiming his plans to 'bring the East to the West' in a spate of interviews in the early 1960s.[31] Aside from the increasing power of the Shaws as a regional player, it is in part this ambition to compete with Hollywood in its own terms, producing products of the necessary aesthetic quality to do so, which ultimately paved the way for the presentation of Hong Kong martial arts films within American and European theatres.

The Shaws' most lavish and successful films of the early 1960s were not, however, action pictures but musicals, love stories and romantic period dramas, often performed as operas in the Huangmei style popular at the time, especially in the Shaws' most lucrative market, Taiwan. Breaking this trend, an October 1965 issue of the Shaws' promotional magazine *Southern Screen* announced a 'new action era' and a 'new *wuxia* century'. In this, they were promising not only a revival of the genre – which they would go on to promote vigorously – but a new, transformed version of the swordplay film very different from its forebears. Indeed, the aesthetic and stylistic innovations of the years following *Southern Screen*'s announcement formed the basis of the changes that would lead from the older *wuxia* pictures to the arrival of kung fu cinema.

The Shaws nailed their new style of action cinema to the mast of 'realism', however paradoxical this notion might be with regard to the representation of superhuman martial arts abilities. The

Southern Screen article proclaimed that 'the fake, fantastical and theatrical fighting and the so-called special effects of the past will be replaced by realistic action and fighting that immediately decides life or death.'[32] Magical flying swords, bolts of energy and the ability to fly or dematerialize at will were (largely) abandoned. In the old films, as the director Hsu Tseng-hung put it, the audience 'would never see blood, even in a swordfight, and people rarely get killed, even after an interminable combat sequence'. By contrast, in the new-era *wuxia*, violence and death became central.[33] The stylized and balletic movements that early *wuxia* had drawn from opera were replaced with more direct combat techniques, and a new generation of fight choreographers was brought in. These drew more directly from the martial arts themselves than from their stage representations, and many of them had served their apprenticeships in the Wong Fei-hung films of the 1950s and '60s. Where physical combat was depicted in the older films, this had tended to be in full frame and with long takes from a static camera, as if the actors were onstage and the cinema viewers were an audience watching the play. The 'new-era' films brought the camera closer into the action, with rapid cuts and changes of angle to heighten visual impact. This also allowed directors to construct the action by editing together separate shots. One shot could show a swordsman making a slash, and then a reverse-angle close-up could show the impact of the blade. A third, from another angle, might then show the opponent falling to the ground. Special effects such as fake severed limbs or spurting stage blood, its redness exaggerated in the Shaws' trademark super-saturated colour process, extended the gruesomely visceral effect of action.

The 'realism', of course, remained deeply stylized, as it would do throughout the era of kung fu cinema. The Shaw aesthetic overall was very different from the naturalism that Hollywood sought. This

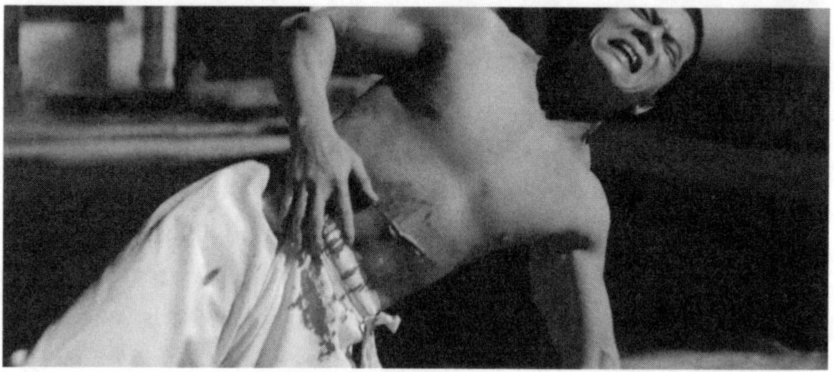

Camerawork and editing in *One-Armed Swordsman* bring the camera close in for visceral effect and construct action through a series of juxtaposed shots implying cause and effect. Note the use of stage blood and a special-effects wound in the final shot.

was perhaps because it drew on a culture much more invested in the artificiality of the stage and even on philosophical and artistic traditions that emphasize the dream-like and unreal nature of life itself. Though sets and costumes were beautifully lavish they remained unashamedly sets and costumes, and the heightened colour of the films only reinforced the deliberate artificiality of the *mise-en-scène*. Characters were larger than life, often aiming at a mythic quality rather than portraits in psychological depth, while plots tended towards melodrama. Fights, too, were exaggerated in their presentation, and it is in this period that the soundtrack of amplified clashing and ringing swords or thudding blows that remained the norm in the 1970s – and is one of the aesthetic pleasures of the kung fu movie genre – was established. As *Southern Screen* promised, the 'new *wuxia* century' would be characterized by 'the "clang-clang" of action'.[34] A useful way to understand the notion of 'realism' pursued by the new swordplays, then, is provided in Man-Fung Yip's concept of a 'sensory realism', which emphasizes the way that viewers are intensively plunged into the experience of their own bodies and the immediacy of the senses (however much this is mediated by cinematic technology itself). If the early *wuxia* 'showed' us action, these films increasingly sought to make us 'feel' it, viscerally.[35]

This emphasis on death, graphic violence and the 'realism' of combat came largely from the Shaw executives' desire to compete with the increasingly violent cinemas coming out of both America and Japan. In Hollywood, Sam Peckinpah was redefining the Western as an increasingly bloody and brutal genre. The global success of Akira Kurosawa's samurai epics provided a further model for emulation. Within Shaw Brothers, the driving force for the redefinition of Hong Kong action cinema in these terms was Chang Cheh, a scriptwriter and film critic whom Shaw took on as an advisor. Chang was ultimately given the job of overseeing the films that started off Shaw's 'new action era' and over the next two decades would also go on to become one of the most prominent and prolific directors in both the swordplay and kung fu genres in his own right. Owing to the impact of his films, Chang has often been called the 'godfather of kung fu'.

Chang argued for a 'modernization' of Hong Kong cinema in the mould of its international competitors. Globally, he noted, it was action that was creating blockbusters rather than romance or music. Chang also argued that while American and Japanese cinema revolved around strong male heroes, and derived its international appeal from this, Hong Kong's star system placed actresses at its centre. Even Hong Kong's action films did so, going as far as to cast actresses across gender in the role of male leads. Audiences would flock, for example, to see Josephine Siao and Connie Chan play alongside each other in swordplays, with Chan in drag taking the role of the male lead and Siao her romantic interest, usually an equally adept swordswoman. This prominence of female characters and stars goes right back to the roots of Chinese swordplay cinema: I have already discussed the character of Red Maiden in the *Red Lotus Temple* films and Butterfly Wu, who played her. The only surviving swordplay film from that era, *Red Heroine*, also takes a swordswoman as its protagonist, played this time by another actress who made her name in such roles, Fan Xuepeng. In contrast, argued Chang, the samurai film and the Western were genres revolving around images of tough manliness, and Hong Kong action cinema, too, now needed to follow a programme of what he called *yanggang* – 'staunch masculinity'. Chang set out to nurture a stable of young, muscular male stars and developed an oeuvre that centred around themes of individualism, machismo, potency, male bonding or competition and the ties of blood-brotherhood.[36] These would increasingly define the landscape of what would become kung fu cinema. Chang's concern with the masculinization of Hong Kong action also played well to the longer anticolonial concerns regarding the feminization of China in Orientalist discourse and its depiction as the 'sick man of Asia', with all the implications that this has of a lack of virility.

The increasingly graphic violence of the genre was also a matter of 'modernization' inasmuch as Chang and his associates self-consciously looked to create a cinema that responded to its historical moment. Like the late 1920s, when the swordplay first emerged, the 1960s were nothing if not a tumultuous decade. Feminism, the civil rights movement and rebellious youth countercultures were growing in America and Europe and were rapidly imported into Westernized Asian cities such as Hong Kong, which had a growing young population that was turning its back on traditional values.[37] Furthermore, the decolonization movement was sweeping the former Third World, and media images of the Vietnam War (and other proxy conflicts in the American–Russian Cold War) were being piped into living rooms by the mass media with a new immediacy created by lightweight cameras and front-line reporting. In 1966, closer to home, Mao Zedong launched the Cultural Revolution in the PRC. As the decade continued, the global wave of student and popular protest that is often remembered as '1968' exploded in both the Eastern and Western Blocs.

Hong Kong itself was not immune to the turbulence of the times. Waves of migration from the mainland had swelled the enclave's supply of cheap labour, and its economy was starting to boom as a centre of manufacture as well as trade and finance. It had, however, remained a deeply unequal society, still run under a systematically racist colonial system that denied the native Chinese population basic democratic rights and in which corruption was rife. Laissez-faire economic policies meant there was little protection for workers, who toiled long hours for little pay and with almost no job security.

For the poor, Hong Kong also largely lacked social security and access to education, healthcare or public housing, and the colony was blighted by vast shanty-town slums.[38] We still see these vividly depicted at the start of *Enter the Dragon* (1973), as the protagonists head through Hong Kong harbour. And this penury was ubiquitous: in 1967, 45 per cent of families were officially recognized as existing below the poverty line.[39] In 1966, a hunger strike against the price rise for the Star Ferry, on which many low-waged workers relied, exploded into a riot that ended in one death and 1,425 arrests. In 1967, even more widespread rioting broke out in the wake of industrial action about factory conditions. Largely led by leftists inspired by the Cultural Revolution, the cause was initially a popular one, but after a draconian clampdown by the authorities, the activists turned to increasingly extremist measures – including terrorist bombings – and alienated much of the island's population. By the end of the unrest, 51 people were dead and 4,979 had been arrested.[40]

In these circumstances, romantic costume dramas – and even the chivalric good manners of the established swordplay genre – seemed to Chang Cheh and his contemporaries lacking in relevance. When putting forwards the concept of 'sensory realism', discussed above, Yip stresses that this is a historically shifting category, and entails cinema's attempts to match the changing sensory experiences of its viewers' real lives. The older films reflected less and less the sensorium of the 1960s, with its rhythms of hard labour or the overcrowded and frenetic city, the shocking intrusion of media images of violence from around the world and the constant threat of political unrest and crime alike. The new martial arts cinema of the era, Yip suggests, is significant in its invention of cinematic affects that echoed and made sense of this new sensory reality.[41] In the 1990s, Chang himself wrote, remembering his career and his motivation in making martial arts pictures:

> The 60s and the 70s were the most energetic periods of Hong Kong – the period when young people exerted themselves. The age of love tales was the past. The masses were striving ahead in a rebellious mood and the colonial administration was receiving a shock to the system. *Yanggang* and the martial arts pictures represented this spirit of the times.[42]

Chang's early films were thus self-conscious attempts to grapple with the extremity of the era and its violence. His debut swordplay for Shaw was a relatively small, black-and-white production called *Tiger Boy* (1966), most notable for introducing Chang's favourite leading man of the following years, Jimmy Wang Yu. Wang was a swimming champion rather than an expert martial artist, though he had taken some karate classes. However, he had good looks and a lean, muscular physique and exuded both a hyperactive athleticism and a brooding machismo.[43]

Chang would soon go on to make his breakthrough with the now-classic *One-Armed Swordsman*. Released during the 1967 riots, this tells the story of Fang Kang (played by Wang Yu), the son of a servant who has died defending his master, a famous martial artist named Qi Ru-feng. Though adopted by the kindly Qi, Fang is bullied by the other – better-off – students in his school. Ultimately, his arm is severed by Qi's daughter. He is nursed back to health by a peasant girl and seems to have left the cruel world of the martial arts behind for a peaceful life working the land with her. However, when he realizes that his old master's school is under attack from the same villainous gang who killed his father, he teaches himself the art of one-armed swordsmanship so he can rescue his teacher and former comrades. Chang was innovative in his use of hand-held cameras, which added mobility to the filming of the fight sequences, creating excitement and energy. He also drew on Peckinpah's use of slow motion to add punch and pathos to violent death. Highly melodramatic, narratively taut, visually lush and drenched in gore, the film was the first to bring in a million dollars at the Hong Kong box office, making celebrities of the director and star alike. Its success convinced the Shaw studios of the value of investing in Chang's 'new *wuxia*' programme.

Chang's next picture, *The Assassin* (1967), repeated the success of *One-Armed Swordsman*, also topping the million-dollar mark. In it, Chang sought deliberately to mirror the events of the 1967 unrest and to explore – and even produce a cinematic hymn to – the extremist psychology taking hold in Hong Kong.[44] At a moment when leftists were undertaking a bombing campaign in the colony, aimed at various establishment political figures, Chang's protagonist is also an assassin. Nie Zheng (played once more by Wang Yu) is a young swordsman from the peasant classes in the chaotic Warring States period of ancient China (475–221 BCE). Though he comes from a subaltern class that seems to have no business with politics, Nie has taken up swordsmanship because he dreams of achieving something significant with his life. When his master is killed in a plot by the encroaching, tyrannical Qin kingdom, Nie undertakes a suicide mission to kill the prime minister, who has done an underhand deal with the enemy. After an extended battle with the minister's palace guard, he dies a heroic death fighting against impossible odds.[45] The final images of Wang Yu, dressed in white but increasingly drenched in hyperreally red blood, set the archetype of the heroically doomed rebel and outsider who is the protagonist of Chang's films, and in fact of much of the kung fu cinema to come. We find similar figures – often marked like *One-Armed Swordsman*'s Fang Kang as being of the wrong class, and often dying stoically heroic deaths like *The Assassin*'s Nie Zheng – in, for example, *Golden Swallow* (1968), *Have Sword Will Travel* (1969), *Vengeance!* (1970),

The New One-Armed Swordsman (1971) or *The Boxer from Shantung* (1972), to mention just a few of the most significant examples.

Despite the deliberate attempt to promote such a 'manly' version of heroism, throughout the late 1960s and early '70s Hong Kong's martial arts cinema was also still packed with images of women warriors, and audiences seem to have been just as excited to see these as their male counterparts. For example, alongside Chang Cheh, the other great auteur and pioneer of the new martial arts cinema of the late 1960s was King Hu, whose films consistently placed strong female protagonists at their heart. Hu's *Come Drink with Me* (1966) paved the way for the success of Chang's *One-Armed Swordsman.* The film's central protagonist was played by Cheng Pei-pei, probably best known to contemporary Western audiences for her portrayal, many years later, of the embittered villainess Jade Fox in *Crouching Tiger, Hidden Dragon*. In the late 1960s, Cheng was *the* role-defining action heroine of the new wave of swordplay films. Trained originally not in the martial arts but ballet, Cheng brought a disarming grace and beauty to her role in action scenes, balanced by a defiant toughness, determination and youthful energy. She is every bit the equal of the male leads she stars alongside in almost all of her films, not only those directed by Hu, but those by others.[46] Cheng's popularity spawned the appearance of a host of other female martial arts stars created in her image.[47] I will return to explore the ongoing tradition of women warriors (in both American and Chinese cinema) who might trace their roots back through King Hu's films later.

In *Come Drink with Me*, Cheng's character, Golden Swallow, is set against a group of ruthless bandits who have kidnapped her brother. To defeat them, she teams up with a seemingly bumbling beggar, Drunken Cat, who of course turns out to be a martial arts master in disguise. In some ways, the film looks back to earlier

Role-defining heroine Cheng Pei-pei in dynamic action as Golden Swallow in *Come Drink with Me*.

precedents, including aspects of the fantastical that *Southern Screen* had promised to reject, and in this regard some critics at the time saw it as only a partial success.[48] But *Come Drink with Me* was also one of the first Hong Kong films to ramp up levels of graphic violence and so to deliver on the promises of *Southern Screen*'s manifesto for a new kind of martial arts action cinema. Just in the film's first five minutes, when bandits attack a column of soldiers transporting a prisoner, we see some nineteen graphic deaths, including bodies pierced through by swords, amputated limbs and spurting blood. Even where Hu's films look back to the past, they were also prescient. Hu, for example, has said that he was never interested in – and knew nothing about – martial arts. Rather, his inspiration for fight scenes was a love of opera, and he conceived them in terms of dance.[49] However, as Stephen Teo has argued, Hu certainly did not simply record the opera stage. Rather, he inventively pursued the ways he could create properly cinematic equivalents for the sense of motion in opera performance, 'modulated' through the medium of film and the 'modernist sensibilities' of its conventions.[50] Because of this, although Hu's attachment to opera, dance and the fantastical seems to draw him away from the direction that the 'new *wuxia* century' and the approaching dawn of kung fu were taking, his invention of new ways of filming fight choreography would nonetheless be highly influential in the coming years. Furthermore, in the larger picture of the history of Chinese martial arts cinema, it is also ultimately Hu's action style – linked as it is to tradition and to the fantastical – that has proved the most enduring. Both the wire-fu films of the 1990s and the international blockbusters of the 2000s (such as those discussed in Chapter Seven) hark back more to his stylistic tenor and thematic preoccupations than to the moment of 'kung fu' as such. In any case, Hu's movies placed extended, visually spectacular fight scenes at their heart, in a way that had not been achieved before this point. Doing so, they redefined the nature of the martial arts film and the role of action within it. This new centrality of fighting – which leads directly to the kung fu genre – is signalled by the fact that Hu claimed, on several occasions, that he was in fact the first person to separately credit a 'martial arts director' (Han Yingjie) on his films.[51]

Overall, Hu was a director with ambitions beyond churning out standard genre fare for a mass audience. Instead, he pioneered what we might call the 'martial-art-house' film, and increasingly his work not only was innovative in its shooting of action but developed an aesthetic seriousness that included an engagement with literary sources and traditions of Chinese painting – landscape in particular – and a concern with both mysticism and political history. Again, we see the influence of these aspirations in the more recent films discussed in Chapter Seven. Though often flawed, Hu's works were of an ambition and richness that defined the martial arts film as a significant artistic form.

After the success of *Come Drink with Me*, Hu felt frustrated within the tight confines of the Shaw system and moved to Taiwan, where he took up a position setting up a production arm for a distributor there, Union Films. Hu's first film for Union was *Dragon Inn* (1967), which, grossing over \$2 million, outdid even Chang Cheh's *One-Armed Swordsman*. Buoyed by this success – and given a new degree of artistic freedom by the studio – King Hu then spent the years from 1968 to 1971 creating what is usually understood to be his crowning achievement, *A Touch of Zen*. At over three hours long, it is a sprawling and genre-defying epic that mixes aspects of martial arts, political intrigue, supernatural horror and Zen mysticism. The original Chinese title of the film, *Xianü*, translates literally as 'lady knight', and it is Hu's most extended exploration of the figure of the woman warrior (this time played by Hsu Feng). It is also remarkable for a pair of dazzling fight scenes set in forests. These later became key reference points for *Crouching Tiger, Hidden Dragon* and *House of Flying Daggers*, each of which includes bamboo-forest action sequences.

Unfortunately, despite its artistic achievements, *A Touch of Zen* was not a box-office success. Seeing its run time as likely to put off audiences, it was heavily cut by the studios, who released it in Taiwan in two parts and in Hong Kong as a single film of much-reduced length (and coherence).[52] Its failure – which meant that Hu would unfortunately never again have access to a similar budget and would often struggle to raise funds for projects – may in part have been because it was too 'arty' for popular audiences. It may also have simply been a matter of timing: between the start of *A Touch of Zen*'s long production process and its conclusion, the swordplay had given rise to the new phenomenon of kung fu cinema, and Bruce Lee had already exploded onto the Hong Kong scene.

THE RISE OF KUNG FU CINEMA

In some respects, the appearance of the kung fu film was a continuation and an evolution of the swordplay, although in others it reversed *wuxia* orthodoxies to create a very distinct new genre. If the 1960s swordplay had increasingly pursued a 'realism' constituted by the viscerality of violent action, kung fu in many respects offered a logical next step. As discussed, the industry had introduced a new generation of choreographers and performers with roots in local martial arts traditions to stage its increasingly complex and spectacular fight sequences, and these had been placed more and more at the centre of the viewing pleasure offered to an audience. Stars, too, were increasingly defined by their ability to perform in these sequences. For example, when Chang Cheh parted company with his leading man Wang Yu, the next stars he fostered were Ti Lung and David Chiang, who often performed in films alongside each other as a duo. Ti had studied wing chun as a young man to protect himself from street gangs, and Chiang was 'discovered' by Chang Cheh while working as a stuntman and fight director. With *Boxer from Shantung*, Chang would also start to work with Chen Kuan-tai, a former world kung fu champion. The kung fu genre continued the cult of the muscular male physique started in Chang Cheh's swordplay films but now increasingly linked this with martial arts abilities.

As action became increasingly central, the choreographers themselves would also play more of an authorial role, often constituting quasi-independent 'second units' within a film for the action sequences.[53] An example of this rising importance of the choreographer can be seen in the career of Lau Kar-leung. Lau traced his martial arts lineage directly, through his father and his father's teacher Lam Sai-wing to Wong Fei-hung, and in fact started his career as a young man working alongside his father on the Wong Fei-hung films of the 1950s and '60s. At the start of Shaw Brothers' 'new *wuxia* century', Lau was signed up by Chang Cheh in his quest for a more gritty action style and worked alongside the Beijing opera-trained Tang Chia to direct the combat scenes for *One-Armed Swordsman.* As the display of kung fu became an increasing box-office draw, Lau's input in his collaboration with Chang grew. This gave him more and more chance to showcase the 'authentic' southern Chinese martial arts in which he was expert, and according to Lau it was his idea to initiate the 'Shaolin Temple' cycle of films that he and Chang made in the mid-1970s.[54] Lau would eventually become a director in his own right, filming martial arts classics such as *The 36th Chamber of Shaolin* (1978), *Dirty Ho* (1979), *Legendary Weapons of China* (1982) and *The Eight Diagram Pole Fighter* (1983). His oeuvre constitutes the most extended exploration of both the physical performance of southern Chinese martial arts and their philosophies, histories and mythologies.

Despite continuities with the swordplay film, the increased centrality of martial arts sequences changed the way action was filmed. Shaw's 1960s *wuxia* films had constructed a sense of the violence of combat through editing. The need to show actual, authentic martial technique meant, instead, a return to longer takes and full-body framing, and the dynamism of combat depended now on physical performance rather than just clever cutting. Cinematic technique would increasingly serve to enhance rather than to substitute for such physical performance. With his interest in showcasing traditional skills, Lau Kar-leung made films (and action-directed sequences) that are the apotheosis of this 'purist' kung fu style.

The action in the films also changed as the combat shifted increasingly away from fencing with swords and towards the 'fist and leg' techniques of the barehanded martial arts. The film often credited as the first to make this shift decisively, launching the kung fu genre and establishing many of its tropes, was *The Chinese Boxer* (1970). This was written and directed by and starred Wang Yu, who after *One-Armed Swordsman* had become Hong Kong's biggest action star. Like the Wong Fei-hung films, *The Chinese Boxer* eschewed the deep or mythical past to set itself in what seems to be the early twentieth century. It tells a basic revenge story, coloured by a nationalist – even xenophobic – sentiment that would also become a regular feature of Hong Kong cinema in the following years. This sentiment was fuelled at the time by an ongoing dispute between China and Japan over ownership of the Diaoyu Islands, an uninhabited but oil-rich archipelago in the Pacific, which became a cause célèbre in the formation of cultural nationalism in 1970s Hong Kong. In *The Chinese Boxer*, Wang plays Lei Ming, who learns the 'iron palm' technique to seek revenge on a group of evil Japanese martial artists who murder his teacher and massacre fellow students at his martial arts school. As well as the anti-Japanese storyline, the plot, based around revenge for the death of a master and the scenes of training in esoteric techniques to achieve this, would provide a standard template for much of the new genre. As kung fu was not only featured on-screen but placed at the film's thematic core, Bruce Lee's biographer Matthew Polly has dubbed it 'the first major movie to devote itself entirely to the art of kung fu'.[55]

The main competitor for the title of first kung fu film is Chang Cheh's *Vengeance!* (1970), which was released just a few months before Wang's offering. Like *Chinese Boxer*, this is set during the early Republican period and is also a tale of revenge. Here, however, this is articulated in terms of the theme of blood-brotherhood, which was becoming an increasingly key concern for Chang in his ongoing exploration of martial masculinity. At the start of the film, opera performer Guan Yulou (Ti Lung) is murdered – in bloody and melodramatic slow motion – by gangsters who covet his wife, and his brother Xiaolou (David Chiang) returns to town to investigate his death. Xiaolou slowly works his way through the network of the rich, powerful and corrupt to wreak vengeance on those responsible for or complicit in Yulou's death. The film's most iconic images are from its finale, an extended battle with knives in which Chiang's beautifully tailored, dazzling white Republican-era student suit is slowly drenched more and more in the gory red of both his enemies' and his own blood. Chiang's student suit locates him on the side of youth, and the film sets him against rich, powerful and corrupt establishment figures. Rather than an anti-Japanese or nationalist tale, this seems an allegory of countercultural revolt. This youthful rebellion would remain another aspect the kung fu genre took from the swordplay and extended. While in some respects kung fu looked back to the 'authenticity' in performance of the Wong Fei-hung films, it is also worth noting the difference between Wong's staid, patrician and traditionalist ethos and the anti-establishment, individualist hero typical of the kung fu film. The fight scenes in *Vengeance!* lack the sophistication of technique we might expect in later kung fu movies, and there is heavy use of knives and hatchets rather than bare-handed combat, but its brutal 'street fight' rawness nonetheless marked a decisive rejection of the fantastical elements that still lingered in the *wuxia* and looked forward to what was to come.

Vengeance! may have come first, but it was *The Chinese Boxer* that stirred the biggest sensation, and while studios rushed to cash in on its formula for success, another pivotal figure in the kung fu story entered the scene. In 1971, Bruce Lee returned to Hong Kong, frustrated by the lack of a decisive breakthrough in his Hollywood career. Lee had been a child star in Hong Kong during the 1950s but was packed off by his family to study in the USA after getting into trouble for street fighting. In America, he dropped out of university to run a martial arts school and pursue a movie career. Lee had some degree of success in both, entering the circles of celebrities such as Steve McQueen and becoming a martial arts teacher to the stars. Lee got a string of small roles and in 1966 was cast as Kato, the sidekick for the eponymous hero in the TV series *The Green Hornet*, bringing kung fu to American screens and becoming a minor celebrity for it. However, due largely to the ingrained racism of the American studios, starring roles eluded him. In the meantime, Lee had become newly famous in Hong Kong: when *The Green Hornet* was aired on local TV, it was known as 'The Kato Show', and Lee was adored as a native son who had broken into the golden kingdom of Hollywood. Lee made appearances on radio and television talk shows – in the latter demonstrating his kung fu to much applause.[56]

When Lee signed a deal with a Hong Kong studio, it was not with Shaw Brothers, whose standard contract was a mere $200 a week for seven years and gave an actor no voice in the films they appeared in.[57] These terms could hardly have been enticing for Lee, who suffered from a strong need for control and was a man with a definite plan for superstardom in both Hong Kong and America. As a result, he was one of the first figures to turn to a new studio appearing in Hong Kong at the time, Golden Harvest. This was led by Raymond Chow, an ex-Shaw Brothers producer who was frustrated with the inflexibility and centralization of Shaw's factory process. He sought instead to set up a more flexible, entrepreneurial form of film production, contracting with independent producers on particular projects and giving stars both more lucrative deals and more creative freedom to lure them in. Lee's deal with Chow – initially $15,000 for two films[58] – would put both of them on the industry map. With Golden Harvest offering similar deals during the 1970s to the comedian Michael Hui and the martial artist Jackie Chan, both of whom turned out to be box-office gold just like Lee, the studio would, by the end of the decade, eclipse Shaw Brothers as the dominant force in the colony's cinema. Their more mobile and responsive form of production proved a decisive advantage over Shaw, where centralized planning was much less nimble in tracking new trends and meant remaining locked into extant formulae by prior investments in sets, props and personnel.

Lee's first film with Golden Harvest was *The Big Boss* (1971). In it, Lee plays Cheng Chao-an, a naive young economic migrant who travels to Bangkok to join a group of Chinese labourers in an ice factory. When two of the workers discover that the ice is being used to smuggle heroin, this sets off a chain of events where all those close to Cheng are murdered by the boss's heavies. Cheng has made a vow to his mother never to fight and spends much of the film holding back from taking part, until finally he sets off to take revenge for his dead comrades and to save the girl he is falling in love with. Though the film was shot rapidly on a shoestring budget on location in Thailand (and its low production values certainly show), it was an enormous success, grossing $3.2 million in a three-week run in Hong Kong alone.[59] Lee was a sensation, in part because of his generally magnetic screen presence and the simmering intensity that he expressed even when not fighting. It was also because of his action performance, the likes of which audiences had never seen, not even in a film like *The Chinese Boxer*. The star of that movie, of course, was not a martial artist of Lee's expertise or calibre. Lee rejected the extended exchanges of technique we see in Wang Yu's film, using the camera instead to display his virtuoso physical performances in short, snappy shots. In these, his trademark lightning-quick kicks dispatched opponents in a single move. As Lee's biographer Matthew Polly puts it, 'Everyone else in *The Big Boss* looks like they are playing patty-cake, while Bruce is a demonic whirlwind.' Hong Kong audiences, familiar as they often were with kung fu, 'knew the real deal when they saw it'.[60] The film also appealed on the level of content: with Lee defending the Chinese abroad, the film touched on the patriotic themes stirred in *The Chinese Boxer*. Setting Lee as a young factory worker against bosses and foremen also activated the tropes of countercultural and class rebellion seen in *Vengeance!*

These patriotic and rebellious themes were extended in Lee's next film, *Fist of Fury* (1972), which drew even more extensively on the themes introduced in *The Chinese Boxer* and *Vengeance!* This tells the story of Chen Zhen, who, like Xiaolou in *Vengeance!*, returns home at the start of the film to mourn a death, and as the film unfolds sets out on a path of revenge. To underline the reference, in the opening scenes he is even dressed in a pristine white student suit redolent of Chiang's. As in *The Chinese Boxer*, the film is set around competing martial arts schools, takes Japanese martial artists as its villains and organizes its revenge plot around the death of a master. However, Lee's film is more historically specific in its location. The dead master is in fact a historical figure, Huo Yuanjia, who headed the Jingwu Athletic Association. Jingwu was a pioneer of the modernizing, nationalistic martial arts movement of the early twentieth century, discussed above as forming a background for the first rise of martial arts cinema in China. Huo, who died in 1910, was made into a patriotic hero by the media, with rumours circulating that he had been poisoned by enemy agents to neutralize the sense of pride and national strength his example inspired. The film is set in the Shanghai International Settlement, an enclave governed by a federation of occupying foreign powers rather than the Chinese state. Given this, and with its nationalist narrative, which depicts the inferiorization of the native population, it is hard not to interpret the film as an allegory of the colonial situation of Hong Kong. In one iconic scene, Lee comes to the gates of a park and is denied entry by a guard, who points him to a sign that reads, 'No dogs and

Chinese allowed'. Taunted by Japanese visitors, Lee explodes into quivering fury, beating his tormentors unconscious and leaping into the air to smash the offensive sign into pieces with a flying kick. In another scene, he single-handedly fights and defeats an entire dojo of judo practitioners to make their teacher physically eat the paper of a sign on which is inscribed the stock insult 'sick men of East Asia', which earlier in the film they have levelled at the Chinese Jingwu students. In local cinemas, which were at the best of times raucous environments, scenes such as this with their potent and emotive anticolonial appeal instigated scenes not far from rioting. Robert Clouse, the director of *Enter the Dragon*, described the response of the audience when he was first shown *Fist of Fury* at a Kowloon screening as 'hysteria', echoing the language of early twentieth-century intellectuals faced with *wuxia* spectatorship. According to Clouse, when Lee spoke the line 'The Chinese are not the sick people of Asia,' the result was: 'Pandaemonium! Everyone rose to [their] feet. Wave upon wave of earsplitting sound rolled up to the balcony. The seats were humming and the floor of the old balcony was shaking!'[61]

Heady nationalism: Bruce Lee takes on an entire dojo of Japanese martial artists in *Fist of Fury*.

The monstrous body of the West: Bruce Lee grasps a handful of Chuck Norris's chest hair in *The Way of the Dragon*.

Lee's third film – his last before the kung fu craze struck the West – was also his directorial debut. *The Way of the Dragon* (1972) was set in Rome, but still not, it would seem, in order to pander to a Western audience. Much as Asia might be used as a colourful backdrop for a James Bond outing, the film treats Europe as an exotic location and offers a specifically sinocentric viewpoint on it. Lee plays Tang Lung (literally 'China Dragon'), who is sent from Hong Kong to Italy to help out a beautiful relative (Nora Miao) who runs a Chinese restaurant that is being targeted by mafia thugs. At first, she is disappointed at his arrival – she clearly expected a lawyer, and Tang appears to be nothing more than a bumpkin with little grasp of the situation he has entered. The restaurant waiters, too, have no faith in Tang's 'kung fu' or their national heritage, having taken up the Japanese art of karate to protect themselves instead. When Lee springs into action, of course, all of that changes. After a series of escalating confrontations, Lee ends up in a final showdown with the mafia's top fighter, played by Chuck Norris, an American practising the Japanese art of karate, so doubly an image of imperialism in the film's terms. Vijay Prashad has interpreted the showdown as an allegory of power and resistance in the East–West relationship. Indeed, in terms of the images of the two fighters' bodies, Norris is large and bulky, seeming to stand for the sheer might of America and the West. The sequence lingers on the hairiness not just of his chest but also his back, and as an image of might, it is also one of monstrosity, reversing the usual ability of Western media to represent its Others in similar terms. Lee, in contrast, is lithe, agile, muscular and intelligent, an image, suggests Prashad, of forms of Asian resistance through guerrilla warfare, as exemplified by the Vietcong or Mao's long campaign against the GMD.[62] This interpretation only gains further credence from the fact that Lee asked Norris, as a condition of his appearance, to put on 20 pounds (9 kg) for the role.[63]

This, then, was the state of play with the kung fu film in Hong Kong as the global craze approached. Through its address of a regional market, pioneered by the canny Shaw Brothers, the Hong Kong film industry had grown exponentially since its early days in the 1930s and was highly outward-looking. In fact, by the time Bruce Lee returned to make films there, it was 'the fourth most active film industry in the world, behind India, the United States and Japan', and 'the most dominant film exporter in Asia'.[64] With Lee and with the local mania for kung fu, action films were commanding the box offices: in each year from 1970 to 1972, all of the top ten highest-grossing films were martial arts pictures.[65] This success, in many ways, was linked closely to the local politics of Hong Kong – and the similar concerns for diasporic Chinese populations across its East and Southeast Asian markets. Kung fu seemed to articulate what the film historian Stephen Teo has termed an 'abstract nationalism': an attachment to the ideas of China and Chineseness that extends beyond particular nation states or modes of government such as those instantiated by the PRC or Taiwan, or even Hong Kong itself.[66] This was fuelled by the rise of youth countercultures, which questioned traditional forms of authority, and also by the anticolonial sentiment that had its roots in the turbulence of the 1960s. Although articulating these in new ways appropriate to the times, it drew on longer histories both of martial arts cinema and of the martial arts themselves as a complex (perhaps even contradictory) signifier of both a national pride embedded in tradition, yet also China's attempt to locate itself within global modernity. Beyond these, it drew on literary, folk and performance traditions that stretch deep into China's past. Its themes, we have also seen, were also articulated in complicated ways around ideas of gender and masculinity. The martial arts tradition was replete with swordswomen but increasingly, under the deliberate programme of 'staunch masculinity', privileged the presence of muscular male heroes who could compete with equivalents from American and Japanese cinema. Both the male- and the female-centric modes of action, in their different ways, and each with rather different implications in terms of the way that gender and national politics might intermesh, can be seen as rejoinders to the feminizing, Orientalizing narrative of the 'sick man of East Asia', which had often been projected onto China throughout the modern period.

The sheer load of particular, local meanings that contributed to the success of the kung fu film in its original market might at first sight seem unpropitious for them to take the box offices in America, Europe and Australasia by storm, as they would soon do. To understand the kung fu craze in its global dimension, then, we will need to understand how these local, national and regional concerns were translated into other situations where they were not abandoned but transformed. I will begin this task in the next chapter, which turns to look at the conditions for the explosion of interest in kung fu in the West.

2
THE AMERICAN CONNECTION

The background of Hong Kong's martial arts cinema and the rise at the start of the 1970s of the kung fu genre is only, of course, a part of the picture. After all, the kung fu craze as I am considering it here was not just a Hong Kong phenomenon. It entailed a sudden explosion of interest beyond the merely local. To understand kung fu's global impact and its 'journey to the West', we need to think about it in terms of its transposition into a series of new contexts. In this task, it is above all the USA, with its dominant cultural place in the world, that we need to consider.

Just as was the case in Hong Kong, this has both a more immediate and a longer-term dimension. As argued in this book's introduction, the kung fu craze takes its place within a broader history of the construction of the interdependent ideas of 'East' and 'West'. This pair of terms, of course, has historically been primarily defined from the standpoint of the West, and was entwined with European imperial projects. Shifting to the more immediate context, 'kung fu' was still a relatively unfamiliar term to most Americans at the start of the 1970s. Indeed, as Paul Bowman has argued, until the 1968–74 period even the broader term 'martial arts' was generally only used by a small and specialist group of enthusiasts fascinated with East Asian fighting techniques and needed explanation beyond this.

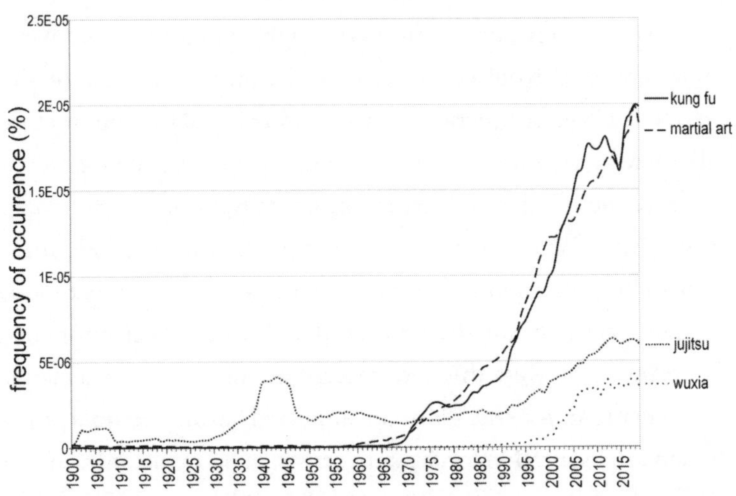

The frequency of usage of the terms *kung fu*, *martial art*, *jujitsu* and *wuxia*. Data from Google Books Ngram Viewer. Corpus: English 2019; data smoothed over three years.

After 1974, the *Oxford English Dictionary* shows, it was not only a transparently everyday term, but alluded to a 'boom'.[1] The novelty of both of these terms, their sudden appearance in the English language around 1972 and their continuing commonness are all also made vivid by the data Google holds on the year-by-year frequency of their occurrence within the books in their digital library.

JUJITSU MAKES ITS MARK

A first context to grasp for the appearance of these terms – and the meanings that attached themselves to them – is a much longer fascination with the East Asian combat arts. These had been, for quite some time, an integral part of how the 'Far East' was fantasized within European and American cultures.

It was the martial arts of Japan that first grabbed the Western imagination. These had reached a broad level of public visibility as early as the end of the nineteenth century, a time when Japan itself, as a growing power, was increasingly significant to the West. Japan emerged from centuries of isolation in the wake of the arrival of a fleet of American warships in 1853, led by Commodore Matthew Perry, whose aim was to forcibly open Japanese ports to trade. Responding to this, especially in the wake of the 1868 Meiji Restoration, Japan underwent a rapid programme of modernization, industrialization and military reform, aiming to compete with the European and American powers that threatened her autonomy. For many in the West, this newly accessible culture became a matter of fascination: from the 1860s on, imported Japanese *ukiyo-e* prints became an inspiration for Western artists, in particular influencing the bold colours and flat spaces of Impressionist painting, and by the 1870s 'japonisme', the study of Japanese art and other cultural objects, had become something of a craze.

With its increasing confidence, Japan was, by the start of the twentieth century, staking out its own imperial ambitions. In 1894–5, their military defeated China's to take Korea and Taiwan as colonies. In 1904–5, they beat Russia in a conflict over rival ambitions in Manchuria. As Pankaj Mishra has argued, this was 'the first time since the Middle Ages a non-European country had vanquished a European power in a major war'. The victory inspired a wave of nationalism across Asia (and beyond) that lasted well into the twentieth century, laying the ground for independence struggles as far afield as China, India and Egypt.[2]

The image of the warlike samurai – increasingly mobilized as a part of Japan's official militaristic ideology – became a stock part of the Western picture of Japan. It presented an ambivalent image, at once fascinating and yet also horrific, of a form of power or strength that contrasted with the technological rationalism of Europe's domination of the globe. It was also one that increasingly presented itself as an alarming competitor. The samurai appeared in the West as emblematic of a feudal otherness coloured with barbaric violence. These connotations stuck with the Asian martial arts through much of the twentieth century and form an important background to the reception of kung fu cinema. As the cultural historian Gary Krug has argued in an essay on the growth of karate in the West, 'The martial arts have been able to function as signifiers of all that Asia was in the imagination.' They were fantasized as 'secret, highly advanced, deadly, and possessing the ability to make the practitioner virtually invulnerable to physical harm. These paralleled beliefs about Asia in general as mysterious, inscrutable, violent.'[3] Wendy Rouse has reinforced such an argument in her work on women's self-defence in this era. While boxing was taken as a manly and honourable pursuit, judo was imagined as underhand, immoral and vicious – 'the physical embodiment of the Yellow Peril'.[4] At this point, where there was any awareness of China's martial traditions, this was in very contrasting terms and usually based on the iconography that had attached itself to the Boxer Rebellion. Although, like the Japanese, the 'heathen and barbaric' Boxers were imagined through yellow-peril anxieties, these were shorn of the sense of a technically sophisticated and effective art of violence, and they were more an image of backwardness, irrational superstition and weakness.[5]

However, as the japoniste craze attests, Japan was not only imagined in terms of violence and cruelty but it presented images of refinement and spirituality, and arts such as jujitsu were also connected to these ideas. By 1898, the Japanese martial arts were being demonstrated, for example, in London by Edward Barton-Wright, and soon after his Bartitsu Club on Shaftesbury Avenue would be teaching them. Barton-Wright, who had been working as an antimony smelter in Japan, brought jujitsu experts back with him to the UK. They taught alongside experts in boxing, stick-fighting and the French martial art savate to create a syncretic self-defence system he named 'bartitsu', adding a Japanese-sounding suffix to the first syllable of his own name. Barton-Wright defined it as meaning 'self-defence in every form'. It was offered to respectable Edwardian gentlemen (and ladies) to protect themselves on the mean streets of London at a moment of a long-standing media-fuelled moral panic about violent crime. This panic itself had its roots in the anxieties of empire, with the violent urban poor imagined in terms of tales of 'Thuggees' in India, violent anticolonial outlaws who, in the media stories, garotted Westerners in acts of robbery and murder.[6] In this regard, the British gentleman's ability to appropriate Asian arts of combat to protect himself was a specially loaded one. Although Barton-Wright's success was fairly brief – his club was closed by 1903 – he nonetheless became something of a media celebrity. *The Times* reported on his system, and the popular *Pearson's Magazine* (which was distributed in both the UK and North America) ran two extended articles on him in 1899 amid a welter of media interest. Above all, the continued fame of Barton-Wright's system is due to Arthur Conan-Doyle's decision, in his 1903 collection of short stories *The Return of Sherlock Holmes*, to make the sleuth's expertise in bartitsu the means by which he escaped death and defeated his arch-enemy Moriarty on the Reichenbach Falls.[7]

Though Barton-Wright's academy was short-lived, the interest in martial arts it piqued was longer lasting. After the Bartitsu Club closed, for example, Barton-Wright's instructor Yukio Tani continued giving public demonstrations and spent time touring the British music-hall circuit under the stage name 'The Pocket Hercules', taking all comers in open challenge. In 1904, he went on, with Taro Miyake, to open a jujitsu school on Oxford Street, where he primarily handled the day-to-day instruction while Miyake toured Europe and the United States giving demonstrations and also teaching in the gym of French physical-culture activist Edmond

A demonstration of bartitsu, from the *Illustrated Sporting and Dramatic News*, 18 March 1899.

Desbonnet. Tani finally came to work at the Budokwai, founded in London in 1918 by Gunji Koizumi and still operational today. The Budokwai also taught judo, a more modernized and 'sportified' version of jujitsu, which became increasingly popular. By 1908, these arts had become so well known that Baden-Powell referred to jujitsu in his *Scouting for Boys*, and it was soon integrated into the Scouts' curriculum – as well as into military and police training.[8]

The growing landscape of Japanese martial arts in London was typical of a more international phenomenon. Just as the Bartitsu Club was closing down in 1903, for example, Yoshiaki Yamashita was introducing judo to the USA. He would soon be teaching no less a man than the president, Theodore Roosevelt, who sought to imagine himself in the image of the 'manly' warrior caste of the samurai.[9] By the 1930s, judo and jujitsu had also become a part of the spectacle of Hollywood cinema. Between 1937 and 1939, for example,

Twentieth Century–Fox churned out eight successful films featuring the Japanese Interpol agent Mr Moto. In these, the protagonist – played by Peter Lorre in what may seem a rather unlikely action-hero role – defeats his opponents repeatedly through his expertise in judo.

In the wake of the Second World War, this familiarity would only grow. Though the conflict with Japan brought the Mr Moto series to an inevitable halt, judo would appear again, for example, as a prominent feature of the film *Blood on the Sun* (1945), made in the closing months of the war. In it, James Cagney plays a heroic American journalist, Nick Condon, who sets out to stop an evil plot for world domination by Japanese militarists during the 1920s. In it, judo appears, when associated with its villains, as a part of the film's yellow-peril imagery of Japan, a mark of their lust for violence. In this the film fits squarely into the pattern described by Krug above, where the martial arts are emblematic of the inscrutability and cruelty of the East Asian Other. However, Condon himself is also first introduced to the viewer while he is training in a judo dojo – imagined now as a space of civilized gentlemanly competition – and his skill at this becomes a mark of his ability to match the Japanese at their own game. The film's climax sets Condon against his arch-enemy, the thuggish Captain Oshima, in a bare-handed judo-cum-boxing brawl. As we shall see in later chapters, Condon is certainly not the last American hero in Hollywood cinema to prove a kind of 'natural' superiority (both moral and physical) to Asian enemies through the appropriation and mastery of their native arts of violence. This trope must have had quite a special emotive appeal at a moment when a long war against Japan was entering its final stages. Nonetheless, in the American consciousness, even as an 'enemy' art, judo does not remain purely a signifier of evil but is also a desired means through which violence and otherness can be conquered, just as was the case with bartitsu.

THE POST-WAR GROWTH OF THE MARTIAL ARTS

By 1949, another film starring James Cagney, Raoul Walsh's *White Heat*, would also feature judo, though now further separated from its cultural origin in Japan and seen in more simply positive terms. In this, Cagney plays the villain, Cody Jarrett, a psychopathic gangster. Edmond O'Brien plays the hero, Hank Fallon, an undercover FBI agent inserted into Cody's gang to bring him down. Judo becomes a part of Fallon's means to survive in this tight spot. Even just a few years after the war, it plays the role of a routine and technical part of the armoury of an agent of the state, rather than being a signifier of 'Japanese-ness'.

The increased familiarity of the American public with judo and jujitsu to which these images testify was to a significant degree due to the increased exposure to the martial arts of servicemen stationed in the Far East. This happened first during the war, then during the American occupation of Japan in its wake, and also during the Korean War, which broke out in 1950.[10] In *White Heat*, Fallon explains his 'fancy wrestling' as having been learned on just such a tour of duty.

The experience of future movie star and karate champion Chuck Norris, who served at Osan air base in Korea from 1958 until 1962, may well be typical of those who brought these arts back to America. Norris recounts how servicemen had three options to fill their spare time: drinking, taking an academic course or the martial arts. Norris – who was by his own account neither a drinker nor a scholar – chose judo and karate by default.[11] With such servicemen returning to America, both supply and demand for martial arts instruction grew. As Michael Molasky's survey of the evidence of phone books shows, while throughout the 1940s and '50s most major American cities would have a single judo school listed, or jujitsu classes in a local YMCA, these expanded rapidly in the 1960s.[12]

Furthermore, this was also the moment when karate appeared as a widely recognized phenomenon. Its popularity soon called for a separate heading within phone books, with karate classes massively outstripping judo and jujitsu in sheer numbers.[13] This rise was largely because the American military set up their most important regional base in Okinawa, whose native martial art is karate.

By 1961, America also had its first magazine dedicated to the martial arts, *Black Belt*, and in 1964, Ed Parker, who had been teaching kenpo karate since the mid-1950s, launched the Long Beach International Karate Championships, offering the emerging American martial arts community an arena for competition. Parker was also a significant figure in the rising public profile of karate in that he was the teacher of one of the biggest celebrities of the emerging era. This was another veteran who had been introduced to the art during his military service, the 'King of Rock'n'Roll' himself, Elvis Presley. Presley famously earned a black belt, integrated the karate kick into his stage performances, opened the Tennessee Karate Institute and, towards the end of his life, even planned a documentary film promoting the art.[14] The extent of karate's penetration of the general consciousness by 1967 is evidenced by the launch of an aftershave, Hai Karate, sold with Orientalist packaging and a long-running series of humorous advertisements, in both the UK and the USA.[15]

In Krug's terms, what we see in this period is the movement away from a culture where there were only occasional glimpses of the martial arts, which could only be interpreted through existing stereotypes about the 'Orient'. Instead, the martial arts were becoming increasingly domesticated, appropriated and absorbed. As more people became involved in their practice, a more extended public vocabulary existed through which to understand them, and to make them carry meaning.[16]

That the martial arts had entered the consciousness of mainstream society in this fashion is further marked by the fact that judo became an Olympic sport in 1964 when the Games were held in Tokyo. This is not to say that the art did not still stand as an image of Oriental otherness, tied to more pervasive stereotypes and fantasies about the East. The same year, perhaps precisely because of the interest in Japan sparked by the Olympics, Australia's Channel Nine presented the television series *Onmitsu kenshi* (literally 'spy swordsman') as *The Samurai*, featuring heroic swordsmanship and ninja intrigue. The surprise hit of the season, this was received enthusiastically by local audiences and – though not widely screened elsewhere – went on to become a cult classic in both Australia and New Zealand. An early embrace of East Asian popular culture here might well be motivated by several factors, including geographical location along the Pacific Rim, which made Japan a near neighbour and so a location of special relevance. With Japan's rapid economic post-war recovery, it was becoming an increasingly significant trading partner, and Australia was, furthermore, undergoing the progressive dismantlement of its 'White Australia' policy, opening the country up to increased migration from Asia and an increasingly multicultural society.

The James Bond film *You Only Live Twice* (1967), released just a few years later, was set in Japan and used judo, karate and kendo (as well as sumo wrestling) as elements of exotic colour, in a manner not so different from *Blood on the Sun*. Like Condon in that film, Bond is set against sly foreign enemies, who now find their apotheosis in the figure of the ninja, introduced for the first time to Hollywood screens in this film. However, ninjutsu also becomes a part of the technical armoury of the spy, alongside Bond's gadgets. Martial artistry of this sort constitutes a stock element of the genre in films such as *Our Man Flint* (1966) and television series such as *I Spy*, *The*

Man from U.N.C.L.E. or *The Avengers*. In these works, although judo becomes deracinated and is made familiar through the figure of the spy, it still carries traces and connotations that connect it to stereotypical ideas about the East. As *You Only Live Twice* underlines, the spy is, after all, a figure connected to the ninja, and the implication is that, like espionage, the martial arts comprise a technique that undermines the 'fair' and 'manly' competition between opponents, allowing the weaker one to win through subterfuge and trickery rather than strength; in this regard, they evoke all of the long prejudices in the West about East Asians as calculating and underhand.

CHANGING IDEAS OF ASIA

However, in this period new – more positive – images of Asia were also developing, alongside seismic shifts in American society and culture. The otherness of the 'Far East' had long served not only as a means to dominate and control Asia or reinforce ideas of Western supremacy. They also stood as counter-images through which European and American thought and belief could be critically examined.[17] For Enlightenment philosophers such as Voltaire, China had provided an image of non-theistic rationality and good government that enabled an all-out attack on the place of the Church in established European society. For Romantics such as Schopenhauer or the American Transcendentalists, readings in Indian thought provided a counter to the materialism of developing industrial societies. But if in the eighteenth and nineteenth centuries these attitudes were played out within the realm of high intellectual endeavour in the face of a more general contempt for non-Western thought and society, the mid-twentieth century seemed to mark a rapid permeation of such ideas into the popular mainstream. For example, after the war, and especially during his stay in the USA from 1950 to 1957, the works of D. T. Suzuki grew in popularity. These translated Zen Buddhism into a Western idiom, presenting it in a manner that chimed well with European and American Romantic traditions.[18] Drawing on Suzuki, Alan Watts also published prolifically on Zen and Chinese Daoism, hosted a popular Californian radio show in the 1950s and even presented a two-season television series in 1959–60. Chiming with these increasingly popular expositions of East Asian thought was the interest of a range of well-known intellectuals such as Carl Jung, Joseph Campbell and Aldous Huxley.[19]

Academic interest in the East was, furthermore, starting to chime with the new post-war countercultural movements. First the Beats and then the hippies used the likes of Suzuki, Watts, Jung, Campbell and Huxley to create an image of Asia that could be used as a counter to the orthodoxies of mainstream American capitalist culture, which they saw as morally and spiritually bankrupt. As Allen Ginsberg proclaimed in a letter to Jack Kerouac in 1957: 'Now the bitter American reality encounters the Oriental century to come.'[20] Reacting against the materialism, conservatism and conformity of post-war society, the Beats stressed a vision of life as a spiritual quest. They discovered in – or projected onto – Zen and Daoism a form of this that could be reconciled with their embrace of psychedelic drugs, sexual permissiveness and their belief in spontaneity and libertarian individualism. Ginsberg's *Howl* (1956) and William S. Burroughs's *Naked Lunch* (1959) both ignited obscenity trials, and the Beats constituted the opening salvo in the culture wars over the values of American society that would in various guises dominate the coming decades. As is underlined by Ginsberg's evocation of an 'Oriental century to come', opposed to the old and 'bitter' Occidental one, the embrace of ideas and images of Asia was a core weapon in this fight.

The new countercultural vision of the East, as popularized in works such as Kerouac's 1958 *Dharma Bums*, opened the door on the one hand to a fascination on behalf of avant-garde artistic figures ranging from John Cage to the abstract expressionists, and on the other to new forms of youth culture such as the hippies. In many ways, although the Beats and their successors reversed the conventional condescension towards the East, the new cultural images retained the outline of well-worn Orientalist fantasies. The East still served as an image of passivity and ancient, unchanging mysticism in contrast to the hard-headed, instrumental rationality and materialism of Western modernity and progress. But now identification with this idea of the East allowed the Beats and hippies to reimagine themselves as others and outsiders, and to make common cause with that which sets itself against the overarching logic of 'the West'. This countercultural revolt increasingly also merged with the struggles of other marginalized groups – the struggles of feminism, civil rights and gay liberation – and pictured itself in the context of global movements of decolonization. In this militant guise, 'the East' also connoted the Vietcong and Mao as exemplary moments of resistance. As the anti-Vietnam War movement grew, all things Asian became increasingly coloured by this association.

Within these countercultures, the martial arts were frequently imagined as a means towards the kind of spiritual quest the Beats and their followers pursued. Eugen Herrigel's *Zen in the Art of Archery*, written in 1948, was translated into English in 1953 and rapidly became a touchstone, drawing others to consider the martial arts in this light. In a half-hour episode of his television series, Watts, for example, took up Herrigel's vision of the martial arts as a spiritual discipline to present kendo and judo alike as antidotes to 'modern life'.[21] Given the extent to which the counterculture saw itself as figuratively at war with establishment values and ways of living, the martial arts must also have offered a particularly attractive image of spirituality, one conducive to militancy. When, for example, Gary Snyder (the inspiration for the character of Japhy Ryder in Kerouac's *Dharma Bums*) outlined a politics of 'Buddhist anarchism' in 1961, he proposed 'gentle violence' as a means to further the agenda of social revolution, alongside 'civil disobedience, outspoken criticism, protest, pacifism, voluntary poverty'.[22] Whether or not Snyder had the martial arts in mind when writing this passage, they would increasingly be seen as embodying the paradox of this 'gentle violence' – a violence very different from that of the burgeoning machine of the Cold War military-industrial complex.

Such shifting attitudes to the East – and the martial arts as a signifier of this – help explain the contrast between the anti-Japanese images of *Blood on the Sun* and the more positive ones offered in *Bad Day at Black Rock* (1955), made a decade later. In this, Spencer Tracy plays John Macreedy, a one-armed Second World War veteran who finds himself pitted against the racism of Midwestern America when he arrives in a small town to visit Komoko, the Japanese American father of a man who saved his life during their military service together. It turns out that Komoko has been murdered in a racist attack, and the town, including its authority figures, closes ranks against Macreedy in his attempts to uncover this. In this way, American society and its establishment are allegorized as conformist, insular, violent and corrupt, in contrast to the outsider Macreedy's cosmopolitanism and pursuit of the truth. Macreedy's openness to otherness is introduced by the fact of his siding with an Asian American, now envisioned as an innocent victim rather than a nefarious enemy. It is amplified in a pivotal scene of confrontation in a bar when the one-armed Macreedy uses judo and karate to defeat an attempt to scare him off through physical violence. Judo here, as a means to overcome violence through non-aggression, figures an 'Eastern' mode of fighting that is morally superior to the

The weak overcoming the strong: the one-armed Macreedy (Spencer Tracy) uses the Japanese martial arts to throw a hired tough guy (Ernest Borgnine) who attacks him in *Bad Day at Black Rock*.

brute strength of its 'Western' counterpart. Macreedy's handicap – he defeats his foes with just one hand – underlines the extent to which the martial arts serve within the film's imagination as a refutation of a logic of sheer force whereby the strong dominate the weak (associated with America and with the corruption of the small town in which it is set).

Bad Day at Black Rock's depiction of the martial arts was echoed in the rise of interest in the samurai movies of Akira Kurosawa among art-house audiences. *Seven Samurai* was released just the year before, in 1954; *Yojimbo* came out in 1961. These drew on the mystique of the samurai in the guise of the *ronin* or masterless swordsman, an exemplary outsider with an inherent appeal within the counterculture. Kurosawa's films mobilized this figure within an anti-militarist agenda that chimed well with the pacifism of the youth movements.

ENTER KUNG FU

These countercultural currents were surely not irrelevant to the growth in the martial arts in the 1960s, and amid this increased interest the Chinese martial arts were starting to appear, too, alongside judo and karate. Pioneers such as Gerda Geddes in the UK and Sophia Delza in the USA – both of whom were embedded in the world of contemporary dance – brought tai chi back from travels in China and started to teach it in the West. In the mid-1960s, another eminent tai chi teacher, Cheng Man-ch'ing, would make something of a mark on the American cultural landscape when he moved from Taiwan to New York. His school was soon filled with 'bearded, long-haired, scruffy hippies' (as one of Cheng's students would later describe himself and his peers) who looked to Cheng as a spiritual guide.[23] One of Cheng's students, Bataan Faigao, would go on to teach no less a luminary of the counterculture than Allen Ginsberg.[24] In San Francisco, by the end of the 1960s, a similar hippy clientele had also been drawn to study with Hong Kong born tai chi teacher Choy Kam Man, who even performed his art onstage at Grateful Dead concerts. At the same time, Chinatown martial arts teachers from a range of styles and backgrounds were starting to take in students from beyond the ethnic enclave.[25] Bruce Lee, in particular, set up a martial arts school in Oakland in 1964, and that year promoted the exotic art of 'gung fu' at Ed Parker's Long Beach International Karate Championships, showing off his one-inch punch and two-finger press-ups. By 1971 he was writing in *Black Belt* magazine to challenge American martial artists to 'liberate' themselves from 'classical karate'.[26]

This growth of kung fu's profile through the 1960s was primarily among the specialist realm of martial arts aficionados, and outside the purview of the culture at large. Lee in particular, however, was also starting to raise a more general awareness of the art. As noted earlier, in 1966 he landed a role as Kato, the sidekick of the eponymous superhero in the TV series *The Green Hornet*, and kung fu got its first sustained outing on American television. The exoticism of his high-kicking performance became a major aspect of the marketing campaign for the show, and Lee received more fan mail than the show's lead, Van Williams. This led to a steady increase in his role throughout the series.[27] As a '*sifu* to the stars', Lee's students included well-known and influential Hollywood figures who helped foster his ambitions as an actor.[28] Lee trained James Coburn, Blake Edwards and Roman Polanski and struck up close friendships with Steve McQueen and the influential screenwriter and producer Stirling Silliphant.[29] With the help of such students, and despite the institutional racism of the era, Lee worked as the fight coordinator for the spoof spy film *The Wrecking Crew* (1968) and landed a series of small roles in television and film. He played a karate instructor in an episode of the TV series *Ironside*, appeared as a villain in the Raymond Chandler neo-noir movie *Marlowe* (1969) and took on a repeated role as spiritual mentor and martial arts trainer to the blind TV detective Longstreet in the series of the same name from 1971. In the last he was given an extended opportunity to present his martial arts philosophy to a broad audience on-screen.

To the conditions outlined above for the emergence of the kung fu film in America – the slow dawning of public awareness of Chinese martial arts and the place that was set for them within the landscape of a growing counterculture – we should also add the changing nature of the Hollywood film industry, which by 1973 had fallen into something of a crisis. This was not, in fact, unconnected to the growth of the countercultures. While the American film industry in its classic era had addressed 'the family' and 'the American public', social change had undermined the apparent unity and transparency of these categories. A 'youth market' had started to grow, and the increasing fragmentation of audiences caused problems for the industry's business model, which had assumed a relatively homogeneous mass audience. The crisis was compounded by the loss of monopoly that the studios had encountered when a 1948 court ruling had separated film production businesses from their distribution arms, letting in competition from abroad. By the 1970s, the major studios had to compete not only with each other – and the rise of television as an alternative means of entertainment – but with European art-house cinema, cinema from the developing world, American independent productions as exemplified by the work of John Cassavetes and exploitation films such as those created by Russ Meyer or George Romero.[30] With their assumption of a uniform public, the mainstream Hollywood studios had been slow to register the concerns and experiences of new audiences and as a result 'largely failed to represent those struggles at the heart of political contestation'.[31] The industry crashed into a recession that hit its peak in the years from 1969 to 1971: for the year 1969 alone, it is estimated that industry losses amounted to some $200 million. A series of high-budget films flopped, bringing a number of the major players in the field close to bankruptcy.[32] By 1973, when the kung fu craze emerged, the studios were casting around desperately for new formulae or products.

Within this field the battle between conservative 'establishment' values and the permissive counterculture was beginning to be felt in the form of struggles over censorship. The year 1968 saw the replacement of the older – and more restrictive – production code and the introduction of a new set of ratings. Alongside the 'R' (restricted) category, these added the 'X' rating, allowing the release (albeit for an age-limited audience) of material that would not have previously been possible. As the kung fu craze approached, the X-rated movie had already become the cultural battleground for controversies regarding the legitimacy of sex and violence on-screen, and American cinema became increasingly bold in its depictions of these.[33]

These, then, were the American sociocultural and industry contexts into which the kung fu film would explode in the spring of 1973. However, laying the ground for the success of these movies were three particular cultural events. The first was the surprise success of Tom Laughlin's film *Billy Jack*, and the second was the emergence of the cult television series *Kung Fu*, starring David Carradine. Both of these inscribed the idea of the martial arts firmly within countercultural imagery and values. The third was Nixon's visit to China in 1972, which marked a new moment of détente between the two powers. This sparked enormous interest from the American public in a land that had for years been sealed to the Western gaze.

BILLY JACK AND *KUNG FU*

The film *Billy Jack*, directed and co-written by and starring Tom Laughlin, was released in 1971. It drew its eponymous hero from a biker-gang exploitation movie of 1967 in which Laughlin had starred, *Born Losers*. In this ultra-violent outing, Laughlin played a half-Native American Vietnam veteran who comes to the rescue of a young woman who is attacked and raped by a biker gang. It was largely from the proceeds of this film that Laughlin funded *Billy Jack*, a film with much grander cultural ambitions. In this, his hero – now also a master of the Korean art of hapkido – defends the pupils and teachers of a liberal 'freedom school' against the prejudice of the inhabitants of a neighbouring redneck town. Billy Jack's particular opponents are the bullying son of the town's kingpin and the corrupt authorities that rally round to protect him, just as they did with the villain in *Bad Day at Black Rock*. In what is probably the film's most memorable scene, after defending a pupil from racial abuse in an ice-cream parlour, Billy Jack calmly takes off his boots and walks barefoot into the town square to take on a dozen enemies, felling them with a blizzard of graceful flying and spinning kicks, filmed in slow motion.

Viewed today, the film looks heavy-handed in its espousal of racial equality, free love and hippy culture. It features extended set pieces calculated to showcase the music and theatre of the movement and long, didactic scenes in which characters mouth the values of the film's director. As a *Variety* review of the time put it, 'The message is rammed down the spectators' throats and is sorely in need of considerable editing to tell a straightforward story.'[34] The film was also controversial in its use of martial arts violence. As Howard Thompson put it in his review for the *New York Times*, 'For a picture that preaches pacifism, *Billy Jack* seems fascinated by violence, of which it is full.'[35] Nonetheless, perhaps precisely because of these qualities, which older critics saw as shortcomings, the film was an enormous success, especially among young

The eponymous Billy Jack takes on small-town thuggery with a barefooted hapkido kick.

audiences. These enjoyed its expression of a cultural position largely ignored by mainstream cinema through a heady combination of agitprop, the celebration of youth-cultural forms and the spectacle of violent revenge against establishment figures. Despite being shot on something of a shoestring, the film took $32.5 million at the box office, which was doubly an achievement since, without the backing of a distributor, it was released initially by Laughlin himself, hiring cinemas privately. It was only its miraculous profitability in these circumstances that convinced Warner Brothers to take it on.[36] The national success of such a moderately funded independent production made the struggling studios sit up and take notice.

More than *Billy Jack*, though, it was the television series *Kung Fu* that prepared the ground for the kung fu craze. Like *Billy Jack*, this featured as its protagonist a mixed-race outsider with martial arts skills, fighting racism and oppression. The story, however, was now set in in the American West in the gold-rush era. In it, David Carradine played Kwai Chang Caine, who is half American and half Chinese and is brought up as a Zen Buddhist monk in the Shaolin Temple, the mythical home of China's martial arts. Having killed the nobleman who murdered his master, Caine has fled at the start of the series to America, where he wanders the land in search of his family, finding himself in each episode in a situation where he must defend the weak and uphold justice.

Much of the mythology of the series would have been new to most of the American public at the time of launch, including the Shaolin Temple and its warrior monks, the very idea that there are Chinese martial arts, and even the name 'kung fu' itself. In fact, this show was decisive in making the term a household one. Despite his long-term interest in karate, it was even a relatively new term for Ed Spielman, the New York-born writer and producer who developed the idea for the show. Spielman has recounted his first encounter with the notion of kung fu within the burgeoning world of American martial arts in the 1960s:

> I discovered this thing sparring with a karate devotee who had – I think he was then third degree – a very good, very strong defence, and he mentioned parenthetically that his wife, his Chinese Hawaiian wife, could put his lights out with not a whole lot of trouble, and I said, 'how could she do that?' and he said 'kung fu', and I said 'huh??'[37]

The exotic term – with its promise of mysterious power in the hands even of the weak – sparked a fascination for Spielman, who started researching the Chinese martial arts and their mythology. Spielman's writing partner, Howard Friedlander, has talked of Spielman constantly 'filling his head' with stories of the martial arts. One day, Spielman brought Friedlander a story he was working on about the seventeenth-century samurai Miyamoto Musashi. In it, one character was a wandering Chinese monk from the Shaolin Temple. For Friedlander, it was this monk who 'resonated', and he imagined him transposed into American history to make the story a Western. From Spielman and Friedlander's collaboration on this idea, *Kung Fu* was born.[38]

Kung Fu, as its creators noted, and as critics of the time were not slow to point out, seemed a deeply unlikely proposition for American television, and its incomprehensible title was the least of its transgressions. The pacifism of its protagonist ('a gentle Shaolin priest from the Far East', as one newspaper advert for the show sold him) made an unlikely recipe for an action-adventure serial. Caine, without horse or gun (both phallic markers of rugged masculinity and power), made a striking contrast to the stereotypical cowboy.[39] He often walked barefoot like a child of the flower-power generation and wore hair that grew longer and longer as the series progressed. The 'spiritual' Caine was usually monosyllabic at best and often remained silent for long stretches of screen time. When he did speak, he did so in enigmatic aphorisms, delivered in a slow, calm, monotone whisper. Just as it was not going to be a series about gunfights, it would also not be carried by witty dialogue.

The series thus seemed to sit at odds with expectations for the Western genre and for its heroes. As Carradine himself put it in an interview:

> I *never* believed it'd really get on TV. I mean a *Chinese Western*, about a half-Chinese, half-American Buddhist monk who wanders the Gold Rush country but doesn't care about gold, and defends the oppressed but won't carry a gun, and won't even step on an ant because he values all life, and hardly ever *speaks*? No way![40]

Carradine's response already suggests that in rejecting televisual formulae, the show was setting itself at odds with an entire set of accepted 'mainstream' tastes and values that the television of the time set out to express and which encapsulated its image of its public. But this was also the key to what turned out to be the programme's success. As I have argued above, this public had been changing rapidly over the previous decades. Cecil Smith commented in the *Los Angeles Times* that 'the wonder of *Kung Fu* is not that it's a hit – its philosophies are very much of these times – but that it's on . . . *Kung Fu* is like nothing television has done before.' Jerry Buck of the Associated Press similarly praised the show's 'new hero, steeped in oriental philosophy, and eschewing such age-old trappings as machismo and retribution. Caine, the mystical hero of ABC's *Kung Fu*, seems to be striking a responsive chord among young people.'[41]

Kung Fu in this regard appealed to the new, countercultural tastes discussed above. The show's episodes interspersed its narrative of Caine in America with flashbacks to his childhood in the Shaolin monastery, giving audiences already fascinated with 'Eastern spirituality' and Zen Buddhism glimpses of an exotic world. This vision of the East enabled the articulation of a set of values that could be opposed to those of the Western world in which Caine found himself – and in which, by extension, the series' viewers lived. Caine's refusal of violence evoked the 'peace and love' of the hippies as set against the rugged individualism of American society. Moreover, for many at the time, the show was transparently legible as an allegory of the Vietnam War in which peaceable Asians are set against more powerful, aggressive and well-armed Americans.[42] Caine's pacifism, spirituality and passivity furthermore served as an antidote to the materialism and violence of modern life. As his lack of horse or gun signalled, his gentleness and refusal to dominate others (or even the natural world) opened an alternative mode of masculinity to the will to power that characterized not only the show's villains, but the heroes of most traditional Westerns.

Posited around these characteristics of its hero, *Kung Fu* seemed to do a much better job of producing a coherent solution to the paradox of integrating combat and conflict into a narrative about pacifism than *Billy Jack*. With Billy Jack's smouldering resentment replaced by Caine's calm solemnity, the narrative tension of *Kung Fu* usually revolved around the attempt to avoid and postpone a battle that is nonetheless forced on the hero and which the viewer, at least, knows is inevitable. In this way, the exotic sight of martial arts remained a central pleasure of the series, but kung fu could nonetheless be coded as a means to avoid the lethal force of the Western's usual recourse to firearms. In the combat scenes, slow motion was used not to emphasize and amplify violence but, paradoxically, to reduce and ameliorate it, making it dancelike and graceful while also reducing the sense of speed and impact. This strategy helped edge the fight scenes past the studio's censors, who remained wary of what could be shown within a prime-time viewing schedule. It also became a means to envision kung fu in similar terms to the 'gentle violence' fantasized back in 1961 by Gary Snyder as a means to his programme of Buddhist anarchism. Despite the existence of a fight at the climax of each episode, *Kung Fu* was praised by the critic Daniel Menaker as exemplary of a new wave of 'grown-up' television that he lauded for its refusal of sensationalist bloodletting.[43]

However, *Kung Fu*'s use of images of China and Chinese martial arts in its articulation of such values was not entirely without controversy concerning its racial politics, despite its reiterated message of tolerance and its unprecedented choice to place a (half-)Asian hero at the centre of its story of the American West. First off was the casting of Carradine as the show's lead, a white actor in 'yellowface' rather than a Chinese American actor, despite a campaign by the Asian American community against this.[44] The playwright and campaigner Frank Chin (probably the most vocal critic of the series at the time) argued that although Caine is a character who breaks the mould of the stereotype of subservient Chinese immigrants, this appears in the show to be symbolically linked to his measure of American blood: the other Chinese characters in the series are either passive, weak and incapable of action – mere victims – or, when they do act, they are corrupt, greedy or foolish. Chin also attacked the cod philosophy of the series, as we find it in the mouths of Caine or his teachers Master Po and Master Kan: 'The Chinese of *Kung Fu* obviously are not the kind of people who'll give anyone directions to the bathroom without a few plodding words so profound they hurt the head.'[45] Here, far from a progressive depiction, Caine and his teachers sit squarely in a line of Orientalizing images of wise

Orientalist imagery and 'plodding words so profound they hurt the head'? Caine (David Carradine) and Master Po (Keye Luke) in the Shaolin Temple in *Kung Fu*.

masters that stretch back to Charlie Chan and forwards to Yoda. For Chin, then, the show remained deeply problematic in its perpetuation of insidious stereotypes. Furthermore, as a left-wing Chinese American periodical of the time complained, nineteenth-century China was imagined as 'a place abstracted from time and space', a locus of Orientalist fantasy rather than political reality.[46]

The familiarity of these stereotypes lay in contrast to all that was new and radical about the show. With all the ways *Kung Fu* departed from tried-and-tested formulae, studios were hesitant to invest in Spielman and Friedlander's vision. Nonetheless, the two scriptwriters got backing from Fred Weintraub, an executive for Warner Brothers who had been put in charge of developing 'countercultural, youth-appealing projects'.[47] (Weintraub in fact had saved Warner from bankruptcy by commissioning the studio's hugely profitable documentary film of Woodstock.) Weintraub managed to bring Tom Kuhn, the head of Warner's television division, on board. Rather than a full series, Kuhn was given the green light to create a 90-minute entry into Warner's made-for-television 'movie of the week' spot. This was aired in the USA in February 1972, serendipitously coinciding with Nixon's visit to China. It received a positive enough response from both the press and ordinary viewers that in April Warner announced that new stories would be appearing at four-weekly intervals.[48] In November another announcement informed the public that the show 'heretofore seen irregularly' would be appearing in a weekly slot.[49] Thirteen regular episodes were aired from January to May 1973, and the show went on to run over three seasons and more than sixty episodes, finishing only when Carradine walked away from the series in 1975. At its height, *Kung Fu* rivalled the hugely popular *Mary Tyler Moore Show* in the ratings.[50] *Kung Fu* was also syndicated internationally, with episodes appearing in the UK, for example, from October 1972.[51]

This, then, was the situation into which the kung fu film emerged in the spring of 1973. The Asian martial arts had steadily grown as a presence in the American (and more broadly Western) cultural landscape. With the TV series starring David Carradine, China (a place of much topical interest) had been cemented in the public consciousness as a place associated with such arts, and the new idea of 'kung fu' had been introduced as a household term, denoting in the Western imagination a sort of Chinese karate, one even more loaded with ideas of spirituality and the miraculous than the more familiar and hence humdrum Japanese equivalent. As well as a growing practitioner base, these arts had increasingly found a place in the media, and the associations they evoked had been transformed by the tectonic shifts that Western societies were undergoing.

With the rise of the counterculture, representations of Asia were increasingly loaded with connotations of anti-imperial resistance, and these coloured the notion of 'kung fu' with a militant glamour. The youthful, anti-establishment and even anticolonial sentiment at the heart of Hong Kong's kung fu films (themselves to some degree influenced by the global wave of rebellion inspired by American youth culture) found a new set of contexts here within which to take on meaning. To these factors we have to add the changing circumstances of the struggling American cinema industry, with its increasingly fragmented markets, the crisis of its older models of production and the controversies around the representation of previously taboo sexual or violent material, facilitated by less stringent censorship.

3
THE CRAZE UNFOLDS

Hong Kong films had regularly had limited releases in specialist Chinatown cinemas for decades, but the first kung fu film to receive wide American release – and to ignite the craze for Hong Kong's martial arts cinema – was *King Boxer* (1972), retitled as *Five Fingers of Death* for the U.S. market. *Variety* records its entry into the charts in its issue of 21 March. The following week it reached the number one spot. So popular was it that nearly two months later, on 16 May, it was still at number three, and it wasn't until 13 June that it slipped out of the charts altogether.

Buoyed by their positive experiences producing the *Kung Fu* television series and distributing *Billy Jack*, it was Warner Brothers who had taken the plunge to take *King Boxer* on as a prospect. In addition to the sense of a potential market that these gave Warner's head, Ted Ashley, the investment required was modest, to say the least. This made the risk of investing in something untried and so far from American audiences' traditional tastes relatively low.[1] Furthermore, initial responses to Hong Kong martial arts films in experiments in European, Middle Eastern and Latin American markets had offered positive indications of their potential for success outside East and Southeast Asia.[2]

KING BOXER

King Boxer was one of the many films that had sought to draw on the success of Jimmy Wang Yu's *Chinese Boxer* by imitating its formula, placing training in unarmed 'kung fu' at its centre and pitting a heroic Chinese protagonist against sinister Japanese enemies. In this regard, it seemed well positioned to capture the fascination with 'Chinese boxing' that had been initiated by the *Kung Fu* television series. Unlike the new leading men of many Hong Kong action films by 1973, its star Lo Lieh, a veteran action hero of 1960s swordplay, was not a truly expert martial artist, but this was less important for an American audience whose yardstick was Carradine's performance. (It is reputed that Chuck Norris once quipped that Carradine was 'every bit as good a martial artist as I am an actor'.)[3] Rather, the film was perhaps selected because of the more than usually adept helmsmanship of Jeong Chang-hwa (aka Cheng Chang-ho), a veteran Korean director hired by Shaw Brothers.

It was surely, however, the film's representations of violence that made it stand out for American and European audiences. These must have looked like nothing they had seen on the screen before – not even the relatively tame fights shown in *Kung Fu* or the brief fisticuffs in *The Green Hornet*. At the most simple level, *King Boxer* included extended scenes of combat and numerous deaths and mutilations. But it was the novel aesthetic qualities of these sequences that marked the film out as striking and new for Western cinemagoers, rather than simply the matter of a quantity of violence. First off, there was the trademark gore of the Shaw Brothers 'new swordplay' style, with buckets of hyperreal red stage blood. In one rapidly notorious scene, as mentioned earlier, a character has his eyes plucked out by an opponent. In another scene, the hero is captured by his enemies and his hands are beaten until his torturers decide

he can be safely assumed to have been permanently crippled. In yet another, the hero strikes an opponent so hard that he flies backwards, leaving a crater in the brick wall behind him. Though in sheer numbers of deaths or injuries *King Boxer* was hardly more extreme than some of the more violent Hollywood offerings of this era, what marked it out was the graphic viscerality of Hong Kong action.

This action was also extraordinary in Hollywood terms for its level of stylization, turning combat into an exotic, otherworldly spectacle. As Verina Glaessner put it, writing in 1974, the kung fu film depended on 'elongated fight sequences that opened up a whole

Larger-than-life combat in *King Boxer*: Lo Lieh traps an opponent's sword between his palms and shatters it with his bare hands.

new perspective on the term "balletic violence" . . . The screen was alive with an ornate choreography.'[4] Even in the first action sequence of *King Boxer*, an elderly kung fu master, surrounded by a gang of thugs, leaps into the air to kick two of them simultaneously. Figures soar above head height with the aid of wires and trampolines, often exchanging blows in mid-flight. Opponents hold elegant – and at the time unimaginably exotic – kung fu postures before bursting into rhythmically intense action. This is to the accompaniment, of course, of the clanging and thudding soundtrack that had become conventional in Hong Kong films by this time. Having learned the mystical 'iron palm' technique, the hero's hands glow red when he fills them with *qi* (life energy) in preparation to strike a deadly blow. In one scene he traps an opponent's sword between his two palms and then shatters it with a bare-handed strike. Everything, in this regard, is larger than life in the film's depiction of combat.

This was of a piece with the Shaw Brothers' broader aesthetic of theatrical artifice and quite at odds with the naturalism that characterized business as usual in 1970s Hollywood. In many ways the kung fu film's depictions of heavily stylized violence would not have been possible within the framework of such a naturalism and would have jarred if set within the familiar world that viewers knew from their daily lives. The setting of the films in an imaginary Orient, far off and perhaps long ago, along with the artificiality of the Shaw cinematic style, signalled for viewers an entry into something like a magical fairyland where the usual rules of cinematic reality might be suspended. Of course, making China such a fairyland is problematic in its projection of these fantasies onto real-world people, and this is something I will return to in later chapters. For now, I shall note that it was only through this Orientalizing fantasy that images of the kung fu film could enter into Western cinematic culture and exert the striking impact that they did, stepping beyond the more measured and restrained language of Hollywood's own products.

In spite of the enormous box-office success of *King Boxer*, reviews were mixed. A write-up in *Variety* at the end of its first week in the charts was surprisingly positive, given the insistent hostility critics would go on to level at the genre more broadly. The reviewer was impressed by the action sequences. They presciently saw it as 'glossed with all the explosive trappings that make for a hit in its intended market' and praised it as 'exquisitely filmed and packed with colorful production values'. Furthermore, 'Direction by Cheng Chang Ho is powerful and direct and he gets top performances from cast.'[5] When it had been released in the UK at the end of the previous year (to some box-office success, though it seems not on the scale of its U.S. response), John Gillett in *Monthly Film Review* had also responded with enthusiasm. Gillett uneasily noted 'a certain delight in close-up violence' and commented on the repeated device of the trampoline leap, which he felt was 'somewhat tedious'. Overall, though,

> The sheer panache of the staging and apparent enjoyment of the participants keep the narrative moving swiftly . . . The present film's portrait of Chinese boxing – which apparently takes in everything from kicks and slaps to eye-gouging – is also highly intriguing, and is accompanied by a veritable symphony of thumps and thwacks on the soundtrack.[6]

Gillett's attention to the soundtrack, the (obviously still new) idea of kung fu and the novelty, extremity and unrealism of the fight sequences seems to have anticipated much of the focus of the critical response to the genre as it developed.

Not all writers, however, were as sanguine about these things. The back page of the issue of *Monthly Film Review* in which Gillett's response appeared also listed three reviews of *King Boxer* in national UK newspapers: each had offered the film a single star out of four.[7] Similarly, Gene Siskel of the *Chicago Tribune*, though acknowledging the excitement of the fight sequences, condemned the film as 'a shoddy, poorly dubbed melodrama stuffed with insane dialog'.[8] Only slightly more generous than his British counterparts, he offered it two stars. Roger Greenspun of the *New York Times* opined, 'I don't know much about karate, but I know what I like. And the karate in *Five Fingers of Death*, for all its slow-motion high leaps, its grunts, its whooshing fists, has the look of the bottom of the barrel. It is all too extravagant, too gratuitously wild.'[9]

THE CRAZE UNFOLDS

Despite the critics' reservations, *Five Fingers of Death* was a hit with the public. It was soon joined in the charts by other kung fu films, transforming the success of a single movie into a broader cultural phenomenon. On *Variety*'s 16 May chart, it was displaced from its top spot to third place by two new entries from Hong Kong. Immediately above it at number two, and climbing to the top spot the following week, was *Deep Thrust/Lady Whirlwind* (1972). This surprised American audiences by taking as its lead performer a female martial artist, Angela Mao Ying, who rapidly became one of the foremost stars of the kung fu craze.[10] At number one, however, was Bruce Lee's debut martial arts picture, *The Big Boss*, which had caused such a stir in Hong Kong, retitled now as *Fists of Fury* for U.S. release. This wasn't in fact Lee's first film release in the USA. In November the previous year, the quite different film originally titled *Fist of Fury* in Hong Kong (note the singular rather than plural 'fist') had been renamed *The Chinese Connection* in the United States and given limited distribution, but, without the prior stir that *Five Fingers of Death* had caused, it had performed only modestly. Initially, then, its dismissal by U.S. critics would have seemed a reasonable assessment: according to *Variety*, it was a 'naive Hong Kong-made meller [melodrama], of little U.S. commercial potential' and no more than a 'novelty act'. Its male lead had an 'aggressive boyish charm' but an appeal limited to 'U.S. femmes'.[11] When *The Chinese Connection* was re-released on 13 June with the kung fu craze already under way, the historical irony in these judgements was rapidly revealed. It soared to number one the following week, remained in the top fifteen until the end of August and was even still lingering in the charts at the start of October.[12]

In spite of the commercial success of both *The Chinese Connection* and *Fists of Fury*, and their contribution to the enthusiasm for kung fu as a genre, Lee himself was not yet the iconic superstar we know him as today and which he already was in Hong Kong. Until the release of *Enter the Dragon* later that summer, he appeared to the American public as one of many similar performers. A measure of how different Lee's fame still was in his Asian and American markets at this stage is given by Matthew Polly in his biography of the actor. This contrasts Lee's two funerals in Hong Kong and the USA when he died in July 1973. Lee's funeral in Hong Kong drew over 15,000 mourners, and when his hearse departed the service, the three hundred policemen attempting to hold back the frantic crowds had to call in reinforcements. At his service and burial in Seattle a few days later, aside from family, friends and students, there were 'fewer than two dozen fans and only a couple of reporters' in attendance. So unsure was the American press and its public of the difference between kung fu stars that when the *Los Angeles Times* published an obituary it made what Polly calls a 'shameful they-all-look-alike mistake', erroneously describing Lee as the star of *Five Fingers of Death*.[13]

Enter the Dragon would soon change that. However, before then a number of other Hong Kong films had already made their impact on the U.S. charts. On 20 June, *Deep Thrust*, *The Chinese Connection* and *Fists of Fury* were joined in the top fifty by two more martial arts actioners.[14] *Duel of the Iron Fist*/*The Duel* was a 1971 Shaw Brothers revenge story directed by Chang Cheh and starring his two favoured stars of the day, Ti Lung and David Chiang. Set in an early twentieth-century gangster milieu, it features blood-drenched fights with knives and hatchets. *Kung Fu, the Invisible Fist*/*The Good and the*

Bad (1972) was an independent (and somewhat cheaply made) production, mixing a similar underworld setting with the genre's almost obligatory anti-Japanese sentiment. The following week, Wang Yu's groundbreaking *Chinese Boxer* was released under the title *Hammer of God*, shooting straight to number one. In the opening weeks of August, two more Hong Kong films followed it into the charts: *Shanghai Killers/The Chase* (1971), one of Golden Harvest's pre-Bruce Lee swordplay films, and *Fearless Fighters/A Real Man* (1971), a Hong Kong–Taiwan co-production whose poster promised an audience they would 'see ten devil weapons used by kung fu masters'. These included the Dragon Razor, the Solar Ray of Death, the Soul Piercer and the Devil Ripper.

ENTER THE DRAGON

Enter the Dragon was Hollywood's first attempt to actually produce a kung fu film rather than merely redistribute Hong Kong fare. When it was finally released, the kung fu craze at the box office had been going on for some four months, and several Hong Kong films had made a sizeable impact on the American charts. However, *Enter the Dragon* itself had been in production for some time, and shooting had already started when *Five Fingers of Death* arrived on American screens. Unsurprisingly, it was Warner Brothers, again, who were behind this. Although the studio had decided against an Asian actor for *Kung Fu*, the producer Fred Weintraub had been enormously impressed by Bruce Lee's auditions for this and had continued to push the studio to find a vehicle for him.[15] When Weintraub saw the box-office figures for *The Big Boss* on its Asian release he realized that Lee's stardom there was such that pre-selling regional rights might allow Warner to finance a film and had a treatment for what would become *Enter the Dragon* drawn up. He asked his studio for half a million dollars for the project and received a promise for half of that, ultimately striking a deal with Raymond Chow of Golden Harvest for the remainder.[16]

The resulting Hong Kong–Hollywood co-production drew on expertise both in front and behind the camera from both industries. The director (Robert Clouse) and scriptwriter (Michael Allin) were American, for example, but Clouse worked with three Hong Kong assistant directors (Chaplin Chang, Chih Yao-chang and Tu Wen). Lee starred alongside two American actors, John Saxon (playing Roper) and Jim Kelly (playing Williams): Warner still clearly did not have faith that the American public would respond to a film carried entirely by a Chinese male lead. With Saxon and Kelly, they sought to maximize the film's appeal by offering a range of potential figures for identification. While Saxon, a white actor, was the most established name, Kelly's inclusion was calculated to appeal to Black audiences and sought to capitalize on the blaxploitation craze of the previous years.[17] Quite how hard Lee had to work to ensure that he was indeed the foremost of these stars is indicated by the fact that Roper is the only one of the three characters offered an arc of character development in the script. Lee's characters in his earlier films navigated psychological as well as physical conflict; in *Enter the Dragon*, the internal dimension of this has largely melted away and Lee remains at the end of the picture the same perfect martial artist he is at the start.[18] It is only by the sheer charisma of his performance that Lee ensures he carries the film's central focus.

Due to the increased control of Hollywood, the film departs markedly from the formula of Hong Kong kung fu films with their rebellious and often explicitly anticolonial narratives. Lee's character in the film is perhaps the clearest indication of this. As the Hawaiian activist and political science academic M. T. Kato has argued, Lee's huge popularity in Hong Kong was to a large degree based on his association with the ethno-nationalist plots of his films and the working-class underdog characters he played in them. In *Enter the Dragon*, however, Lee is cast as an agent co-opted by a British secret-service organization in a Bond-type plot, making him ultimately a 'lackey' of imperialist masters – just the kind of character otherwise vilified as a traitorous villain in typical kung fu films.[19] This may well go some way to explaining why *Enter the Dragon* – although it was the runaway success of the American kung fu craze – performed much worse than Lee's earlier films in Hong Kong, despite the wave of emotion that had been unleashed by the star's recent death.[20] The film's villain, Han, also reverts to the 'yellow-peril' stereotype established by Fu Manchu or typified by Dr No in the Bond films. For Kato, this pairing of hero and villain in Hollywood's rather than Hong Kong's terms sets up the film as an 'imperialist narrative' projected by Warner Brothers.[21]

But as Kato also goes on to explore at length in his chapters on *Enter the Dragon*, which examine its production in detail, the film is much more complicated and contradictory than this. The term 'collaboration', in fact, fails to capture the fraught process through which it was created, and the final movie is best considered as a compromise between clashing viewpoints, especially with regard to the battles between Lee and the director and scriptwriter over their visions for the film, which by all accounts were heated, to say the least.[22] As well as balancing the input of cast and crew from Hong Kong and America, it was, moreover, produced through the pressures of two very different markets with very different expectations. It ultimately offers a complex double optic on its world, viewing it at once from America and Hong Kong.

Some scenes certainly reiterate an anticolonial and antiracist perspective viewed from the position of the underdog, as with Lee's previous films. For example, in an early scene, a white martial artist, Parsons, is bullying some of the Chinese workers on the boat taking the fighters to Han's island for the film's tournament. Lee steps in, tantalizing Parsons with the promise to show him the style of 'fighting without fighting' and tricking him into getting onto a small dinghy, ostensibly for a contest. Then, instead of joining him, Lee lets the boat's rope out, stranding him. He hands the line over to the workers whom Parsons was tormenting, placing his fate in their hands. Lee has in effect fulfilled his promise of showing Parsons the art of 'fighting without fighting' – from which this book draws its title. As imagined in *Enter the Dragon*, this phrase might be taken as emblematic of kung fu as a means that the poor and weak have of overcoming the strong not through a direct contest of strength but through skill and guile. It is clearly imagined here as a means of justice and resistance, and a way of transforming the relationship between the 'East' and the 'West'.

Similarly, Han as an opium dealer can be placed within a longer thematic of kung fu films where the drugs trade became a shorthand for China as the 'sick man of Asia'. His drug dealing resonates with the history of China's subjugation to the 'unequal treaties' of the Opium Wars in which it was forced to accept the British import of narcotics. When Lee and his associates free the seemingly drug-addled and passive men in Han's prison, and they rise against his hired thugs in the film's climactic battle, we can understand him as an archetypal liberator of the enslaved and oppressed, and the film seems to imagine these slumbering masses finally rebelling against their subjugation.

This interpretation of the film is amplified by the presence of Williams, an African American martial artist. Williams is introduced to the audience as involved in a Black Power karate dojo and then depicted defending himself from assault by racist white policemen. Towards the start of the film, as Williams and Roper are rowed through Hong Kong's Aberdeen Harbour, the camera lingers on the poverty of the island's slums. Williams's line responding to the panorama speaks for the film as containing a message of global solidarity for the world's poor: 'Ghettos are the same all over the world. They stink!' For Kato, the appearance in a Hollywood film of the actuality of this scene of Hong Kong life amounts to 'the everyday reality of the oppressed seeping through Hollywood's fantastic aesthetic grid'. He suggests that its manifestation was necessitated by the 'third world' budget and conditions of the film's production and the director's need to conjure visual richness from what was to hand.[23] It must, however, have presented a welcome message not only to Black American audiences, but to those from Hong Kong and the global south, and to the fans from the counterculture of *Billy Jack* and *Kung Fu*.

Nonetheless, the perspective of this very scene can be construed differently, too. The camera's lingering, documentary-like attention on the Hong Kong poor also comes close to an ethnographic viewpoint, offering knowledge of a fascinating foreign world to a Western audience. It is through the eyes of the story's American characters that we are brought into this scene, and this has been

The tourist gaze? Roper is rowed through Hong Kong's Aberdeen Harbour in an early scene from *Enter the Dragon*, amid colourful images of exotic poverty.

set up in the images that accompany the film's titles. These depict Williams and Roper disembarking from an aeroplane at the island's airport and follow them through the exotic streets of Hong Kong towards the harbour. We are offered the voyeuristic perspective of, as Kato puts it, a 'tourist gaze', lingering on the alien and colourful. This gaze is further addressed in a later scene, which occurs once the martial artists have arrived at Han's island. There, a feast is laid on for them, and the viewer is treated to a veritable barrage of Orientalist images: as well as unfamiliar, inedible food, there are lion dancers, jugglers, sumo wrestlers and dancing and serving women in exotic dress (intimating, perhaps, the image of the harem). The set, moreover, is peppered with caged birds, a sight that had fascinated Clouse in his own navigation of the Hong Kong streets.[24]

These more familiar Orientalist images and perspectives may well go some way to accounting for the success of the film in the USA. In addition, its narrative structure and style of direction – overseen in both cases by American crew – were more closely attuned to domestic tastes and expectations than the previously released Hong Kong movies. The film was also shot directly in English, rather than being released with the dubbing that so many critics derided in reviews of the time. Overall, the final $850,000 budget, though meagre in Hollywood's terms, was of an entirely different order from most Hong Kong productions and offered to an American audience the production values much closer to those they were used to.[25] Finally, with Warner not only distributing but producing the film, their added investment gave them all the more motive to promote it and ensure its success.[26]

Whatever the balance of these factors, the film was a resounding hit. John Saxon has recounted how, riding in a limousine to the Los Angeles premiere of *Enter the Dragon*, his progress was slowed by 'lines of people, and the lines didn't end'. When he asked his driver what the big event was, he was surprised to hear that he was looking at the crowds for his own film.[27] The anecdote suggests not only the level of sheer enthusiasm *Enter the Dragon* inspired but how unexpected this was in terms even of the most successful Hong Kong imports to this date. The fact that it was a surprise in this way even to those involved in its production underscores just how out of the blue this degree of success was. Opening that week on 22 August in a limited number of venues, *Enter the Dragon* entered the charts at number seventeen. The following week, with a full nationwide release, it shot to number one. It was still in the top ten over two months later on 24 October, and it still lingered in the top twenty on 7 November.[28] By the end of 1973, it had grossed $90 million worldwide.[29] This was despite the fact that it was not released in many European countries until the following year.[30] As Matthew Polly has put it, describing the development of the kung fu craze, 'While the TV series *Kung Fu* and Shaw Brothers' *Five Fingers of Death* . . . cracked open the door, it was Lee's performance in *Enter the Dragon* that blew it off its hinges.'[31]

Along with the film, an avalanche of products cashing in on Lee's sudden posthumous superstardom appeared. Bruce Lee fan magazines were soon joined on the shelf by memorial albums and hastily penned biographies. In a 1975 article on this 'posthumous industry', the film critic Kenneth Turan cites as evidence of the sheer adulation Lee rapidly inspired a letter to *Black Belt* magazine. In this, the writer professes, 'I loved Bruce Lee as one of my family and would gladly have taken his place in death.'[32] Lee's widow, Linda, made a deal to license his image in almost every imaginable medium, including 'posters, T-shirts, beach towels, stationery, trophies, lamps, men's cosmetics, karate garments, dishware, glassware, jewelry, games, and toys'.[33] Meditating on not only the outpouring of Bruce Lee fandom but the wave of merchandise it elicited, Turan concludes that 'not since James Dean died in the crash of his silver-grey Porsche . . . has any Hollywood star received this kind of send-off to Valhalla.'[34] As Fred Weintraub put it in interview, before 1973, 'every town in America had a church and a beauty parlor. After *Enter the Dragon*, there was a church, a beauty parlor, and a karate studio with a picture of Bruce Lee.'[35]

As noted in this book's introduction, the sheer fact of Lee's superstardom as a Chinese male lead – in America and across the globe – was a fundamentally unprecedented event. The door blown off its hinges by his performance in *Enter the Dragon* was not just that of the kung fu craze. Rather, Lee's stardom changed the image of Asian masculinity and even opened a space for a more pluralistic culture. Lee's success transgressed and exploded Hollywood's expectations, norms and ways of working. He forms an important chapter in the longer narrative of the rupturing of hierarchies of race and ethnicity that over the last half-century have turned the global order of cultural production and consumption – once modelled on a colonial world view – inside out.

Alongside *Enter the Dragon*, a number of other films hit the charts that autumn, marking a continued enthusiasm for the broader genre, most notably the two Angela Mao vehicles *Hapkido/Lady Kung Fu* (1972) and *The Opium Trail/Deadly China Doll* (1973). These were joined by *The Chase/Shanghai Killers* (1971), *Fist to Fist/Fists of the Double K* (1973), *The Water Margin/Seven Blows of the Dragon* (1972), *Survival of the Dragon/The Thunder Kick* (1973) and *The Avenger/Queen Boxer* (1972).[36] But as the year came to a close, fewer and fewer Hong Kong films were visible in the charts. February 1974 saw the first week without a single martial arts picture to be seen in the top fifty. Bruce Lee's *The Way of the Dragon*, released in the summer, made a million dollars during its first five days in New York alone, attesting to the continued pull of his stardom. However, this was very much an isolated case.[37]

Nonetheless, it was not the end of kung fu's presence in the broader cultural landscape. As its mainstream audience melted away, the kung fu film increasingly became a more specialist or subcultural interest, moving to 'inner city theatres, second-run houses, small-town double bills, and drive-ins'.[38] In New York, for example, the kung fu movie remained, throughout the 1970s, a permanent fixture of the seedy landscape of the grindhouse screens of 42nd Street and as many as thirty different 'chopsocky' films might be playing in these cinemas at one time.[39] Already by 1970, there were some nine hundred screens across the U.S. specializing in 'exploitation' cinema, and kung fu became a core part of the programmes offered at such venues.[40] However, once films were made cheaply for distribution on these circuits, and with profit ensured on the scale of these limited releases, quality control plummeted.

Nonetheless, if for cinema scholar David Desser the 'death knell' of kung fu had sounded by the end of 1973,[41] this is only because he is viewing the phenomenon purely in terms of the film charts. In contrast, as a broader cultural phenomenon, the fascination with kung fu was clearly an ongoing one for some time after. Indeed, as Paul Bowman notes with regard to Britain, '1974 was arguably a bigger year for the consumption of martial arts texts . . . than 1973.'[42]

For example, Carl Douglas's hit single 'Kung Fu Fighting' was released only in August 1974. The fad for kung fu in comics was similarly belated with regard to cinema. It was just as the cinematic boom was receding, in December 1973, that Marvel released *Hands of Shang-Chi: Master of Kung Fu*, which ran successfully for ten years. Marvel followed this up in April 1974 with *Deadly Hands of Kung Fu*, a publication that ran over 33 issues until 1977. It included comic-book stories, film reviews, interviews with martial arts teachers and movie stars and even instructional material on martial arts. In May 1974, the character Iron Fist also made his debut in *Marvel*

Carl Douglas performing his hit song ‘Kung Fu Fighting’ in 1974.

Premiere and appeared in stories in a range of the company's comic books over the next decade. Following several steps behind box-office statistics, there also remained an outpouring over months and even years of martial arts novels, instruction systems, magazines, posters and assorted merchandise. These all outlived the economic viability of kung fu as a broadly distributed cinematic genre with mass appeal. Even though film sales had slumped, the kung fu craze had introduced a vocabulary of words, ideas and images that would, as we shall see, have a lasting impact. A marker of how far their image had become ubiquitous, and in fact synonymous with 'Chinese culture' in the USA, is given by the fact that in June 1974 when the Chinese government sent a goodwill cultural mission to the USA to follow up on Nixon's visit to Beijing, this took the form of a tour not by a symphony orchestra or theatre troupe but by the national *wushu* team. This culminated in a performance for the president on the White House lawn that included the eleven-year-old Jet Li.[43] That same month, a martial arts tournament and demonstration in New York sought to fill the 20,000-seat Madison Square Garden arena, looking forward to the giant success of mixed martial arts events in the 1990s after the launch of the Ultimate Fighting Championship.[44]

THE CRITICAL RESPONSE: KUNG FU AND MORAL PANIC

The massive interest in kung fu films was all the more striking in the face of near-universal hostility from the critical establishment. Analysing the reception of kung fu in the trade press, Desser writes of an 'inability, which seems like a genuine unwillingness, to see the appeal of Hong Kong films'.[45] *Variety* magazine, in the very first weeks of the kung fu craze, discussed the films as a 'rash' of imports, as if their appearance were symptomatic of a sickness of the American film industry, or of society itself.[46] The *New York*

Times critic Vincent Canby complained that such movies 'make the worst Italian Westerns look like the most solemn and notable achievements of the early Soviet Cinema'. Bemoaning the sheer level of gore in them and their lack of dramatic 'coherence', he cuttingly concluded that 'kung fu movies are to cinema what roller derbies are to theater.'[47] Howard Thompson, reviewing *Enter the Dragon* in the same paper later that year, complained that the 'bone crunchers from China' were 'shoddy productions'. In contrast he singles out the technical achievements of the Hollywood version: he praises the 'pounding pulse of Clouse's direction' and its 'crisp dialog', judging the film 'expertly made and well-meshed; it moves like lightning and brims with color'. He nonetheless complains,

> It is also the most savagely murderous and numbing hand-hacker . . . you will ever see anywhere . . . Arms, legs and necks snap like kindling, and the predominantly young audience cramming Leow's State 2 yesterday applauded, laughed and ate it up. Anyone over 30 will have plenty to think about.[48]

Another review, this time of the Angela Mao vehicle *Deadly China Doll*, attacks the film as 'distinguishable from its predecessors principally by means of its title' and makes a judgement that 'the dialogue and most of the performances are as deadly as the principals.'[49]

Such criticism wasn't entirely universal. The kung fu phenomenon gained a number of supporters, too. Prominent among these was Tony Rayns, who, among several colleagues at Britain's *Monthly Film Review*, was generally upbeat about the energy and the forceful expression of the best kung fu films, developing an appreciation of different directorial visions.[50] Verina Glaessner of London's *Time Out* also wrote sympathetically about Hong Kong movies, going on to produce the 1974 book *Kung Fu: Cinema of Vengeance*, which offered fans a knowledgeable and enthusiastic account of the genre, introducing key films, stars and directors, and placing these in the context of the Hong Kong industry.

Nonetheless, negative responses dominated the press of the day. Critics condemned the kung fu film in the first place as marking a degradation of formal and aesthetic quality in cinema. Within this perspective, the films were characterized by substandard acting, poor dialogue, laughable dubbing, misshapen plots and overblown action scenes that departed from the bounds of the proper suspension of disbelief. These characteristics marked them as valueless cultural trash, fit only for the credulous and those with an uncritical appetite for sensationalist spectacle. In many ways, this echoed the responses of Chinese critics to the first martial arts films in the 1920s, as discussed earlier. In 1970s America, this collapse of aesthetic standards (and of the audience's capacity to make properly dispassionate aesthetic responses) was also viewed as a moral collapse in the films and their viewers alike. It was seen as symptomatic of a growing hunger for the pornography of violence, and consequently kung fu not only was a 'craze' or a fashion but rapidly became a moral panic, too.

Debates around the violence of kung fu took part within the larger disagreements around censorship or permissiveness that had grown from the broader conflicts between liberal and conservative visions of American culture. These had gravitated to both the art house and the grindhouse extremes of the cinema of the time. Stanley Kubrick's *A Clockwork Orange* had, for example, been withdrawn from British screens in 1972 after claims about copycat crimes. The same year, Francis Ford Coppola's *The Godfather* had been a blockbuster hit despite – or perhaps because of – the controversies about its depictions of cinematic violence. Jerry Gerard's *Deep Throat* shocked conservative America by bringing pornography into the mainstream, making its way to the top of the charts in the face of a ban in many parts of the country. The kung fu film – featuring a level of stylized brutality that situated it a long way from the 'gentle violence' of Gary Snyder's Buddhist anarchism – drew on these new tastes for transgressive cinema but also pitched itself into the existing controversies initiated by the counterculture to which Snyder belonged. Where, as we have seen, the *Kung Fu* television series could still be hailed in May 1973 for its pacifist qualities as 'grown-up' television, by April 1974 the kung fu movie genre was being criticized in an article by Marya Mannes as 'part of a screen violence which absolves the audience from real horror by being sanitized'. Mannes, furthermore – like many contemporaries – saw this as having dangerous real-world consequences. She proposed that it was 'unarguable that there is a clear connection between the daily diet of violence on the screen and the tidal wave of senseless killing on our streets'.[51]

These anxieties soon spilled beyond the culture pages. After a riot in Queens in February 1974, even the generally liberal *New York Times* found itself blaming kung fu and blaxploitation films in the nearby Cambria Theater for getting local youths 'hopped up'.[52] When a front-page article from the same paper in November that year sought to analyse the reasons for a rise in youth crime in the city, it turned, again, to 'the influence of movies and television with their violence and their two-fisted hero-policemen and Kung Fu fighters'.[53]

These fears were about not only the films themselves, but their audiences. These were envisioned by – generally older and more middle-class – journalists as young, lower-class, male and often marked by ethnic and racial difference. These anxieties are visible in some of the earliest scholarly responses to the kung fu phenomenon. A pioneering essay from 1974 by Stuart Kaminsky, for example, interprets the kung fu film as a 'mythic' expression of the experiences and (supposed) values of the 'ghetto kid'. For Kaminsky these films eschew the 'bourgeois' concerns with pacifism and justice still to be found in the Carradine television series. Instead, he argues, they offer fantasies of 'the satisfaction of revenge', the commanding of 'respect' and a 'superhuman agility' through which one might destroy one's enemies. From this standpoint, kung fu films amount to an asocial and amoral embrace of violence ('graceful, dirty fighting') by those whose lives are marked by the experience of a dog-eat-dog world where there is no sense of a larger benign cosmic or civic order to which one might appeal.[54] Kaminsky certainly recognizes something significant in the difference between the fantasies of violence involved in the earlier television series and the altogether more bloody films that followed, and in the shift in the audiences that these addressed. However, his suggestion that the kung fu film is not concerned with morality or with the social seems to bespeak at the least a lack of familiarity with the Hong Kong context from which the films emerged and the politics they implied within this. It also, I would argue, stems from a set of prejudices about the urban poor that were clearly widespread at the time. That these anxieties were also fuelled by the racial stereotypes of the era is evidenced in Kaminsky's comment, for example, that 'the number of black youths who practice pseudo-Kung Fu is strikingly evident on urban streetcorners'.[55] Though to an extent written with a degree of sympathy, Kaminsky's essay evokes an image of a dangerously lawless, amoral, antisocial and violent underclass of racial others.

It wasn't just the critics who came up with this kind of picture of the kung fu audience. It was, as Desser has observed, something ingrained into the very marketing and distribution of the films that made the phenomenon. The previous years had seen the surprise success of the blaxploitation genre, which had given the exploitation-movie formula of sex and violence an ethnic twist. *Sweet Sweetback's*

Martial arts within the blaxploitation genre: Youngblood Priest (Ron O'Neal) takes a karate lesson in *Super Fly*.

Badasssss Song (1971) and *Shaft* (1971) were followed by the runaway success that was *Super Fly* (1972), another Warner Brothers release. In *Super Fly*, the Asian martial arts were given a prominent place, with one scene showing its hero taking a karate lesson and another showing him using this art to defend himself. It was through this lens that Warners seem to have imagined the kung fu film as a product, and they marketed it accordingly. The decision to include Jim Kelly as one of the trio of stars for *Enter the Dragon* is symptomatic of this. Kelly had recently made his movie debut in another blaxploitation film, *Melinda* (1972), where he played the protagonist's karate instructor. Treating the kung fu film on the blaxploitation model, Warner 'double-billed many of its martial arts offerings after 1973 with blaxploitation films (including re-releases), and advertised its product along familiar generic and exploitation lines. Other distributors followed suit.'[56] For Desser, though, the success of the films among a Black youth audience was a contributing factor not only to the genre's success but to its 'precipitous decline'.[57] Its association with exploitation cinema and with young, Black inner-city audiences may well have been a reason for journalists' 'almost immediate critical dismissal' of the genre and their unwillingness to see aesthetic value in it.[58] It may well have been the relative distance from these American debates that offered British critics a more positive perspective on the genre, in addition to the earlier appearance of kung fu films there, allowing critics' attitudes to develop further before the existence of a 'craze' through which to interpret them.

CAMP PLEASURES AND IRONIC CONSUMPTION

The responses – both positive and negative – of mainstream audiences, too, may well have been marked profoundly by these associations. Even the popularity of the films at their height seemed to involve a certain dismissal of their value. One of *Variety*'s first reviews discussing the genre, for example, noted that as well as being due to hardcore action fans ('black and white'), the runaway success of *King Boxer* was due to its crossover appeal to 'camp followers who find the dubbing and excessive mayhem food for giggles'.[59] This ironic appeal is also clearly visible among the pleasures described by the genre's more sanguine critics: Derek Malcolm, for example, in a review of the Shaw Brothers/Hammer co-production *Legend of the Seven Golden Vampires*, described the film as 'good fun for total idiots' but added the caveat, 'I can say that in full freedom having rather enjoyed it myself.'[60] Carl Douglas's disco hit 'Kung Fu Fighting' seems very much on the register of lighthearted parody, with its leitmotif Orientalist riff, its over-the-top 'Huh!'s and 'Ha!'s and its lyrical play on cliché. This was further reflected in Douglas's performance and costume. If kung fu was dangerous and violent, it was also approached as a little bit ridiculous, and fun only because of that.

It seems to me that this ironic consumption involves a complex and ambivalent relationship to two groups. The first is the original Hong Kong producers and consumers of the kung fu film abroad and the second is the Black and otherwise marginal underclasses to whom the kung fu film was so strongly marketed at home. On the one hand, kung fu films gave mainstream, white audiences a chance to step for a moment into other positions and identify with those whom the American mainstream had largely excluded up to this point. To this extent they remained a part of the longer project of the 1960s counterculture. It entailed an opening and pluralization of identity, wresting the white, male subject from the centre of his universe. However, the ironic mode of this identification also marked a limit to this. It recuperated the loss of a central position through forms of distance, superiority and mastery over otherness.

The concept of 'camp' can be of help in analysing this. As described famously by Susan Sontag, what defines camp (as much as it can be defined) is its deliberate overvaluation of the object of enjoyment.[61] In Sontag's account, camp strategies had an emancipatory function as they emerged in particular from the subculture of sexual minorities. Ironic consumption becomes a means of appropriating the images of mainstream culture and making them signify anew, stripped of what may originally be oppressive meanings. But as 'camp' became a mainstream taste in the 1960s, these politics reversed: 'camp' enjoyment often involved the appropriation by an intellectual elite of the popular culture of those beneath them: camp reasserted a form of cultural superiority, taking ironically that which one's naive cultural inferiors take seriously.[62] In this regard the 'deliberate overvaluation' of the kung fu film is a twentieth-century version, if you like, of a Victorian aristocrat 'slumming it' at a music hall or dive bar to experience the frisson of 'passing' among the dangerous underclasses. In 1973, such a fantasy took as its reference points first the dangerous developing-world East Asian who in the wake of Mao and the Vietnam War threatened the superiority of the Western subject with spectacular forms of violent anticolonial revolt, and second the races and classes from the 'ghettos' at home, who threatened riots, violent criminality and social disorder.

The kung fu film and the spectacle of the East Asian martial arts, then, remained ambivalent cultural phenomena. In many ways, it would seem that the power of the genre – its ability to produce on the one hand fanatical enthusiasm or a desire for emulation and on the other moral panic – was due to the way it provided an aesthetic form that resonated with and gave expression to a series of vivid contradictions or tensions at the heart of life, identity and society in the early 1970s. Because of this, 'kung fu' had rapidly become much more than cinema: it was also a shorthand for anxieties about social violence, a subcultural fascination, a booming physical exercise trend, a popular path of spiritual discipline counterposed to modernist rationality and a new figure for the East more generally, among other things. Though these movies were often denigrated by critics, there were a series of other, more properly artistic reasons why the films 'stuck', too: their heady staging of the primal cinematic spectacle of the body in motion; the sheer novelty and visual splendour of Shaw Brothers' *mise-en-scène*; and the intense and magnetic physical performances of stars such as Bruce Lee and Angela Mao, for example. Greenspun's complaint that the genre was 'all too extravagant, too gratuitously wild', quoted earlier, can be treated in a more positive light as a description precisely of its vibrant energy and joyous excess.

As I've examined it over the last chapter, my focus has been on how the kung fu film articulated ideas about the East and the West, in particular through the motif of violence. By the end of the craze, the idea of 'kung fu' seems to have taken a somewhat different function to that which it served when David Carradine first hit television screens as Kwai Chang Caine, and this can be understood as a result of shifts in the cultural landscape. *Kung Fu* had seemed like the culmination of the pacifist youth culture of the 1960s, with its outward-looking social attitudes. However, the American adoption of Hong Kong cinema seemed to express a less idealistic moment, engaging with more fully marginalized subcultures and producing an image of those subcultures for the broader parent culture. The kung fu film's images of violence remained at the heart of this engagement.

4
ENTER BLACK DRAGONS

The kung fu craze marks a significant moment in the longer 'encounter with Asia', which opened up the West to a world outside itself. This encounter in turn sent ripples through society, offering new ways of imagining identities as these were being changed by the social upheavals of the time, and the upcoming three chapters will go on to explore some of these transformations. But it was not just the white Anglo-Saxon Protestant identities dominantly associated with the West that were at stake. Thinking about the relation of kung fu to Black popular culture allows us to understand the ways martial arts cinema and its iconography served as a means by which people from ethnic minorities could renegotiate their identities and place in society. To understand this, we need to take the American and European experience within the wider context of an enthusiasm for kung fu that wasn't merely limited to the developed West but spread across the developing world, riven as this was at the time by the struggle for decolonized independence. However, we will start where we left off at the end of the last chapter, with America.

We have discussed the African American audience in the kung fu craze and even its role in determining the rise and fall of the phenomenon. But this does not even come close to fully doing justice to the intimate link between the kung fu craze and Black American popular culture. In many ways it has been in this relationship that the most significant and lasting effects of the craze can be traced.

It is not simply that Black audiences were especially receptive to kung fu films; the other side of this coin is the fact that kung fu remains an important touchpoint within Black popular culture. For example, when in 2011 the Black British artist, designer and activist Jon Daniel set out to make a set of poster images celebrating his political and cultural heroes and inspirations, Bruce Lee found his place in these alongside such figures as Fela Kuti, Maya Angelou, Marvin Gaye, Malcolm X and Martin Luther King.[1]

The link between kung fu and African American audiences was already signalled in the appearance of Carl Douglas's hit single 'Kung Fu Fighting'. Douglas was a Jamaican artist, and the disco style which his song did so much to bring into the mainstream was itself derived from 'Black' dance genres such as soul, funk and R&B. The commonness of this association between kung fu and Black popular culture is further evidenced in the decision of Hanna-Barbera in 1974 to have their cartoon character Hong Kong Phooey voiced in a caricatural African American accent by the Black actor and singer Scatman Crothers.[2] The ongoing strength of the link is highlighted by its parody (and celebration) in *The Last Dragon* (1985), which was produced by Motown music mogul Berry Gordy. In this, Black martial arts student Bruce Leroy (Taimak) walks the streets of New York in stereotypical Chinese attire and battles the 'Shogun of Harlem', Sho'nuff (Julius J. Carry III). Gordy self-consciously brought kung fu together with a soul music soundtrack, casting Taimak alongside the Prince protegé Vanity, and included images of breakdancing and body-popping, too.

The lasting nature of the association, in any case, can be traced more broadly in cinema. The appearance of Jim Kelly in *Enter the*

Dragon opened the door for a line of Black martial arts performers that stretches from Ron Van Clief (who appeared as the 'Black Dragon' in a string of Hong Kong movies in the 1970s) down to Michael Jai White today. When Hollywood turned again to Hong Kong action in the late 1990s, it was often in combination with images, stars and motifs from Black American culture. Jackie Chan's breakthrough to the U.S. market, *Rumble in the Bronx* (1996), locates him amid a multi-ethnic New York ghetto, and the media theorist Gina Marchetti has interpreted this as part of a larger strategy in Chan's work to recognize and address a significant Black contingent in his global fan base.[3] The success of this film was followed up two years later by Chan's breakthrough Hollywood production, *Rush Hour* (1998), which sees him in partnership with Chris Tucker. Its cop-buddy formula pairing a Chinese martial artist with a Black comedian was soon picked up in the TV series *Martial Law* (1998–2000), which brought together Sammo Hung and Arsenio Hall. When Jet Li started to star in American films, it was also often in partnership with Black co-stars: in *Romeo Must Die* (2000) he appears opposite R&B artist Aaliyah; in *Cradle 2 the Grave* (2003) alongside rapper DMX. More generally, Black heroes are repeatedly associated with the martial arts, from Jim Jarmusch's casting of Forest Whitaker in *Ghost Dog: The Way of the Samurai* (1999) to Wesley Snipes's performances in *Blade* (1998) and its sequels.

Above all, though, it is through the medium of hip-hop and rap that kung fu's association with Black American popular culture is most evident. This is most spectacularly visible in the output of the Wu-Tang Clan. Their name itself is a reference to the mythology of kung fu movies and their work involves an extended play on the iconography of these films. So closely is their music associated with the martial arts that when in the late 1990s Xenon Film bought up the VHS distribution rights to a portion of the Shaw Brothers and

The 'Black connection': Jackie Chan locates himself amid the multiculturalism of the inner city in *Rumble in the Bronx*.

Golden Harvest back catalogues, these were re-released within series whose names made close reference to Wu-Tang songs; some films were even retitled to add appeal to hip-hop fans.[4] RZA, the driving force behind the group, has gone on to direct a movie that pays homage to 1970s martial arts cinema, *The Man with the Iron Fists* (2012). He also scored the soundtracks for *Ghost Dog* and *Kill Bill* and since 2016 has been performing a series of live shows where he re-scores the film *The 36th Chamber of Shaolin* with a DJ set.

The Wu-Tang Clan are far from an isolated case of hip-hop's love affair with kung fu cinema, however. Kendrick Lamar has created an alter ego for himself as 'Kung Fu Kenny', based on a character from Jackie Chan's *Rush Hour II*. Gangsta rappers Mob Style named an album *Game of Death* (1992) after the Bruce Lee film. Jeru the Damaja, whose debut album was *The Sun Rises in the East* (1994), styles himself a 'Taoist Professor'.[5] His video for 'Ya Playin' Yaself' (1996) was shot in Hong Kong and pays tribute to (and casts himself within) its martial cinema. Dead Prez use a symbol from the Chinese divinatory text the *I Ching* within their logo and repeatedly combine martial arts imagery with reference to the history of radical Black politics within their work. This is to name just a few prominent examples of hip-hop/kung fu crossovers. Beyond specific cases, hip-hop, with its 'rap battles', 'wild styles' and 'grandmasters', has pervasively used a vocabulary drawn from martial arts cinema to provide it with the metaphors through which it imagines itself. As the martial arts scholar and cultural theorist Paul Bowman has noted, the reverence with which kung fu references are handled within rap music makes a stark contrast to the role that they take on in rock videos of the same era, where martial arts are primarily played for camp effect.[6]

But the success of the kung fu film with Black audiences and its lasting impact on hip-hop culture is not just a matter of lucky marketing on behalf of Warner Brothers and similar studios. They had picked up on a pre-existing concern with the martial arts in Black American culture, and when the kung fu craze exploded, a series of meanings had already accrued to them from there. These meanings determined the ways in which kung fu imagery would work its way into the kinds of cultural products we have been discussing. Thinking about these meanings and histories will help us understand the particular needs that images and ideas from kung fu cinema met for this audience and how they were used to negotiate the realities of ethnic identity and experience.

MARTIAL ARTS AND BLACK POWER

Discussing this pre-existing interest in an essay on the early reception of Hong Kong action cinema by Black audiences, Frances Gateward has argued that in fact 'African Americans had their own kung fu craze, prefiguring the mania that would sweep the mainstream.'[7]

As evidence for this, Gateward reproduces advertisements by Chinatown cinemas in newspapers specifically targeted at Black audiences, which promoted kung fu double bills and appeared weeks *before* the release of *King Boxer*. The ads sit on pages alongside marketing for jazz music events and reruns of blaxploitation films. Part of the explanation for the Chinese cinema-owners' decision to advertise in these publications can be discovered in the fact that blaxploitation movies such as *Super Fly* and *Melinda* had also flirted with the imagery of the martial arts. The poster for the latter even showed its protagonist, played by Calvin Lockhart, in a karate pose.

As a result, the imagery we see close to the start of *Enter the Dragon* where Kelly appears in a karate school infused with militant Black Power ideology and his confrontation with corrupt and racist white cops which follows would already have been a familiar one for audiences of the time. It also had roots in a certain social reality. As Vijay Prashad has emphasized in his book on the history of interconnections between Black and Asian experiences and struggles, many African Americans were among those exposed to the martial arts during military tours of duty in the mid-century decades, and some of these went on to be prominent in the burgeoning martial arts scene of the 1960s. They included the man who plays Jim Kelly's instructor in *Enter the Dragon*, Steve Sanders. Sanders learned karate while stationed in Okinawa and came home from Vietnam disillusioned with the war in which he had been asked to fight. This, alongside his experiences of pervasive racism in American society, drew him increasingly to radical ideas. Sanders, along with Jerry Smithson, Don Williams, Fred Hamilton and Cliff Stewart, founded the Black Karate Federation (BKF) in 1968, inspired by ideas of Black Power, civil rights and collective self-defence.[8] Its logo borrowed the Black Power clenched-fist salute (sometimes with the added words 'power to the people'), along with a cobra and a band in Marcus Garvey's pan-Africanist colours of red, black and green.[9] Aiming to promote Black cultural consciousness and historical awareness alongside the martial arts, the BKF 'sought to preach the path of karate as the path to a disciplined and just community'.[10] Stewart, for example, had opened a dojo in Los Angeles in 1960 and made karate accessible to local kids who could not afford sporting equipment, offering free training for those who kept off drugs.[11] With Sanders taking a cameo in it and with the BKF graphics decorating the space in which it is filmed (presumably this is Sanders's actual school), Kelly's dojo scene in *Enter the Dragon* offers a nod – for those in the know – to the work of the BKF.

But if the work of organizations like the BKF brought the agenda of the civil rights movement to bear on the practice of karate as both individual and collective empowerment, Prashad also suggests that the connection between the martial arts and Black militancy was more deeply ingrained and systematic. The Black Panther Party, after all, reversing Martin Luther King's principle of non-violent resistance, was initially officially named the Black Panther Party for Self-Defense. Though this self-defence was notoriously armed

Black Power and karate combine in the dojo visited by Williams towards the start of *Enter the Dragon*. The uniforms the students wear include the BKF logo.

rather than a matter of karate's 'empty hand', there is a rhetoric here that ties militancy to the martial arts. Indeed the Panthers – and a number of other similar Black Power organizations – took up the provision of martial arts training as a part of their community programmes.[12]

In this environment, the relation of the martial arts to their origins in Asia – and the changing awareness of Asia brought by the Cultural Revolution and the Vietnam War, as discussed earlier – had a further impact on the way kung fu was taken up. The countercultural associations of anticolonial Asian conflicts had a particular charge within the sphere of Black militancy in the late 1960s. Movements such as the Panthers set up close ties with Asian communist organizations. In Carmichael and Hamilton's 1967 manifesto *Black Power*, decolonization in the developing world was taken as a model for Black struggle in America. Similarly, in setting up the Black Panthers, Huey Newton and Bobby Seal drew on Chairman Mao for inspiration and sold his 'little red book' on university campuses to raise funds. The Panthers included prominent East Asian members and embarked on a strategy of coalition with leftist groups across Black and Asian communities, including the Red Guards in San Francisco's Chinatown and I Wor Kuen in New York.[13] Representatives of the Black Panthers even met with Vietcong representatives in Montreal, embracing them publicly in an act of mutual identification as 'yellow panthers'.[14]

As Prashad argues, 'For U.S. radicals, the Vietnamese became a symbol of barefoot resistance.' Activists saw an echo of their own struggle in the image of popular resistance to the technological might of the American military and government.[15] The martial arts – dependent on the human body rather than firearms technology and promising by means of skill to level out the advantage of sheer power – fitted neatly into the imagery of 'barefoot' struggle against imperial domination. They seemed to many at the time analogous to the logic of guerrilla resistance, using flexibility, camouflage, precision strikes and improvisation – Bruce Lee's 'fighting without fighting', perhaps – to overcome conventional military force.[16] This mythology condensed around karate as the art of the 'empty hand' rather than the sword. Its origins were in Okinawa, a string of islands to the southwest of Japan, where bladed weapons had been forbidden to all but the samurai classes during Japanese occupation. Bruce Lee's iconic *nunchaku*, for example, is drawn from the armoury of this art and is in essence a repurposed rice-thresher, a farm tool turned into a weapon of resistance.[17]

KUNG FU CINEMA AND GLOBAL RESISTANCE

There were a number of ways in which plots of kung fu films, too, seemed to draw on a similar iconography. Their heroes were often lone underdogs fighting the rich and powerful. Often, as with *King Boxer*, *Fist of Fury*, *Hapkido* and *The Chinese Boxer*, the anti-Japanese plots were legible – if through a process of translation – as narratives of anticolonial resistance. As stories of ethnic struggle, they may well have had palpable relevance to those across the world who faced discrimination, exclusion and exploitation on the basis of race. For example, Warrington Hudlin, founder of the Black Filmmaker Foundation, has discussed the resonance for Black audiences in America of the famous scene in *Fist of Fury* where Bruce Lee's Chen Zhen smashes a sign on a park gate declaring 'No dogs and Chinese allowed.' Such audiences may have recognized the existence well within living memory of similar signs in the USA barring Black and Latin Americans – alongside canines – from spaces of privileged white leisure.[18]

It is the Hawaiian scholar and activist M. T. Kato who has probably pursued this argument the furthest, arguing that the kung fu film draws essentially on the folklore of China's Boxer Rebellion, 'from the perspective of those who fought against imperial conquest' and hence 'articulated the power of the masses in its active role in making history, defying subjection to the dominant power'.[19] Kato's case here is overstated, but it is lent certain credence when we consider the roots of Chinese martial arts cinema in the turmoil of the early twentieth century. When Verina Glaessner interviewed a Shaw Brothers executive for her 1974 book *Kung Fu: Cinema of Vengeance*, she asked him about his audience. The response came: 'There are a lot of poor people, a lot of illiterate people in Hong Kong . . . They go to the movies.'[20] Made for a dispossessed underclass in one part of the globe, the films translated well into the conditions of those elsewhere. (Or, to quote Williams from *Enter the Dragon* one more time, 'Ghettos are the same all over the world.')

In his account of the entanglement of Black karate organizations in a politics of global radicalism that united the Vietcong and the Black Panthers in a sense of shared struggle, Prashad also reflects on a formative personal experience of kung fu viewing that helps further understand the genre's global reception. Prashad first became a fan of Bruce Lee when he was a young Marxist militant in Calcutta in 1974, hanging a poster of the Hong Kong superstar on his bedroom wall. Lee became, for him, an icon of revolution in the developing world, and Prashad recounts his own reading of the films, which was coloured by the light of his political position. For him, Lee in *Enter the Dragon*, wearing his Chinese peasant suit, recalled the 'army in black pyjamas' in Vietnam who were giving the American military a run for their money and inspiring decolonization struggles across the world.[21] For Prashad, Lee's stand-off against the white American martial artist Chuck Norris in *The Way of the Dragon* was a 'perfect allegory' of the possibility of victory even within the terms of asymmetric power: Lee's smaller, more

An East–West confrontation: Lee prepares himself for combat against Chuck Norris in *Enter the Dragon*. Can Lee's honed physique in this scene be interpreted as an allegory of anticolonial resistance?

honed and disciplined body is set against Norris's monstrous, hairy bulk and eventually triumphs against it through adaptation and intelligence.[22] It offered an image of hope for those who felt they were pitted against the gargantuan military-industrial complex of the West.

M. T. Kato proposes kung fu cinema as a matter of globalized 'popular cultural revolution' and notes the 'unprecedented transcultural popularity of *Fist of Fury* in Asia and Third World countries beyond the confinement of the Chinese world' even before the release of the film in the USA. He argues that this was due to the degree to which it served to 'contest the symbolic kernel of imperialist culture'.[23] The kung fu craze, for example, also swept South America, Lebanon and Iran, in the last of these cases so successfully that the national film industry itself was threatened with collapse.[24] Its prominent role within Tanzanian post-independence youth

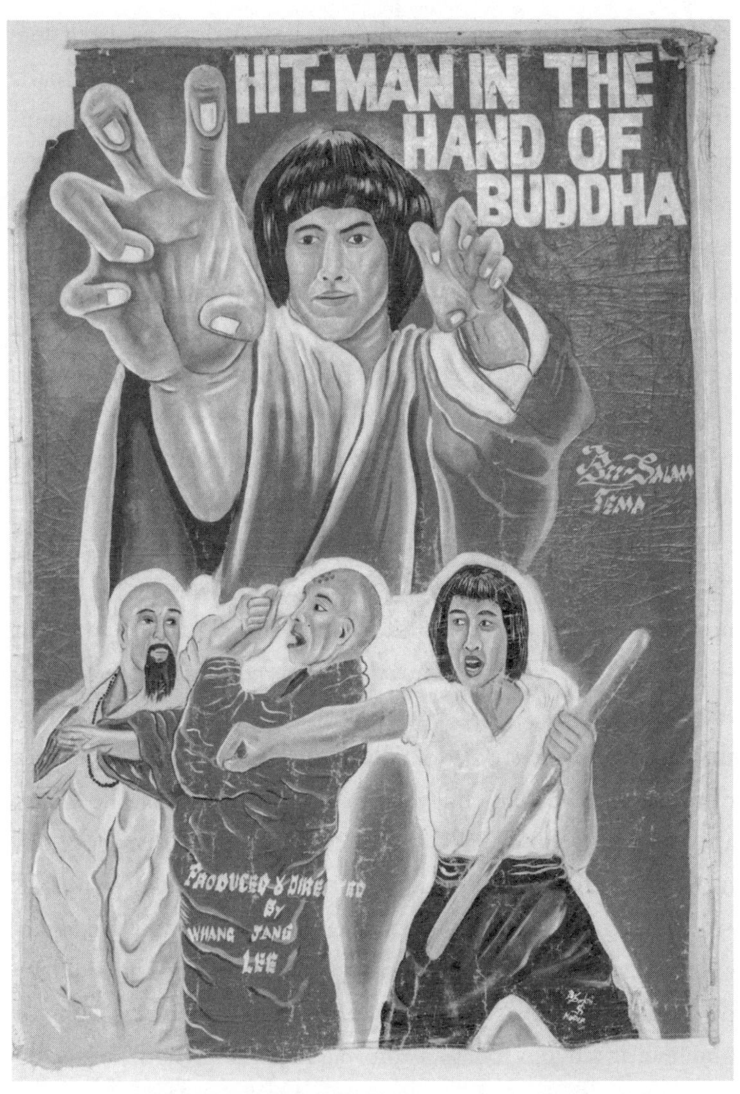

Death Is Wonder, *Hit-Man in the Hand of Buddha*, hand-painted poster from Ghana (date uncertain), oil on canvas.

culture – to take just one example from East Africa – has been documented by May Joseph.[25] A broader account of the response to the arrival of Asian martial arts cinema, in production and consumption across the continent from Egypt to South Africa, has also been offered by Ivo Ritzer.[26] To give one vivid example, so popular have kung fu films been in West Africa that in the 1980s an entire genre of hand-painted vernacular poster art developed to advertise travelling public showings of them through VHS tapes from the back of vans.[27] These informal screenings were the primary access that many rural populations had to cinema, and kung fu was a solid favourite in this business. A good deal of the global popularity of such films within all these developing-world contexts must surely, indeed, be a result of the ways that their contents speak to shared conditions.

The kung fu phenomenon, of course, had a very particular significance for Asian and Chinese Americans at just the moment when the Asian American movement was getting off the ground. As Hsiung-Ping Chiao has put it, Bruce Lee was the 'Oriental on the world's screen who had finally graduated from the stereotypes of the vicious Fu Manchu, the obese, inscrutable Charlie Chan, and the mob of unidentifiable farmers and railroad workers'.[28] For many young Asian American men, Lee's scintillatingly powerful, modern and cosmopolitan image of Chinese identity reversed years of bullying and created new, more positive images of a masculinity they could aspire to.[29] For many other Asian Americans, kung fu nonetheless remains today an ambivalent phenomenon, producing a new series of stereotypes even as it undermines older ones.

KUNG FU AND BLACK AMERICAN IDENTITY

As we can see from his global popularity, Lee, and the kung fu film more generally, enabled a much broader affirmation of ethnic pride, which could translate into a range of contexts for a range of people beyond the specificity of Asian or Chinese American masculinity. Perhaps within the racialized imaginary of mid-century America, there was something all the more exciting about the performances of ethnically Chinese stars such as Lee, precisely because the stereotype of East Asians pictured them as the submissive and dutiful 'model minority' who stayed in their place and were the least likely to rebel. They were those whose self-assertion entailed the most shocking upturning of an entire symbolic system.

The film and literary theorist Bill Brown has argued that Lee's significance for young Black Americans was to a large extent a matter of 'generic ethnicity' – the signification of difference (whatever that difference may be) to a white mainstream.[30] As David Desser puts it, 'Outside of the blaxploitation genre it largely replaced, kung fu films offered the only nonwhite heroes, men and women, to audiences alienated by mainstream film and often by mainstream culture.'[31] In a DVD commentary to *The 36th Chamber of Shaolin*, RZA has recounted just this experience and the effect that it had on him. He recalls coming to 42nd Street theatres for the first time and suddenly encountering a whole history that sat outside the Eurocentric narratives of the past he was being taught in school, narratives which not only excluded him, but rationalized his social and economic marginalization. To suddenly find a world – cinematic and historical – that did not revolve around the heroic deeds of white people offered him a sense of profound liberation and a basis for all kinds of new and self-affirming fantasy identifications.[32] These fantasies then formed the basis of the iconography that he would use as organizing tropes in the work of the Wu-Tang Clan.

For Brown, this identification with a 'generic ethnicity' rather than the particularity of Blackness – fuelled as it was by understandings of the parallels between struggle in the developing world and racially grounded oppression in developed-world inner cities

– opened up to new forms of identification beyond the nation state. They entailed an 'international *class* longing', albeit, Brown proposes, a 'failed' one.[33] Becoming figuratively Chinese through the medium of kung fu was a way of rejecting 'Americanness', with all its disabling effects for people of colour. It also, perhaps, offered a means of stepping out of the narrow boxes within which racial identity was defined. In this regard, kung fu may have offered more empowering possibilities of identification for Black audiences than for Asian American ones, who may well have found themselves fixed in place rather than embracing a new mobility in self-imagination.

For Brown, then, the 'postnational' bodies and identities kung fu conjured made it 'a figure for imagining how the circulation of the commodity-from-elsewhere can animate a new kind of sensuous collectivity' that cut across borders.[34] To put this another way, the global distribution of cultural products such as movies offered an awareness of a shared vocabulary of images, sensations and feelings between people from different nations and even continents. Watching these films, one could imagine oneself undergoing an experience that many others from very different backgrounds in very different parts of the world might recognize. From this awareness emerged an increased solidarity, which cut across previous national and ethnic divisions. In the case of kung fu, the powerful 'sensuousness' of this feeling of collectivity was amplified by the possibility of taking up a martial art, and the shared experience of the intense physicality of martial training.

By the 1970s, the nation state constituted less and less the horizon in relation to which identities could be defined. The sense that audiences had of Hong Kong films as coming from 'elsewhere' may have been a powerful part of the pleasure of watching them. If kung fu itself could be imagined as somewhat like guerrilla warfare, then the cheaply made film from the periphery of empire, too, placed up against the technological might and intensive capital of Hollywood's slick offerings, may also have seemed something like guerrilla film-making. Mainstream critics (as I noted in the last chapter) accused inner-city audiences of a lack of aesthetic sophistication in their consumption and a blindness to cut-price production values. Far from being blind to this fact, such audiences may well have experienced do-it-yourself cheapness as a virtue rather than a vice.[35]

Much of the above seems to bind the kung fu film to radical and highly politicized currents in Black American culture, speaking as it does to an experience of discrimination, disenfranchisement, poverty and oppression. We nonetheless need to be cautious in reading too direct a correlation between movies and politics. By the time the kung fu film appeared, the heyday of the civil rights and Black Power movements had already passed. As the music journalist Jeff Chang has put it, 'As the '60s drew into the '70s, King and X were gone, the well of faith and idealism that had sustained the movements . . . drained, and a lot of Black dreams – integrationist or nationalist – simply burned.'[36] The FBI's concerted campaign against the leadership of Black militant groups decimated them and sent the remainders into a spiral of self-destructive infighting. Their influence in poor urban areas was often replaced by a rising gang culture, and the optimism of radical politics gave way to despair, frustration and anger.

Further putting the link between the kung fu craze and Black radicalism in question, the blaxploitation films that paved the way for the appearance of Hong Kong martial arts films on American screens and to an extent determined how the public received them were themselves highly controversial within the Black community, drawing strong criticism from activist groups such as the NAACP. In spite of offering a rare chance for African American audiences to cheer on a non-white hero, their protagonists – usually criminal, amoral, macho, violent, oversexed and sexist – nevertheless played up to negative stereotypes.

The kung fu film, if free of some of the worst and most regressive images of ethnic difference we see in early blaxploitation cinema, may well still have been – as Brown puts it – more a matter of 'displacing' than 'fulfilling' the promise of the post-national imagination.[37] Though these films seemed to echo the concerns of Black radicals, they were now represented as a spectacle for passive consumption rather than a prompt to political solidarity. Like most cinema, they also tended to promote the lone and exceptional individual rather than the group, and Stuart Kaminsky, in his account of the kung fu film as 'ghetto myth' (discussed earlier), is not entirely wrong to see in them a dominance of narratives that emphasize personal revenge or resentment rather than collective liberation, even if this does flatten out the genre (and its audience) somewhat. The path to action from the kung fu film was most immediately a matter of individualistic self-improvement, returning the viewer to work on their own body through the practice of martial arts rather than a route to politics. The philosopher and film theorist Kyle Barrowman, for example, has discussed Bruce Lee not in terms of a collective struggle or ethnic identity but through the lens of the individualistic ethos of the perfectibility of the self, as espoused by Ralph Waldo Emerson and Ayn Rand.[38]

Brown's arguments about the 'postnational' identifications of the kung fu craze, discussed above, come from an essay that primarily offers an extended analysis of a short story, 'China' (1983), by African American author Charles Johnson. This story helps us further understand what kung fu has to do with the shift from the 'political resistance of the 1960s' to 'the consumer pleasures of the seventies and eighties' and 'how collective radicality becomes transcoded into a privatizing politics of consumption'.[39] In Johnson's story, Rudolf, a middle-aged Black postal worker, starts reinventing himself though an encounter with a kung fu film and the subsequent decision to take up martial arts training. Though Rudolf's wife, Evelyn, is dismayed at his new obsession ('You can't be Chinese!'), it offers him what Brown discusses as a 'project of self-salvaging', restoring his health, his sense of agency in the world and his sense of masculinity, bruised as this is by menial work, low pay, an unfulfilling marriage and having been turned down for military service.[40]

In many ways, as Brown argues, African American masculinity has often been experienced as all the more fragile and threatened than its white counterpart by experiences of systemic exclusion and by the denial of access to the means to achieve a white set of ideals. This is linked to structural forms of economic marginalization that operate in terms of race. For those excluded from access to economic success or professional status and the independence and control these offer, the assertion of physical strength in acts of violence becomes all the more attractive as a means to prove to oneself one's potency in the world and one's masculinity. Kung fu, as a cinema focused around violence and permeated by narratives of the transformation of powerlessness into strength through means of the body alone, appeals in particular to these experiences. Rudolf's interest in kung fu in Johnson's story responds to this, as he reaffirms himself in terms of stereotypical Black masculinities – defined as these often are in terms of hyper-muscularity, aggression and physical prowess – but also by an identification that transforms these. Overall, despite the ways in which it may reiterate certain ideas about race and gender, the story seems a positive one. In it, a character whose sense of identity and self-worth has been crushed by the racist world around him surmounts this through his identification with the Chinese martial artists he discovers on the cinema screen. In doing so, Rudolf seems to step out of the position that society has prepared for him as fate, wresting his destiny into his own hands. Furthermore, kung fu's 'counternation' (as Brown calls it) also stands as an alternative to paths to masculinity through patriotic identification with the nation that are problematic for Black subjects already marginalized within it.[41]

However, as Brown emphasizes, Rudolf's triumph is an entirely personal one, rather than one that offers any collective or political promise. It happens through the medium of consumption: through martial arts classes, nutritional supplements, books, training equipment and movies. What this marks is the movement from 1960s radicalism to the 'search for self' typical of the postmodern culture that developed in the 1970s and '80s, within which 'this year's radical symbol or slogan will be neutralized into next year's fashion.'[42] Rather than changing a damaging system, it makes overcoming this damage the individual responsibility or burden of its atomized victims. In this regard, Prashad's projection onto his Bruce Lee poster discussed earlier, discovering in him an icon of radical struggle, was a relatively rare experience compared to the ways that posters of Lee have functioned as signposts in the 'search for self'. Think, for example, of Italian American Tony Manero (John Travolta) in *Saturday Night Fever*, getting dressed to go out, watched from his wall by a poster of Lee, alongside one depicting Sylvester Stallone's Rocky. White martial arts writers such as Matthew Polly or Davis Miller similarly pay tribute to Lee as an inspirational figure through whom they redefined their self in the face of sometimes crushing feelings of inadequacy by embarking on journeys of physical transformation through martial arts training.[43] Although in Johnson's short story Rudolf's search for self is inflected by race differently, it nonetheless follows much the same pattern. What it demonstrates, at the very least, is the extent to which struggles around identity themselves, at just the time that the kung fu film arrived, were increasingly being fought not collectively but individually. The way that martial arts cinema and its iconography would be taken into Black popular culture in the wake of its appearance on Western screens has been profoundly marked by this shift.

BLAXPLOITATION AND THE MARTIAL ARTS

Perhaps the first and clearest sign of the embrace of kung fu by Black American popular culture – aside from attendance at the films – was in the field of cinema production itself. At its height, the kung fu craze largely eclipsed the blaxploitation genre. Since kung fu films successfully reached the same audiences, it was far cheaper for studios to buy up Hong Kong productions than make their own. However, as the kung fu boom receded in 1974, a new wave of blaxploitation movies with martial arts more firmly at their centre started appearing, and these mark the first attempt by the American industry to produce their own version of the kung fu film. Pioneering this, released in January 1974 and produced by Warner Brothers executive Fred Weintraub (who had been instrumental in the development of both *Kung Fu* and *Enter the Dragon*), was *Black Belt Jones*.[44] This reunited *Enter the Dragon* director Robert Clouse with the film's co-star, Jim Kelly, and featured choreography supervised by Bob Wall, who had played a prominent villain in that film.

Black Belt Jones revolves around a Los Angeles karate school – very much on the model of the BKF – that provides instruction for impoverished youths and offers them a route away from the pervasive crime of their neighbourhood. The school is threatened when a (white) mafia organization seeks to acquire the land it is on. When the mafiosi send a group of local thugs in to expropriate the school, Kelly's hero, Black Belt Jones, has to act to rescue it. Black Belt is a maverick cop – an ace operative who is nonetheless suspicious of his (white) superiors. They in turn rely on his exceptional talent but treat him as expendable. In many ways this uneasy relation to authority echoes that established in *Enter the Dragon*, where Lee, too, is cast as a somewhat sceptical agent of international law enforcement. At the end of *Enter the Dragon*, the helicopters Lee calls in arrive, like the cavalry rushing in to save the day at the end of a Western, but by that time Lee has already had to solve the problem himself. The powers that be are similarly inept or uncaring in *Black Belt Jones*, and at the end of this film, too, the police arrive too late to be of any use. There seems to be a message in both films that those from outside the privileged elite are fundamentally on their own in looking after themselves.

Nonetheless, there is something striking in Kelly's rather more 'wholesome' role – as a clean-living representative of law and order – compared to the controversial 'negative' depictions of Black masculinity that dogged the pre-kung fu version of blaxploitation. This in fact became much more the pattern that developed in the wake of *Black Belt Jones*. Rather than chancers out to make their big score, the heroes of these films are concerned with justice and, in particular, defending the Black community. For example, in *Three the Hard Way* (1974), Jim Kelly, along with Jim Brown and Fred Williamson, foils a plan by white supremacists to poison the water supply with a toxin lethal only to Black people. In *Twist the Tiger's Tail* (1976), Kelly reprises his role as Black Belt Jones, travelling to Southeast Asia to foil a corrupt wing of the U.S. military. In *Black Samurai* (1977), he works as a Bond-like secret agent penetrating the island fortress of an evil crime lord.

These more positive roles could be understood as overdetermined by a range of factors. We can understand them as the result of the campaigns against negative stereotypes in blaxploitation cinema by organizations such as the NAACP. They might alternatively be

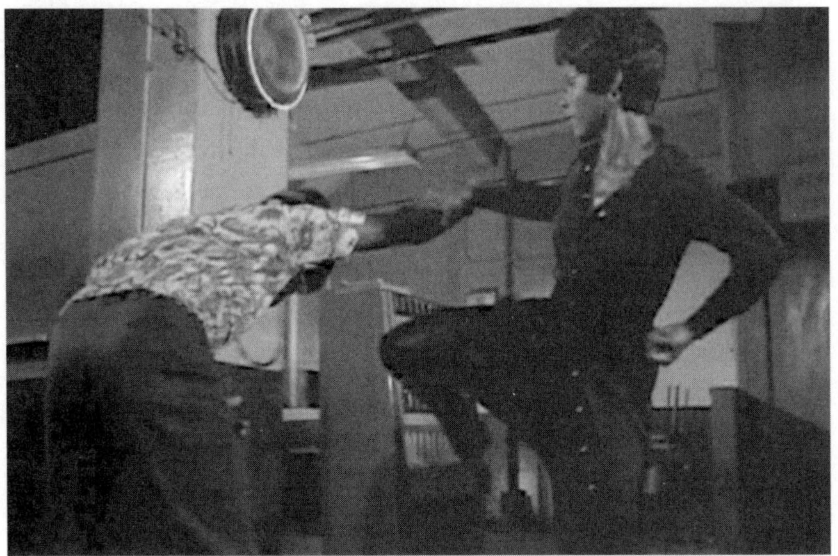

Sydney (Gloria Hendry) slips off her shoes and karate kicks a gangster in *Black Belt Jones*.

seen as defusing the danger to white society of criminal heroes like *Super Fly*'s Youngblood Priest. Their images of Black heroism are also closely linked to the histories of African American martial arts and the ties to the civil rights movement and to the themes of community empowerment and ethnic pride that I have been describing here. They also emerge from the patterns established in *Enter the Dragon*. And, more simply, the broader images of discipline, health and personal development that had been established around the martial arts sat increasingly uneasily with a figure such as *Super Fly*'s drug-addicted pusher, Priest.

Interestingly, the karate-inflected blaxploitation genre – though falling far short of today's standards of political correctness – also rebutted a degree of the persistent sexism for which its precursors were also criticized. *Black Belt Jones*, for example, introduces the character Sydney, played by Gloria Hendry, who turns out to be just as much a karate expert as Black Belt himself. In one memorable scene, she enters a pool hall run by the film's villain and, slipping off her heels, proceeds in stockinged feet to dismantle a roomful of thugs. When Black Belt suggests to her that she stay behind and 'do the dishes' while he takes on the villains, she pulls out a gun and blasts them to ceramic smithereens instead: 'They're done!' she quips. Hendry's performance had been anticipated by Tamara Dobson's eponymous role in *Cleopatra Jones* (1973), which appeared at the height of the kung fu boom. This involved a female special agent fighting drug gangs and taking them out with martial arts, among other methods. The sequel, *Cleopatra Jones and the Casino of Gold* (1975) extended the martial arts connection by sending its heroine to Hong Kong and pairing her with a local female cop, played by Tian Ni. We will return to the question of the images of women that surrounded the kung fu craze – ethnic and otherwise – later.

KUNG FU AND HIP-HOP

As these films were making their mark, kung fu was also integrating itself into the landscapes of new urban cultures then developing in New York, which would soon themselves have a global impact. As the kung fu craze exploded, a cycle of gang warfare, which had lasted since around 1968, was drawing to a close. In 1973 and 1974, a new party scene was starting to take off in the Bronx. Figures such as DJ Kool Herc and Afrika Bambaataa, who had himself formerly been a gang 'warlord', were pioneering inclusive events that transcended prior neighbourhood, gang and racial affiliations. These displaced violent rivalries into the realm of culture and laid the foundations for what would soon become recognizable as hip-hop, which is usually discussed as encompassing within it the elements of DJ-ing, rap, breakdancing and graffiti. Over the preceding decades, projects such as Robert Moses's Cross-Bronx Expressway, the development of vast housing projects and an overall policy of ironically named 'benign neglect' (the systematic abandonment of urban neighbourhoods by politicians and planners) had decimated the economic and social fabric of many inner-city areas. Districts such as the South Bronx faced rising levels of poverty and crime, leading to massive 'white flight' to the suburbs. Hip-hop would flower as the culture of the remaining youths growing up in these harsh conditions, in a distinctively post-civil rights era.[45] Ironically, it could be argued that it is precisely the same processes of globalization that brought images of inter-ethnic, global solidarity into local cultures and carried the kung fu movie as commodity into the American urban landscape that had caused these impoverished conditions. They were set in motion by the flight of manufacturing economies from the inner cities of the West and the rising dismantlement of social support as developed-world metropolitan centres sought to restructure themselves as hubs of both finance and the white-collar service industries.[46]

This changing urban landscape was not unconnected to the growth of an inner-city exploitation movie circuit, such as that on 42nd Street, in which kung fu and blaxploitation flourished alongside each other. The traditional audiences of cinemas in the centre of town disintegrated as the (mainly white) middle classes abandoned the city. Television allowed suburbanites to entertain themselves without having to expose themselves to the dangers of urban mixing. Inner-city theatres increasingly became the territory of the youth subcultures who were also in the process of developing the hip-hop scene. As an integral part of this landscape of urban youth culture – and one that persisted throughout the 1970s – kung fu seems to have left its mark on hip-hop in a number of ways.

Most obviously, this is visible in the emergence of breakdance. Breakdance had a number of origins, but as Jeff Chang notes in his book on hip-hop, even before the kung fu craze 'the line between dance and martial arts was thin.'[47] One origin of breakdance was in ritualized gang confrontations, which would often start with gang 'warlords' facing off against each other in an 'uprock'. In this, each sought to undermine or out-faze their opponent with complex Muhammad Ali-esque footwork and symbolic feints with the hands. According to Chang, 'Sometimes a dance was enough to settle a beef, sometimes the dance set off more beef. This was style as aggression, a competitive bid for dominance.'[48] Breakdance retained the uprock's basic scenario of symbolic battle as its primary form, whether this be between individuals or 'crews'. The hands, for example, were usually held up in something like a guard rather than being lifted above the head or dropping down by the sides in free abandon. One practitioner involved in the scene in the mid-1970s, interviewed by Chang, describes a 'straightforward, aggressive' flavour retained in breaking, unlike other forms of dance he had come across: 'A lot of times in my neighborhood I didn't see smiles in their faces. They were on a mission to terrorize the dancefloor.'[49] With this aggressive, competitive approach, it seems hardly coincidental that the kung fu movies that breakdancers were watching in inner-city cinemas were soon cannibalized for their most spectacular movements and integrated into the language of the dance. Moves such as the 'windmill' extended spinning scissor kicks from kung fu's groundwork. 'Carp flips' brought the combatant-dancer from the horizontal to the vertical, and the 'suicide dive' reversed this, drawing on martial arts breakfalls.

Hip-hop took these elements of battle – of aggression sublimated into dance and always, perhaps, threatening to spill back out into real violence – as a more fundamental poetic principle for all of its forms. Competition also lay at the heart of DJ-ing, rap and graffiti. The clash of 'styles' these staged was articulated in potent metaphors of rival-school narratives from kung fu films, while DJs, rappers and b-boys called themselves 'Grandmaster', envisioning themselves within the iconography of martial arts hierarchies. When seminal breakdancer Crazy Legs set out to assemble a group around himself (this would go on to be the Rock Steady Crew), he explicitly took kung fu film plots as a model for his 'quest', setting out to travel the city, challenge all rival 'masters' and build a group of disciples around himself.[50]

Initially existing as a local subculture below the mainstream's radar, hip-hop would not break through into the consciousness of a global culture beyond its margins until the late 1970s and early '80s. When this breakthrough came, it was primarily rap music that presented it in a commercial form. Rap, as many commentators have argued, articulates a series of contradictions: underlying many of these is its status as at once a spectacular commodity for mass entertainment but also a medium for the cultural expression of a minority group. In terms of this latter (especially in the 'gangsta' rap which developed in the 1990s) it arguably replicates a number of problematic aspects lodged within this experience – toxic modes of masculinity, violence, sexism and homophobia – but it has also been lionized as telling the stories of the marginalized and silenced and narrating Black experience and history. At its best, rap offers a critical standpoint on this for the 'hip-hop generation' of the 'post-civil rights' era, who continue to live under conditions of discrimination and exclusion.[51]

Through its collage-like processes – for example, by means of sampling or simply through the flood of references made within song lyrics – rap and hip-hop are often concerned with assembling a form of Black cultural history, providing the basis of a sense of collective identity from the fragments of the past. It is unsurprising that kung fu, entwined as it has been with this Black experience, finds a prominent place within the montage that rap presents. Rap's invention of Black cultural history is complicated by the traumatic shattering of continuity by slavery and diasporic life, and in such circumstances, 'kung fu', as a form that itself evokes tradition or ancient wisdom, has an added appeal. Here, the (fantasized) connection to a deep Chinese past serves as a substitute for an unbroken thread leading back to a pristine African origin. In this regard, kung fu, with its chain of transmission from master to student, a theme prominent in many films, offers a metaphor for the desired relationship to the legacies of Black cultural history which rap often seeks to take up.

The figure of kung fu plays a range of roles within this. Rap's most intensive engagement with its iconography is probably, as mentioned earlier, in the music of the Wu-Tang Clan. Released in 1993, their debut album, *Enter the Wu-Tang (36 Chambers)*, pays homage in its title not just to Bruce Lee but to the kung fu classic *The 36th Chamber of Shaolin* (1978). Its tracks are peppered with movie samples and quotations, and the Shaw Brothers' signature sound effects of clashing blades and bodies become a percussive element within their beat. Videos for the singles from the album, such as 'Da Mystery of Chessboxin'' (1993), featured group members posing with martial arts weapons. This concern with the iconography of the martial arts has remained a key part of their repertoire right up to the present day.

The Wu-Tang Clan is primarily the brainchild of Robert Diggs, better known under his stage name, RZA. Drawing on formative experiences in 42nd Street cinemas, RZA and his collaborators interwove in their lyrics a gritty narrative of small-time criminal life in Staten Island with a heady kung fu mysticism.[52] (Staten Island itself is rechristened in their music 'the slums of Shaolin'.) This in turn was mixed with science-fiction elements and the quasi-biblical symbolism of the Five Percenters, a splinter group of the Nation of Islam. In this collision of references an Afrofuturist Black nationalism is reimagined through the combined spirituality and violence of martial arts cinema. Images of Black and Asian culture become hybridized once again in tracks, at their best, of near hallucinatory intensity.[53] The result is a body of work with a dazzling sweep of references and registers, ranging from the sublime to the ridiculous and encompassing the mythic and poetic, social commentary, tragic narratives of urban poverty or violent crime, obscenity and sheer male posturing – including a not-insubstantial dose of misogyny and homophobia. Kung fu becomes a medium through which the violent confrontation of street gangs slides (as it often does in hip-hop) into the symbolic competition of the rap battle, where the tongue can be reconfigured as a weapon (a 'liquid sword'). But this can also be flipped around: kung fu becomes a means to articulate this symbolic self-assertion within the limits of a hyper-macho and aggressively competitive masculinity.

Posing with butterfly swords in the video for the Wu-Tang Clan's 'Da Mystery of Chessboxin".

RZA's use of kung fu narratives, however, extended beyond the confines of the lyrics themselves (or even the videos that accompany the work) and became a metaphor through which the group's very business strategy and mode of organization were developed. The figure of the 'clan' – and in particular that of the Wudang swordsmen depicted in the film *Shaolin and Wu Tang* (1983) – became the basis for this. It foregrounded an ideal of loyalty and collectiveness antithetical to the individualism of the world of rap music at the time and combined this with an embattled 'us against the world' mentality that marks all of their work. This collectiveness had an artistic function, producing tracks where a range of contrasting voices and styles rapidly gave way to each other, and this variety became one of the things that made them musically distinct from their competitors. It also had a business function, with RZA initiating a 'five-year plan' for the group, which sought to launch individual careers while maintaining a commitment to the greater whole where individual earnings were ploughed into the shared project and vice versa. Individual image was subordinated to the creation of an overall brand, which was monetized in forms as diverse as Playstation games and the Wu Wear clothing line.

There are other ways in which rap has plumbed the history of Black American culture's fascination with kung fu. One of the most visible examples of an articulation of the martial arts' connection to radical Black histories is in the 'conscious' rap of the duo Dead Prez, comprised of Khnum Muata Ibomu and Mutulu Olugbala (who perform under the names stic.man and M-1). In their lyrics, Dead Prez draw together revolutionary Black nationalism, pan-Africanism and socialist anti-imperialism. In word and image they weave an iconography that evokes the Black Power movement of the 1960s. As a part of this, we see coordinated displays of martial artistry in their videos (such as that for their biggest hit, 'Hip Hop', 2000), evocative of the paramilitary drilling of the Black Panthers. The martial arts, however, perform an extended role within their work. They are repeatedly referenced within their lyrics, often becoming the central topic of a song, such as in 'Way of Life', a hymn to the discipline of martial arts training. At other moments, this image of discipline is used to articulate a militant attitude. In 'Walk Like a Warrior', the mystique of the martial arts and their 'journey' is retooled as a metaphor for the transformation from acquisitive gangsterism to conscious revolution. But the associations between the militant and the martial arts run in both directions, offering a radical glamour to practices of individual physical training, which can now be imagined as in themselves emancipatory in nature. This training takes its place within a broader concern in their music to evangelize wholesome living and diet, abstinence from alcohol and even veganism (for example, in the song 'Be Healthy'). Expanding from the music, Ibomu started up the RBG ('Revolutionary But Gangsta') Fit Club in 2011, an organization promoting healthy eating and exercise, and he has authored a series of lifestyle books such as *Eat Plants Lift Iron* (2015).

But just as the personal becomes political, the political becomes personal, and Ibomu's concern with the transformation of the body echoes Rudolf's journey in Charles Johnson's 'China'. Dead Prez's hope is clearly that this new subject is not just a consumerist one but becomes capable of autonomy, militancy and collective action. In this, they echo the desires of the early twentieth-century martial arts reformers in China, for whom kung fu, against the background of Western and Japanese imperialism, was a means to re-engineer the collective body of the nation, through the bodies of its individual citizens, as fit and capable of struggle. Now, however, this individual/collective body is divorced from the state and articulated in terms of the (still impossible) 'international class longing' Brown discovered in the kung fu craze.

In their use of martial arts imagery, Dead Prez and the Wu-Tang Clan share a concern with self-transformation, which was also a core concern of the kung fu film and more broadly a fundamental aspect of the meaning that the martial arts have taken on in Western cultures. While for Dead Prez, it is the health benefits and discipline of martial training that have a regenerative effect on the self, for the Wu-Tang Clan it is more the power of movie narratives to offer opportunities for new fantasy identifications. Here, the kung fu film offers an image of the individual and the clan surviving in a hostile world through a code of action. The group's music often draws on its own self-mythologization, recounting the passage of lives initially immersed in low-level crime towards collective musical endeavour – becoming a rap 'clan' and outcompeting all rivals – as a means to exit the ghetto. In this much, the Wu-Tang Clan can be understood as offering an aspirational model. The story their music tells of transcending the limitations of social disadvantage certainly owes a lot to a Black nationalism, especially in the Nation of Islam tradition, where personal growth and economic advancement are lauded. Like many of the other rappers influenced by the Nation's offshoot the Five Percenters, the Wu-Tang Clan's storytelling perhaps seeks to position them, to some degree at least, as 'poor righteous teachers' (and in this kin to the vagabond masters of kung fu cinema). But it is also notable that, contrary to Dead Prez's radical rhetoric, the collective nature of the Wu-Tang Clan remains firmly within the confines of a capitalist ethos, as much like a corporate entity as a revolutionary cell.

Though very differently, the Wu-Tang Clan and Dead Prez both seem to find in kung fu a means to explore (or assert) an experience of contemporary Black identity and experience. Both draw on the history of kung fu's entanglement with Black popular culture. Because of the historical link to the civil rights and Black Power agendas from the 1960s, images of the martial arts resonate with the legacy of those heady times and with the hope for change contained within them. However, kung fu cinema itself emerged into Western culture contemporaneously with the new cultural forms of the generation that came in the wake of these movements, a generation largely bereft of the hope of the civil rights era. In rap, kung fu iconography is often used in a less optimistic or idealistic fashion to negotiate (and register anger at) the continuing marginalization of Black people within American and global culture and their continued vulnerability to the systemic violence that has propelled recent movements such as Black Lives Matter. As a means to assert ethnic difference to the white mainstream, kung fu also offers the chance to 'turn East Asian' and to escape, in fantasy at least, the often uninhabitable place that Blackness signifies in present-day Western culture. In such cross-ethnic identification, it also, perhaps, has the potential to offer the hope – signalled in the works of Brown, Prashad and Kato discussed above – of global solidarity beyond national borders and ethnic or racial identities. This potential is complicated by the fact that these global identifications are themselves the product of the intensification of capitalism's atomizing processes of globalization and the commodification of culture, which accelerated rapidly at just the moment the kung fu craze occurred. This in turn initiated the 'postmodern' shift of politics into the realm of consumption and the sphere of the individual.

The fact that Black popular culture itself is reproduced commercially means that its significance is not limited to what it means to Black people in America, or even Black people across the world. Rap in particular, as Tricia Rose has emphasized, is significant not only in terms of its 'black cultural address' but in how it speaks to 'the thousands of young white boys and girls who are critical to the record sales and successes of many of rap's more prominent stars'.[54] Black popular culture, with this double address, also carries messages about race, ethnicity, masculinity and identity to white audiences. As one of the most prominent places where kung fu cinema has been received and processed in Western culture, in many ways rap has determined what the Asian martial arts mean there, too, stamped as these are now not only with connotations of 'Asian-ness', but 'Blackness'.

5
WHITE MEN, ASIAN ARTS

The kung fu craze engaged Black audiences in the West through a sense of a shared ethnic difference to the dominant white culture. It allowed identification with narratives of anti-imperialist rebellion and articulated an experience of being impoverished and oppressed. But this raises the question of what white audiences enjoyed in these films and how these forms of enjoyment were bound with – or had an impact on – white identities.

After all, the typical kung fu film asserted a fierce cultural nationalism in the face of China's long brush with the West's imperial ambitions, stemming back to the Opium Wars of the nineteenth century and the Boxer Rebellion at the dawn of the twentieth. This included the ongoing colonial occupation of Hong Kong itself by Britain. Within these films' narratives Westerners are often depicted as the bad guys. We have discussed, for example, Bruce Lee's *The Way of the Dragon*, in which the hero, Tang Lung, (literally 'China Dragon') travels to Rome to defend the owners and workers of a Chinese restaurant from the Italian mafia, leading to the film's final East–West showdown with white American martial artist Colt, played by Chuck Norris. Similarly, in *Fist of Fury*, we find the towering Robert Baker (one of Bruce Lee's American Jeet Kune Do students) taking up the role of Petrov, the Russian

Bruce Lee overcomes the monstrous West, in the guise of Robert Baker, in *Fist of Fury*.

henchman of the nefarious Japanese occupiers, whom Lee's character, Chen Zhen, must defeat in a climactic battle. The spectacle of Lee's triumph over these hulking white bodies seems calculated as a core pleasure for the original Hong Kong audiences of these movies.[1] Even where there are no white villains, the Japanese often still seem to stand in for them as foreign imperialists. They are there as antagonists in *Fist of Fury* as well as other prominent examples in the first wave of kung fu films that entered the West, including *King Boxer* (the film that launched the kung fu craze in America), Jimmy Wang Yu's genre-defining *Chinese Boxer* and prominent Angela Mao vehicles such as *Deadly China Doll*. Even in these films – and certainly within the kind of picture of the world sketched out by the identification of Black and Asian struggles explored in the last chapter – the most obvious place where white cinema-goers could find themselves reflected on-screen might not be an appealing or comfortable one.

One explanation is that the films appealed in terms decidedly distant to the whole politics of race and identity. The film historian Stephen Teo has argued that while Chinese audiences responded enthusiastically to Bruce Lee's ethno-nationalist narratives, the American response was more a matter of 'narcissism'. In other words, this is at the level of the individual and their self-image, and in terms of desire for power and perfection in the body or self, rather than in terms of ethnicity.[2] The narratives of kung fu cinema also appealed to the broader psychology of adolescence, and adolescent males in particular.[3] Their anti-imperialist storylines could be taken up by young viewers as representing the rejection of parental and societal authority, the assertion of independence and the embrace of the position of the outsider typical to the phenomenon of the 'teenager' as it developed in post-war society. As we have seen, the youthful heroes of Hong Kong's rising action cinema were themselves highly influenced by the arrival of teenage rebellion in the colony and the consequent rise of a market for movies that addressed this.

Even here, however, the idea of race as signifying an outsider status is not irrelevant. Asian kung fu movies shared the charge of transgression and danger offered by Black music and style – central as this has been in white youth subcultures throughout their history.[4] My argument here is supported by the success of the precursors to the kung fu craze such as *Billy Jack* and *Kung Fu*, with their deliberate appeal to young and countercultural audiences. As I have already argued, the image of Asia within these films served as a means to reject values and ideals these audiences saw as Western. White viewers' awareness of the growing place of kung fu iconography within Black popular culture itself as the craze unfolded would only have cemented these associations.

Questions of race, after all, are not irrelevant to the ways other identities, such as class, gender and generation, are articulated, intertwined as these different aspects are with each other. The same goes for the 'narcissistic' concern with self-esteem. White youths' negotiation of their place in the world through kung fu movies, or even through taking up a martial art in imitation of martial arts stars, will have been inflected by ideas about race and ethnicity.

These identities were also changing rapidly at the time the kung fu film became popular. There is already a significant difference between the conceptions of masculinity represented by Caine's gentle pacifism in *Kung Fu* and Bruce Lee's explosive muscularity. And the kung fu craze occurred at the pivot point between the liberalizing politics of the 1960s (without which the non-white heroes of kung fu cinema would be unimaginable) and the resurgence of more conservative values in the later 1970s. As this unfolded, Hollywood's interest in kung fu and blaxploitation films and its taste for 'the exotic, the avant-garde and the countercultural' gave way to a return to the mainstream and the spectacular (and, we might add, the white) in films such as *Jaws* (1975), *Star Wars* (1977) or *Superman* (1978).[5] *Star Wars* in particular borrowed extensively from Asian martial arts cinema. It most explicitly reworked Kurosawa's classic samurai film *The Hidden Fortress* (1958) but also drew eclectically on the warrior mythology of kung fu. However, it relocated its narrative to outer space, offered its audience white American stars to identify with and toned the violence down to make it acceptable family viewing. In the same period, older ideals of tough masculinity, which had been challenged by the advent of feminism, were also returning, as evidenced, for example, in the rise of the muscleman-heroes of the 1980s.[6] Making sense of the response of white, male audiences to the kung fu craze – and what it is that their fandom represents – from the evidence of Hollywood film itself is difficult because of the belatedness of the appearance of American martial arts films outside of the blaxploitation genre. It is not until the late 1970s that white American martial artists began to appear truly as stars in their own right, first with the success of Chuck Norris and then, in the 1980s, with the rise for a brief period of Jean-Claude Van Damme and Steven Seagal as A-list celebrities before they lapsed into the territory of straight-to-video productions. As the 1980s progressed, the martial arts were the subject of both mainstream films like *The Karate Kid* (1984) and B-list video-store fare such as the cycle of ninja movies kick-started by *Enter the Ninja* (1981).

MARTIAL ARTS, VIETNAM AND THE 'ORIENTAL OBSCENE'

The first of these Hollywood martial arts productions featuring white protagonists was *Good Guys Wear Black* (1978), starring Chuck Norris, the former world professional middleweight karate champion who had taken up the role of Bruce Lee's antagonist in the iconic Colosseum fight in *The Way of the Dragon*. As the film historian and journalist Barna Donovan puts it, with this movie Norris 'revived the martial arts on [Hollywood] film at a moment they might have faded into obscurity. The revival, though, was possible for an American audience because Asians were removed from the lead roles in films featuring Asian martial arts.'[7] The all-American, white martial artist would step in to take this place.

Good Guys established a series of tropes that have remained mainstays of the genre. In it, Norris plays John T. Booker, a Vietnam veteran now studying for a PhD and teaching at a university. Booker uncovers a plot by corrupt military officials and politicians, who are bumping off soldiers from the elite commando unit he led to cover up their misuse of the unit for illegal missions during the war. This plot links Booker to Asia and to America's history of military involvement in the region and explains his skill in martial arts. It also positions the film ambivalently between countercultural and conservative ideals. It picks up on the counterculture's distrust of the establishment, and Booker himself is associated with its values to the extent that as both a veteran and martial artist he is immersed in non-Western cultures and experiences. But as Sylvia Shin Huey Chong has noted in her book *The Oriental Obscene*, the plot hedges its bets, allowing ordinary Americans – and American soldiers in particular – to remain good and heroic. These soldiers and citizens represent an idea of America to which traditional patriotism remains due. They take the role of justified victims in the face of the corrupt elites in the film – and, symbolically, in the face of all the real-world guilt of involvement with Vietnam.[8]

In raising these ideas the film is hardly unique. Vietnam returns as a concern in Norris's output, for example, in the *Missing in Action* trilogy (1984–8), which revolves around missing POWs from that conflict. Vietnam also throws its shadow over the broader history of American martial arts cinema and the list of its heroes who are veterans is too long to do more than offer a few indicative examples. Notably, Steven Seagal's breakthrough *Above the Law* (1988) also envisions its hero Nico Toscani as a former Vietnam special operative, somewhat like Booker. As a police sergeant, Nico finds himself opposing a CIA drug-smuggling network that has imported corruption back from the field of war into American society, allying itself with the mafia. A further example, *Blind Fury* (1989), casts Rutger Hauer as another veteran, blinded in Vietnam and nursed back to health – and taught the deadly art of swordsmanship – by kindly villagers.

For much of *Good Guys Wear Black*, the action is provided – as in the majority of American cinema – by cars, explosions and guns, and Norris's martial arts really only come into play in his final confrontation with the assassin employed by the film's sinister cabal of villains, an ex-officer of the South Vietnamese military named

Mhin (*sic*) Van Thieu. According to Chong, 'The end fight between Mhin and Booker is the mirror image of the fight between Norris and Lee in *Way of the Dragon*: here the large white body defeats the small Asian body.'[9] The allegory of triumphant ethnic pride and resistance to the global might of the West suggested in Lee's work is reversed. Where Norris appears hulking and grotesquely hairy in the Colosseum in contrast to Lee's idealized physique, his body is now heroic, virtuous and normal in opposition to Mhin, who appears the very image of abnormal evil, disguised in racial drag with a blonde wig. Norris is made into the legitimate or 'natural and organic' possessor of the Asian martial arts, as is proved by his victory. For Chong, the film represents 'a triumphant cannibalization of the oriental other under the banner of white American masculinity, reinvigorated by its cultural miscegenation with oriental violence'.[10]

This scene in *Good Guys* prefigures a pattern discussed by film critic Sean Tierney as prevalent in American martial arts pictures of the 1990s.[11] He argues that this pattern belies any sense that Western take-up of the martial arts, certainly as we see it through cinematic representation, is a 'benign instance of cultural exchange'.[12] Plots insistently imagine white protagonists being made the inheritors of Asian martial arts traditions. As proof of their legitimacy, they are pitted in battle against Asian opponents, whose nefarious nature marks the moral superiority of the white hero and whose defeat demonstrates the hero's physical superiority. A series of repeated motifs recurs throughout these films. The hero often picks up the Asian martial art in question with prodigious speed and to an exceptional level of achievement, making him the favoured successor of the wise Asian master and attesting to his special destiny. Furthermore, the Asians in the film 'bifurcate' into two kinds: the wise and kindly, who help the hero, and the evil xenophobes who oppose his right to mastery.[13] The films fundamentally seem to support ideas of whites' superiority and their supposed 'natural' place as leaders. They insist on the 'entitlement' of white people to own and sample other cultures at will. This depends on an asymmetric 'universality', whereby white people's ethnicity is invisible and allows them to take on aspects of other cultures in a way that people of other ethnicities cannot, fixed as their identities are by essentializing representations.[14] Certainly as we often see it in American action cinema, taking up martial arts serves as an extension of a mindset that transforms other cultures into exotic possessions that can be mastered from a position of privilege.

However, a more nuanced and historicized account of the nature of this appropriation can be given. As mentioned above, many American martial arts films of the late 1970s and early 1980s, like *Good Guys*, take Vietnam as a point of reference. In this, they fit into a larger pattern of U.S. culture at the time in which Vietnam had become an organizing part of America's imaginary relation to the world and its picture of race. The American martial arts film – and in fact the earlier fascination with kung fu itself – was linked to the many other films of the era which sought to come to terms with America's disastrous involvement in Vietnam, from *The Deer Hunter* (1978) and *Apocalypse Now* (1979) to the *Rambo* trilogy (1982–8). Chong terms this complex the 'oriental obscene'. In this, East and Southeast Asia had become, in popular consciousness, places of a traumatic encounter with violence, one that had been piped into homes on a daily basis by the news media and was represented by the appearance of damaged Asian bodies. Though Chong associates the appearance of this imagery specifically with Vietnam, there is a much longer pattern of this association of Asia with 'obscene' violence. Its history includes the Boxer Rebellion, Pearl Harbor, the Pacific front of the Second World War, Hiroshima and the

Korean conflict – and even the anxiety about Indian 'Thuggees' that informed British debates on self-defence in the late nineteenth century. In the case of Vietnam, it was a violence that resulted in a moment of national humiliation, where America's self-image as potent, unified and in charge of its own destiny had been shattered by both military failure abroad and the spectacle of discontent at home.[15] The resultant images opened up a range of positions, not least the cross-ethnic identification of the Black Power movement with Asian anti-imperial struggle discussed in the last chapter, and the growth of the Asian American movement, too.[16] In this and other cases, the Vietnam War served to draw together images of the divides within American society. On the one hand, it linked a range of countercultural movements through mutual recognition. On the other, it presented these for conservatives as manifestations of a single threat to traditional values and hierarchies, emerging simultaneously from both within and without.[17]

Chong interprets the Western interest in kung fu – and the narratives of the American movies that later took up the martial arts – as stemming from the questions raised by the Vietnam War. The kung fu film extended the fascination with obscene Asian violence into the realm of the cinema, its images of killing and violated bodies echoing the newsreel footage that had become so familiar,making these safe by aestheticizing them.[18] As a review of *Five Fingers of Death* in the *Village Voice* put it at the time, only half-jokingly, 'They beat us over there (or at least we didn't beat them), and . . . we demand to know why.' The article goes on to suggest that depictions of the 'secret weapon' of kung fu offered cinema-goers an imaginary answer to what it was that allowed a Vietnamese peasant army to win against America's technological and economic might.[19]

For Chong, then, kung fu is approached by American audiences as a 'style of violence'. Understanding it in this way, 'Asian martial arts stars such as Angela Mao, Lo Lieh, and Sonny Chiba do not serve as direct points of identification, but are conduits for this style of violence that flows through them and into the audience as kinetic energy.'[20] As exemplified in Booker's victory over his Vietnamese opponent in *Good Guys*, this 'style of violence' – the very thing that had threatened white American masculinity – could be adopted, even 'owned', in a manner that allows it to reassert itself in its old terms and to overcome its prior humiliation. In doing so, it short-circuits the empathy and imaginative self-transformation that identifying with Asian martial artists would involve. To underline the point, Chong proposes that there is a difference between a fan's imitation of Bruce Lee and stars such as Marilyn Monroe or Elvis Presley. While 'becoming' Monroe or Presley involves dressing up, dyeing or coiffing one's hair and changing one's appearance, 'becoming Bruce Lee' doesn't. Rather, it involves taking on a set of gestures, a style of movement, a 'swagger' and a 'physical virtuosity'.[21]

Becoming Bruce Lee – Jason (Kurt McKinney) strikes a Bruce Lee-like posture, drawing on Lee's 'swagger' and 'physical virtuosity' and appropriating his 'style of violence' in *No Retreat, No Surrender*.

Of course, impersonating Monroe or Presley involves a degree of physical performance or mannerism, too, but in becoming Lee, the balance is altogether towards skills of movement rather than 'dressing up'. In this much it could be seen above all as a matter of action, rather than identity.

In Chong's account, the obscene violence associated with Asia is registered as a threat to the white male subject, and we see this in the repeated image of the traumatized or disabled veteran, who is imagined as abject, emasculated and, as Chong puts it, 'incontinent' – in other words, unable to regulate the boundaries of their physical or psychic self. One of the fantasies of kung fu training is to shore up the male subject against the threat of his 'incontinent body', and the techniques of violence are taken up not only to defeat a feared enemy but to produce a 'body mastered' and so restore the integrity and self-possession by which the white, male subject defines himself.[22]

Seen in this light, the idea of the Asian martial arts (outside their use by minority groups) serves not as a challenge to older forms of white, masculine identity and power but rather as a means for white men to repair the damaged virility involved in their identity in the wake of Vietnam, feminism, civil rights and the counterculture. This offers one way of explaining, for example, Davis Miller's account of his overcoming of chronic insecurity through fandom and imitation of an Asian martial arts hero in his memoir, *The Tao of Bruce Lee*, or Matthew Polly's account in *American Shaolin* of his decision to travel to the Shaolin Temple in search of kung fu mastery, also driven by feelings of masculine inadequacy.[23]

But I am not so sure that the idolization and mimicry of kung fu stars by young white men like Polly or Miller is because such stars are *only* 'conduits' for a 'style of violence' that can be taken up without any impact on identity. It is the concept of 'mimesis' that best helps us understand this.

MIMESIS: BECOMING OTHER THROUGH KUNG FU

'Mimesis', in its most basic definition, refers broadly to processes of copying, imitation and representation through similarity. However, in his book *Mimesis and Alterity*, the Australian anthropologist Michael Taussig sets out a specific definition of the term, drawn from the ideas of Walter Benjamin and the circle of surrealist artists and thinkers with whom he was associated. For these, 'mimesis' refers not simply to copies that one might decide to make at the level of one's rational mind, but to a primal faculty, deeper and more primitive than conscious thought and older than humanity itself. This is the faculty through which living beings accommodate and adapt themselves to their environment by replicating it in themselves. For Roger Caillois, for example, the mimetic urge lies behind the tendency for camouflage or for butterflies to take on images of predators' eyes on their wings. Benjamin and the Surrealists proposed that this faculty underpins our human abilities to represent, to mimic and even to grasp similarities between things. Benjamin himself wrote that 'the gift of seeing resemblances is nothing other than a rudiment of the powerful compulsion in former times to become and behave like something else'.[24] Taussig puts it more straightforwardly: mimesis is 'the compulsion to become the Other'.[25] The startling thing in Benjamin's observation is that what may seem rational and intellectual (and within our control) turns out, at its root, to involve something sensual, irrational and corporeal. Mimicking an Other is not just something through which we come to know, understand or even control them. It stems from a 'compulsion' that seizes us and involves not only the desire to 'behave like' but even to 'become' them. A profoundly destabilizing experience, it involves 'slipping into Otherness, trying it on for size'.[26]

This seems to have a special relevance to martial arts, which place the copying of another at their core as a means of learning and also often include the mimicry of animals (in tiger, crane, monkey, snake, mantis or eagle styles, for example) or even divine beings (gods, dragons and so on).[27] The address of the kung fu film to our bodies through the pleasure of movement extends this function into cinema viewing.

These ideas offer a different way to interpret the adventure recounted in Matthew Polly's autobiographical *American Shaolin*. Going beyond the acquisition of a 'style of violence', this did not only involve him learning to punch and kick. Inspired initially by David Carradine in *Kung Fu*, Polly studied Chinese language and philosophy at college and moved to the Shaolin Temple, 'going native' there at a time when Westerners were a rare sight. There, he pursued martial arts as well as, for example, meditation. Though an extreme case of cultural immersion, his experience is of a piece with the broader experience of many Western students of the Chinese martial arts. Even if they first turn up to classes for exercise or self-defence, a proportion of them become increasingly absorbed in aspects of a broader culture. The martial arts scholar Douglas Wile, for example, calls tai chi (just one of the martial arts styles achieving mass popularity in the wake of the kung fu craze) 'China's cultural ambassador to the world'. He argues that, 'Touching the lives of more Westerners, and perhaps more deeply, than books, films, museums, or college courses, t'ai-chi ch'üan is often the entrée to Chinese philosophy, medicine, meditation, and even language.'[28] The reduction of these experiences (privileged as they may still be) to the appropriation of a 'style of violence' would hardly seem to do justice to the processes of mimetic becoming that they involve.

Many American films – such as *Good Guys Wear Black* – seem calculated in some degree to refuse such becoming, allowing martial

Jason's discipleship of the spirit of Bruce Lee begins with a lesson in language and morality in *No Retreat, No Surrender*.

arts to remain an activity that in no way makes its heroes less 'white'. Nonetheless, other films do also involve characters who increasingly transgress the boundaries of their identity. One of these is *No Retreat, No Surrender* (1986). Significantly an international co-production, made for the American market with largely American actors but directed by Hong Kong industry veteran Corey Yuen and initiated by the producer Ng See-yuen, *No Retreat* tells the story of Jason, who sees his father, a karate instructor, humiliated and crippled by mafiosi. Moving to a different city, Jason pursues the martial arts secretly on his own, first visiting the grave of Bruce Lee and then learning kung fu in a series of dream-revelations from the dead star. This tutelage allows him, finally, to defeat the very villain who crippled his dad and, as Chong puts it, 'restore the privileges of whiteness that Jason temporarily lost with the emasculation of his father'.[29] But we do not need only to see the film as turning Bruce Lee into an honorary American father figure. Jason can also be seen as becoming 'Orientalized' through his imaginary relationship with his hero, whom he calls 'Lee da ge' (big brother Lee).[30] Lee's first lesson for Jason is the meaning of the Chinese character *wu* (martial), making his education cultural, linguistic and philosophical rather than just a matter of a 'style of violence'. Furthermore, Jason's pursuit of the martial arts throws him into further 'multiracial affinities', as he becomes best friends in particular with R. J., an African American whom he defends from bullies.[31]

CHANGING MASCULINITIES

Just as I feel that white fans' mimesis of kung fu stars *was* more than a mere appropriation, I'm also not so sure that traditional ideas of Western 'masculinity' remain untouched by the identifications involved. After all, masculinity itself is not always a comfortable fit and for most men does not entail something easily and naturally assumed, but is a struggle. If kung fu's narratives of training, discipline and self-mastery dramatize the struggle to achieve masculine power and identity, they serve not only to celebrate the result but to express the very struggle itself. In so doing, they reveal masculinity not as biological destiny but as something to be achieved.

It is worth noting the differences between the images of masculinity offered by Asian kung fu stars and their Western counterparts. The very opposition between Lee and Norris in *The Way of the Dragon*, discussed earlier, points us towards this. Lee's is a masculinity not determined by sheer bulk but by a trained, agile, quick, precise and intelligent body. As the media theorist Yvonne Tasker has observed, despite the influence of Lee's muscular torso on the American bodybuilders of the 1980s, Hong Kong stars offered something fundamentally different to their white Western counterparts in terms of physical performance. While the kung fu body is marked by its extraordinary mobility, she proposes, the muscular Hollywood action star remained 'top-heavy, almost statuesque', a figure who 'essentially strikes poses within an action narrative'.[32] The typical image here is the star walking towards the camera, unmoved, in slow motion, filling the frame, while spectacular explosions ravage the world behind him.

In this stoic immobility, the U.S. action stars of the 1980s looked back more to John Wayne than to Bruce Lee, and this was also the case for martial arts performers such as Norris and Seagal. Norris's acting was, in the words of Donovan, 'inexpressive, taciturn, if not downright stiff', but this was actually an advantage for him in the roles he played.[33] This is in contrast to Lee's melodramatic facial exaggerations, which betray emotions that might easily be seen as 'unmanly' in a Western movie star. For Donovan, Norris's performance 'exudes a crucial, very solidly masculine presence' in his roles and is characterized by 'obvious hardness'.[34] The reference to Wayne rather than Lee became increasingly prominent in Norris's career as it developed. His association with cowboy mythology, for example, led to his role as a Texan lawman in the film *Lone Wolf McQuade* (1983), which was then elaborated in the television series *Walker, Texas Ranger* (1993–2001).

Seagal, though an outlier for the stars of the time in his lack of a muscular physique, outdid Norris in deadpan, inexpressive delivery. His one-liners are often barely mumbled, and he extended the Hollywood action star's immobility into his style of martial arts performance. Here, his movements are often deliberately minimal, emphasizing the way that his body remains the still centre around which an arc of violent motion revolves: he hardly seems to move, while his opponents are sent crashing through space or bone-crunching injury is inflicted upon them.

Given these differences, the interest of young men in Hong Kong's kung fu stars may well be significant precisely because it offered a means of imagining their masculinity differently from the stars offered by Hollywood. Mark Gallagher in fact opposes the stoical white American action hero to performances he terms 'hysterical'. For him it is Jackie Chan's 'burlesque' kung fu that marks the height of hysterical subversion.[35] These feature comic exaggeration of emotion and an emphasis on physical vulnerability (where Chan is often set against opponents much stronger than him and often takes a beating), and he displays a prodigious gymnastic mobility and flexibility. Chan is often presented in situations and environments that are quite out of his control, and the action often entails flight rather than fight, for example in extended chase sequences. Gallagher argues that these features may seem to 'feminize' him in the familiar terms of American cinema. Though Chan may be an extreme case, the earlier films of the kung fu craze already also depart from Hollywood norms significantly and offer male audiences a means to do masculinity differently, 'hysterically', even.

In this perspective, Hollywood's 'action movie narratives . . . tend to represent for the viewer a kind of masochistic trial of masculinity and its body'.[36] It is the ability to resist and master the disordering feelings and effects of pain that marks the properly masculine hero. This said, the American genre is not entirely homogeneous: for example, Bruce Willis's performance in *Die Hard* (1988) is deeply hysterical, even if Willis seems at first glance the very archetype of the tough American action star.[37] This should make us suspicious of drawing too stark a division between Hong Kong's kung fu heroes and their American counterparts.

Nonetheless, the Shaw Brothers studio's relish for garish stage blood and dismemberment perhaps already signals that masochism is highly prominent in kung fu cinema. Director Chang Cheh, in particular, fascinated Western critics with his repeated motifs of blood-soaked and disembowelled heroes fighting on with their intestines hanging from their body and recurrent images of protagonists' naked torsos pierced by their opponents' weapons, represented in a manner that drew combat into the realm of the homoerotic.[38] Rather than simply overcoming or mastering masochism, these films surely also allow us to tarry with its seductions.

DAREDEVIL, NINJAS AND THE INCONTINENT BODY

Within American culture, the masochistic martial body can be seen particularly vividly in the Netflix television series *Daredevil* (2015–16). This draws on a set of stories set out in comics from the early 1980s which pit Daredevil against a secret occultist ninja organization called 'The Hand', intent on taking over the world in typical yellow-peril style.[39] This comic series appeared during a wave of fascination with the ninja – a minor 'ninja craze' echoing the kung fu craze a decade earlier. This encompassed films such as Chuck Norris's *The Octagon* (1980), *Enter the Ninja* (1981) and its two sequels (1983–4), and the *American Ninja* franchise (1985–93). In these, the ninja is a paradigm of the threatening alien Other of Orientalist fantasy: unseen, lurking, hostile, deadly, often swarming, their individuality cloaked in a uniform that hides their face. In line with stereotypes of the Asian and in contrast to Western norms of self-interest, cinematic ninjas pursue duty without human feeling and unto death.

But in his confrontation with The Hand, Daredevil, too, is masked, a virtuoso acrobat and a proponent not only of the martial arts but of stealth. He is their opponent as well as their uncanny mimetic double, constructed in their image. It turns out that Daredevil's special fighting abilities stem not from his heritage as the son of a boxer but from his training by another ninja group, 'The Chaste', The Hand's sworn enemies. In this much, *Daredevil* can be seen as typical of the 'white mastery' plots discussed earlier, whose heroes outperform their nefarious Asian opponents on their own ground and are cast as the proper inheritors of their arts.

However, what is particularly striking in the Daredevil character is his physical vulnerability. This vulnerability is linked to the very fact that his superpowers of enhanced sensory perception emerge from disability: he is blind. In this, Daredevil makes a stark contrast to characters such as the monstrously strong Incredible Hulk, the armoured Iron Man or even the bulletproof Luke Cage. Against these, what stands out throughout *Daredevil* (both the TV series and the original comics) is the spectacle of the hero's body as bruised, penetrated, cut open, bleeding and suffering. It is in terms of his vulnerable, mutilated and leaky – that is, incontinent and masochistic – body that *Daredevil* hails the desires and identification of its audience.

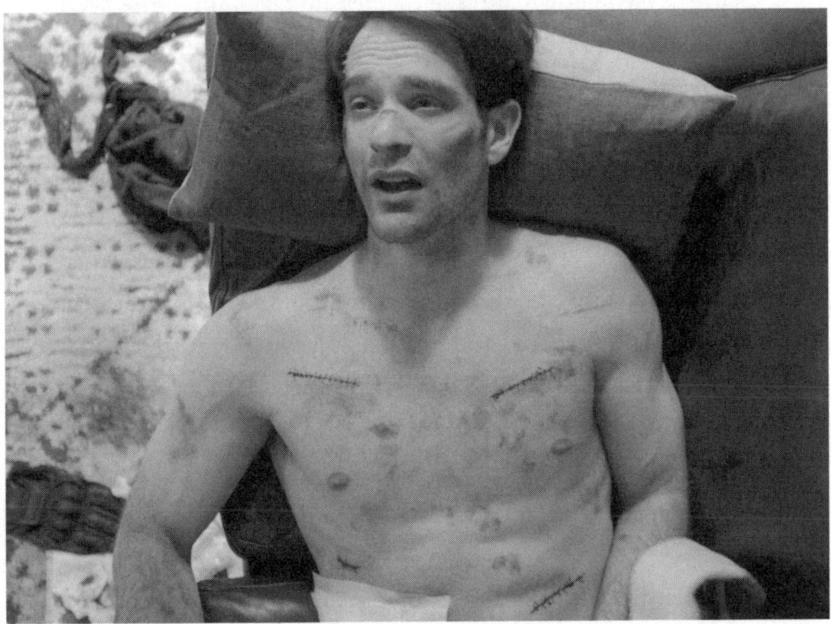

The incontinent body: Matt Murdoch lies injured, bloody and scarred after his confrontation with the ninja Nobu in *Daredevil.*

These themes of blindness and mutilation have their roots in Asian martial arts cinema itself. Among the films that launched the Hong Kong industry's return in the 1960s to swordplay cinema, as discussed earlier, was Chang Cheh's *One-Armed Swordsman* (1967). This in its turn drew on a craze for disabled heroes prompted by the success of the Japanese film series featuring the blind swordsman Zatoichi, which comprised 26 movies, starting in 1962. Zatoichi sparked a wave of copycat films across Japanese, Korean and Hong Kong cinema. These have been interpreted as responses to 'the profound social fractures caused by the twin processes of modernization and colonization' in the region.[40] Disabilities come to allegorize experiences of dispossession and disempowerment, with the miraculous skills of the blind swordsman signalling 'a desire to be healed and restrengthened'.[41]

Much changes when these themes are taken up in the West. Here, blind martial artists have featured, for example, not only in the television series *Kung Fu* (in the character of Caine's teacher, Master Po), but in the Rutger Hauer vehicle *Blind Fury* (1989), a loose remake of a Zatoichi story transposed into modern-day America. This is not to mention Donnie Yen's role in the *Star Wars* spin-off *Rogue One* (2016). The resultant images in *Daredevil* are complex and ambivalent in their relation to Asia. While the original ninja craze appeared at the moment Japan became the world's second-largest economy, *Daredevil* was produced at a moment when China was adopting this mantle and was being increasingly demonized by Donald Trump's electoral campaign, and its rerun of the 'oriental obscene' is redolent with the paranoid politics of the times.[42]

But beyond its topical relevance, *Daredevil* also points us to a more general and long-running aspect of the fantasies invested in kung fu. These may be as much about masochism as about the 'body

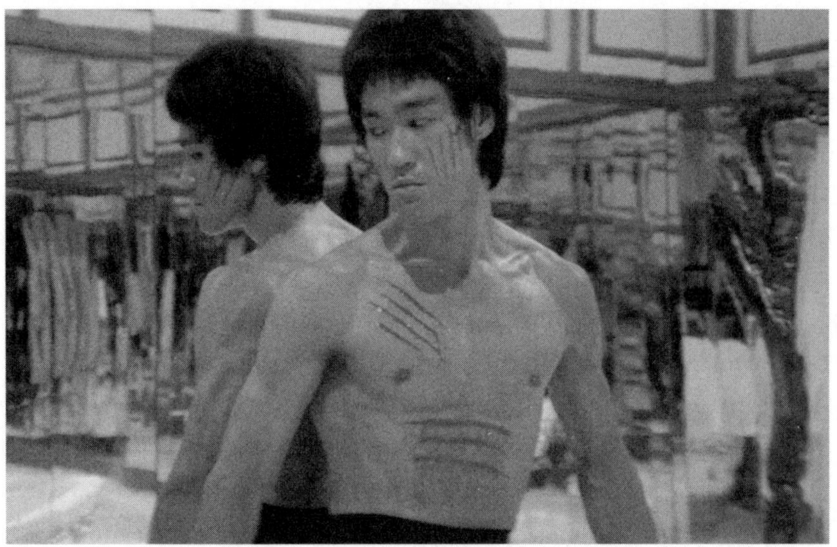

Lee's scarred torso in *Enter the Dragon*.

mastered'. For example, the famous poster of Bruce Lee from *Enter the Dragon*, which adorned so many adolescent walls during the 1970s, presents the star's torso and face alike bleeding with gashes from Han's prosthetic claw.

Even Lee's frequent display of his naked torso was itself unusual in Hollywood at the time (though not for Hong Kong). It presented the male body as a potentially erotic spectacle, marking it with a 'to-be-looked-at-ness' which feminist film theorist Laura Mulvey, writing two years after Lee's death, famously associated exclusively with women under Hollywood's dominant 'male gaze'.[43]

The American martial arts films we have been discussing seem largely to go against the 'hysterical' potential in kung fu cinema to challenge masculine stereotypes. But even here, the images of masculinity are not cut from a single cloth. Jean-Claude Van Damme, for example – 'the muscles from Brussels' – combined martial arts performance with bodybuilding credentials, so we might expect him to have taken up a persona more like the hypermasculine Arnold Schwarzenegger. Instead, he rejected the standard 'grim, humorless' style of delivery in favour of 'boyish charm'.[44] Further distancing him from the masculine stoicism of his contemporaries, 'an equally distinctive feature of his iconography was the lingering close-up on his large, soft eyes, long lashes moist with tears.'[45] Rather than sheer bulk, Van Damme's films frequently emphasize the flexibility of his physique, an aspect often associated with femininity. His ability to perform the splits is a recurrent motif – one, again, with 'feminine' sexual overtones in its opening and exposing of the groin. *Kickboxer* (1989), for example, includes a training montage sequence involving an apparatus of ropes and pulleys to pull his legs open, with distinct suggestions of sadomasochism. Van Damme was also shown nude in his films far more frequently than other bodybuilder or martial arts stars. Quite aside from his female fans, he built a significant gay following, becoming, in the words of Jeffrey Brown, a 'polymorphous sexual icon', attractive 'to men *and* women, heterosexual

Sadomasochist sexualization? Jean-Claude Van Damme is trained for high kicking exploits by being tethered to a system of ropes and pulleys that force his legs open and expose his groin in *Kickboxer*.

and homosexual', emblematic of 'how flexible contemporary presentations and readings of sexuality and gender have become'.[46] Van Damme's film persona is often constructed around images of 'suffering',[47] and the pitching of such imagery towards masochistic identification may open questions, at least, about the extent to which his performances evoke the 'incontinent' body of Chong's 'oriental obscene'. Though one way of interpreting *Kickboxer* would be as a film where a white man travels to Asia, becomes the true physical and spiritual inheritor of their combat arts and defeats an evil, non-white villain who stands in his way, we can alternatively understand it as a story of 'American hubris and re-education' in which its hero 'slowly transforms or "assimilates"'.[48] This kind of plot is typical of many internationally produced action films, which seem inherently drawn to tales of '"contact" between rival ways of life',[49] perhaps because – especially beyond the mainstream – they require multiple audiences across the world to make them commercially viable.

THE KARATE KID: MARTIAL MASCULINITY IN SUBURBIA

The Karate Kid (1984) offers another interesting example of masculinity in the genre. Its plot is once again archetypal of Western fantasies of the martial arts. Daniel (Ralph Macchio), a weak outsider bullied by the strong and entitled, takes up the martial arts to reassert his masculine potency and 'get the girl'. The absence of Daniel's father in his life as a role model and the appearance of the wise (if gnomic) karate master Mr Miyagi to fill this gap fit squarely within the common pattern of stories involving the appropriation of an Asian 'style of violence' in order to restore the white male subject. But Daniel's outsider status is also linked to his ethnic difference as an Italian American and this already aligns him with Miyagi against the more obviously Aryan bullies he faces. More importantly, the particular 'style of violence' he takes up is markedly different from that of his foes from the Cobra-kai dojo. While their karate is functionalist, brutal and powerful, Miyagi teaches Daniel a more 'aesthetic' (and philosophical) form, emphasizing the 'art' of martial arts. Chong, in her analysis of the film, links this with traditional Western associations of Japan with japonisme and the 'feminizing' dimensions of this.[50] Miyagi's japoniste karate becomes a means for Daniel to assert a masculinity distinct from the 'hardness' of its more usual Western incarnations. The particular kind of male potency Daniel regains through his elegant crane kick in the film's climactic battle is altogether different to that which he might have acquired if this had been a film featuring bodybuilding or even boxing. (The film's director, John G. Avildsen, was best known at this point for *Rocky*, 1976.) Macchio, whose training was in tap-dancing, was surely chosen precisely for his slim, unassuming physique and for his ability to perform an altogether more sensitive and vulnerable masculinity than is usually hymned in Hollywood action cinema.

The Karate Kid's location in suburbia should also remind us of the significance of middle-classness in all this. It seems, after all, hardly surprising that *The Karate Kid* appeared in the wake of the syndication of Hong Kong movies through cable television in Saturday afternoon slots such as 'Black Belt Theater'. These had opened new audiences for them, placing kung fu cinema in reach of suburban kids whose parents saw trips to inner-city exploitation cinemas as dangerous.[51]

The Karate Kid's suburban background should also remind us of the ways in which martial arts, as a leisure pursuit, were also becoming a means for middle-class, white-collar men who didn't work with their bodies to engage with fantasies of 'masculine' physical violence. Participation in martial arts allowed these men to shape their bodies according to normative ideals and develop self-discipline, even promising defence against the nightmare of criminal attack from the underclasses.[52] In this middle-class environment, the association of the martial arts (especially more esoteric martial arts such as tai chi or aikido) with 'Eastern wisdom' defined them as a cultural and intellectual rather than just a physical pursuit. Because of this, they could be used to assert social distinction and, in their non-Western origin, helped define the practitioner in terms of the liberal and globally oriented values of the late twentieth-century middle class.[53]

Alongside the old images of tough, violent masculinity that predominated in the American martial arts cinema of the 1980s, part of the legacy of the kung fu craze has been its role in these changing ideas of masculinity. It is also worth noting, though, the ways that these new images serve to reinforce class hierarchies. And however 'progressive' they may be in terms of masculinity, they still often rely on projecting onto other people a very familiar set of Orientalizing ideas of the East. This remains a seat of ancient, unchanging wisdom counterposed to Western modernity, and Asians are still imagined as more 'feminine' (or less 'masculine') than their Western counterparts. *The Karate Kid*'s depiction of Mr Miyagi (short in stature, reticent, passive, gentle) again serves as emblematic for this.[54] Asia remains, then, a lingering fantasy in which men from the West seek to partake, if in very different ways, to construct their identities.

6
WOMEN WARRIORS

Hong Kong's martial arts cinema – drawing on much longer literary and theatrical traditions – has long been replete with warrior women. In spite of the concerted drive within the Hong Kong industry to promote *yanggang* ('staunchly masculine') stars and stories, female protagonists and the actresses who played them continued to abound within the kung fu genre as it developed in the 1970s. In spite of Western expectations of action cinema as a 'male' genre, many of these 'high-kicking heroines' made their mark within the craze here, too. It is to this phenomenon that I turn in this chapter.

The most prominent of the women kung fu stars was Angela Mao Ying, and the extent of her importance in the first wave of martial arts films released in the West might well surprise us, given her relative obscurity today. In contrast to Bruce Lee, Lo Lieh or even Gordon Liu, at the time of writing Mao's most influential films are not available on major streaming services, nor on DVD release. However, hot on the heels of *King Boxer*, at the very start of the kung fu craze, her film *Lady Whirlwind* entered the U.S. charts on 16 May at number two, right behind Bruce Lee's *The Big Boss*, which it knocked off the top spot the following week. Though with some ups and downs along the way, *Lady Whirlwind* was still at number three on 13 June, a month after its first entry, and still in the top fifty on 4 July.[1] Released on 5 September, at the height of *Enter the Dragon*'s reign over the U.S. charts, Mao's *Hapkido* (1972) nonetheless hit number one on 19 September, and a week later her film *Deadly China Doll* (1973) was released in the USA. It also rapidly climbed to number one and went on to gross $400,000.[2] Mao, owing to her huge popularity in Hong Kong, was cast as Bruce Lee's sister in *Enter the Dragon,* and she puts in a remarkable – if brief – performance in it. A sense of her status in contemporary eyes is given by the fact that Verina Glaessner's 1974 book *Kung Fu: A Cinema of Vengeance* accords her a chapter to herself – a privilege shared only by Bruce Lee and Jimmy Wang Yu.[3] Mao was surely among the biggest and most recognized kung fu stars of the moment, in the West as well as in Asian markets. She was every bit the equal of her male counterparts when it came to the box office, just as she was in the performance of deadly spinning kicks.

Angela Mao Ying shows she can kick with the best in *Hapkido*.

When American distributors mined the back catalogue of Hong Kong martial arts pictures, they seem to have hardly scratched the surface of the reserve of films featuring female leads, obviously preferring male stars.[4] Mao was nonetheless far from alone in making this leap from Asian to Western screens. Judy Lee, for example, hit the U.S. top fifty in October 1973 in *Queen Boxer* (1972). When the British studio Hammer sought to cash in on the kung fu craze with a genre-bending horror–kung fu co-production with Shaw Brothers, *Legend of the Seven Golden Vampires* (1974), it cast Shih Szu in a prominent action role, alongside David Chiang and Peter Cushing. In July 1974, Cheng Pei-pei, the swordswoman supreme of the Shaw Brothers *wuxia* era, also saw a U.S. release of her kung fu outing *Attack of the Kung Fu Girls* (1973), which was a self-conscious attempt by Golden Harvest to rebrand her as 'the female Bruce Lee' in a movie that imitated the plot of *Fist of Fury* and was filmed by the same director, Lo Wei. In 1975, at the tail end of the kung fu craze, Western critics and art-house audiences were introduced to Hsu Feng in her role as a powerful swordswoman when King Hu's masterpiece *A Touch of Zen* (1971) was belatedly screened at the Cannes Festival, where it was both nominated for the Palme d'Or and awarded the Grand Technical Prize.

After the first explosion of the kung fu craze was over, of course, the Hong Kong industry did not stop producing martial arts pictures featuring strong women leads. Japanese studios soon also looked to imitate the formula, and in 1976, *Sister Street Fighter* (1974), with Etsuko Shihomi, was released in the United States, followed by its two sequels. Arguably, though, it was Kara Wai Ying-hung who took up Angela Mao's crown as queen of kung fu, appearing first in a range of supporting roles in the work of director Lau Kar-leung throughout the 1970s before being promoted to an increasingly central position, in particular taking up the titular roles of *My Young*

Auntie (1981) and *Lady Is the Boss* (1983). In the 1980s, a cycle of films featuring women as police officers would bring a further generation of martial arts actresses to the fore, including Michelle Yeoh, Cynthia Rothrock, Moon Lee, Yukari Oshima and Cynthia Khan. (Rothrock, after a highly successful career in Hong Kong – where she stood out as a white, female performer in a landscape dominated by Asian men – came back to make a number of films in the USA, although many of these were straight-to-video affairs.[5])

These depictions of strong fighting women were all the more striking in the context of a Hollywood in which such roles were altogether more scarce. As Neal King and Martha McCaughey note, on Western screens 'white women don't pick up guns in remarkable numbers until the 1980s.'[6] Further, the roles of fighting women in kung fu films were noteworthy in the extent to which their violence is endorsed as positive: it is 'less to do with aggressivity, sadism, or villainy and more to do with skill and the will to defend life or honor, and usually only when provoked . . . The women warriors of the kung fu genre are the films' heroes rather than villains.'[7]

Containing these new images, the kung fu movie seems to have offered Western audiences a new vocabulary for imagining female heroism. In fact, when in the following decades women did appear increasingly often as action protagonists in Hollywood films, starting with blaxploitation actresses such as Tamara Dobson, Pam Grier and Gloria Hendry, kung fu cinema often seems to have offered a blueprint for them. Aside from the models of female heroism Hong Kong cinema contained, the martial arts themselves provided a set of technical means through which women could be depicted as fighting equally with men. The kung fu kick became an essential part of the armoury of any self-respecting action heroine, in film or television, as directors brought in Hong Kong-style choreography and stunt doubles trained in the martial arts. Think of *La Femme Nikita* (both the 1990 film and the 1997–2001 TV series), Uma Thurman's role in *Kill Bill*, the film version of *Charlie's Angels* (2000), Trinity in the *Matrix* films (1999–2003), Max in *Dark Angel* (2000–2003) or *Alias*'s Sydney (2001–6). We similarly encounter female martial artist characters in superhero dramas, for example Melinda May in *Marvel's Agents of S.H.I.E.L.D.* (2012–20), Colleen Wing in *Iron Fist* (2017–18) and *The Defenders* (2017) or Elektra in both the film of the same name of 2005 and *Daredevil* (both the movie of 2003 and the television series of 2015–18).

Xena: Warrior Princess (1995–2001) and *Buffy the Vampire Slayer* (1997–2003) took particularly clear inspiration from Hong Kong cinema. Sarah Michelle Gellar's primary stunt double for the first four seasons of *Buffy*, Sophia Crawford, got her start in the Hong Kong industry in a range of martial roles before seeking her fortune in Hollywood, where she was eventually hired for the job of making the eponymous Vampire Slayer convincingly capable of taking on monsters and demons.[8] The physical performance skills she brought with her were central to defining the character and even facilitating the central premise of the series: the contrast between Buffy's appearance and her capabilities. If Gellar's acting created Buffy, it was Crawford who made her 'the Slayer'.[9]

Though *Xena*'s producers Sam Raimi and Robert Tapert didn't directly hire expertise from Hong Kong as Joss Whedon did with *Buffy*, they were nonetheless fans of its cinema and explicitly sought to imitate its high-flying wirework with the skills and resources available in New Zealand, where the series was shot. They even used mix tapes of action sequences from 1990s Hong Kong swordplay films as a means to pitch their vision and raise money for the series. Raimi and Tapert settled on Zoë Bell – trained in both gymnastics and taekwondo – to perform star Lucy Lawless's spectacular fight scenes.[10]

Making Sense of Kung Fu's Fighting Women

Critics have made sense of this profusion of women warriors, and the Hong Kong martial arts heroine in particular as a potential source for them, through the changing status of women in society.[11] 'Second wave' feminism, which had emerged in the 1960s, was very much at its peak as kung fu hit Western screens. Women were taking an increased role within the world of work, asserting their independence and expressing the desire for freedom and equality. Images of martial arts heroines such as Angela Mao acted as vehicles for both the excitement and the anxieties that the idea of the independent, strong woman evoked during these changes. In the newspaper articles of the era that touch on the martial arts outside the realm of film itself, questions around gender often seem close to the surface. When a Chinese *wushu* team toured the UK in 1974, for example, *Guardian* journalist Angela Neustatter was fascinated by the inclusion of women within the troupe. Noting the growing 'cult' of kung fu, she remarks,

> In Australia the liberated women are threatening to take up the ancient art as protection against rapists. To the Chinese troupe this is old hat – their women already practise Kung Fu and it would be a foolish fella who tried messing with them.[12]

In terms of Chinese culture itself, the reasons for this profusion of images of female martial artists would seem much more complex than an association with feminism. Certainly, the martial arts movies of the 1960s and '70s had as a context the growing independence of women within Hong Kong society, just as was the case in the West. Even further back, a significant background for the prominence of female martial artists in Shanghai's silent cinema of the 1920s was the rise of a modernizing agenda in the Republic in which the equality of women served as a marker for progressive credentials. This ideology had spread to the martial arts themselves: the most prominent and influential martial arts organization of the era, for example, was the Jingwu Athletic Association, which demonstrated its patriotic and modernizing agenda by promoting the inclusion of women within its classes and activities. Many other schools were quick to imitate this.[13]

However, the existence of stories of female martial artists within the Chinese literary canon is much older than this and belongs to a culture marked much less by the cause of women's equality. The tradition on which Hong Kong cinema draws accepts a much greater variety of figures who might be able to fight than Western culture, which associates this possibility only with young, virile males and the main protagonists of a story. Within the conventional universe of Chinese martial arts fiction, women, too, are quite capable of fighting, and not only the exceptional heroine but 'utterly common female characters in supporting roles – middle-aged mothers, sisters or wives who can stand up for themselves in the most spectacular ways'.[14] As a result, martial arts mythology is replete with legendary women fighters, such as the Buddhist nun Ng Mui and her student Yim Wing-chun, after whom the well-known martial art wing chun is named.

Furthermore, women warriors feature in the oldest existing martial arts literature. For example, a Tang Dynasty (618–907 CE) short story, adapted in 2015 for the cinema as *The Assassin* by Hou Hsiao-hsien, introduced the female martial artist Nie Yinniang. Mulan, who disguises herself as a man in order to go to war in place of her father, appeared in one of China's most famous poems even before this. Similar women are seen in a range of operas, for example the cycle telling the story of the generals of the Yang family, whose wives, daughters and mothers repeatedly take up arms to avenge their menfolk's deaths in battle and preserve the reputation of the clan.[15] As the Hong Kong-based cultural theorist Siu Leung Li has argued,

> In contrast with European opera and drama, the woman-warrior role-type in Chinese opera is unique in its widespread presence in the general repertoire and in its imposing representation of the power of women . . . The Chinese women warriors appear as a fabulously strong female sex that is a potentially disruptive force in the patriarchal order.[16]

Others are less optimistic about the subversive function of such images, arguing that these representations may well not have had a progressive effect within late imperial China's patriarchal culture, which accorded real women few chances to be like the figures shown on the stage or page. Theatrical and literary images served to reinforce a model of masculinity that the women warriors must imitate in order to act, shedding their 'femininity' in the very moment they take on the garb and the role of men. As fictions, these tales demarcated a 'fantasy realm' that only confirmed the constricted place of women in real life.[17] Whatever the precise way in which we understand the gender politics of images of martial women in imperial China, their tradition, as it is echoed in martial arts cinema, seems to offer a particularly rich vein for more contemporary culture to tap in its depiction of women's changing status in the modern world, in both Hong Kong and the West. Old images have taken on new meaning, posing us with the problem of interpreting not their origins but what they have become. After all, audiences in Europe, America and Australasia who were first confronted with the performances of Angela Mao and her contemporaries would have had little foreknowledge of the East Asian cultural histories through which the pictures on-screen had been formed. Even in Hong Kong, martial arts cinema reworked the stories of the past to address a new, modern, urban audience increasingly attuned as much to the norms and conventions of a global popular culture as to the models of national tradition.

The question, then, has been whether these new images provided by kung fu movies bolster women's freedom by offering empowered and active role models, capable of holding their own against men, challenging the conventional parts allocated them in fiction and life alike, or whether they remain fetishized and sexualized products of male fantasy.[18] In many ways, it is undeniable that some degree of the latter is an essential aspect of these images, since these films are ultimately the product of primarily male authors who envisioned a primarily male audience, so its images of fighting women emerge from these men's concerns and fantasies.[19]

LADY WHIRLWIND

When critics have examined Angela Mao's *Lady Whirlwind*, for example, they have often stressed the extent to which it not only offers a striking image of a powerful female martial artist but, through its narrative form, seems to seek to contain and ameliorate this. In the film, Mao plays Tien Li-chun, who at the start of the story arrives in a small town seeking revenge on Ling Shi-hao, the man who jilted her pregnant sister, leading to her suicide. However, she finds that Ling has now turned over a new leaf and has vowed to rid the town of the villainous gangsters who not only dominate its gambling but are enslaving women and selling them into prostitution. Ling also has a new girlfriend, Hsuang Hsuang, whom Tien rescues and seems to develop a sisterly affection for. When the lovers beg her to hold off on her revenge until Ling has completed his vow, she relents and ironically finds herself protecting Ling's life from the film's villains, as in order to get revenge she must make sure nobody else kills him first. Eventually, after Tien helps Ling triumph over his enemies, Hsuang Hsuang begs her to spare his life, and she turns on her heels, abandons her revenge and stalks off into the sunset.

Certainly, Mao offers a remarkable image of a powerful, independent woman. Her performance – as in many of her other films – is marked by her grim determination and her operatically furious intensity, as well as her explosive movement in the action scenes. Of all the fighters in the film, she sits at the pinnacle of virtuosity, clearly the superior of all of the male characters. As one character in the story describes Tien, 'She fights like a man, even better.' At the start of the film, Mao, a lone female in a world of men, walks calmly into the gang's casino, exposes its crooked gaming tables and proceeds to defeat its entire staff of heavies in a whirlwind of kicks and chops, 'leaving the bank broken and the croupier cowering under the table'.[20]

But though Ling is more vulnerable, he seems to draw our sympathy and identification more, and it is he who ultimately drives the 'heroic' plot of the fight against evil and injustice, in contrast to Tien's desire for personal revenge. If this divides the heroic role, Mao's presence as a leading lady is also contained by her pairing – which we often find in martial arts films that have female leads – with the more conventionally 'feminine' Hsuang Hsuang, who serves as a love interest for Ling and offers a safer and more acceptable object for the male audience's heterosexual desire. In the film's universe, the final shots of Tien walking into the landscape alone seem fated by her taking up the 'masculine' role of the warrior rather than the 'feminine' one of wife. It may appear that only the latter path leads to a 'happily-ever-after' ending. However, it is quite within the normal pattern of a swordplay film that the hero rejects love and domesticity for a life of roving adventure. In any case, if

Tien had ended up with a marriage this might equally have been interpreted as a moment betraying her potential as an independent woman.

Hapkido, Mao's next film released on the American market, similarly refuses to offer Mao quite the same position as her male counterparts. While the film takes up the anti-Japanese, 'rival schools' plot of Bruce Lee's *Fist of Fury*, the heroism Lee represents on his own in that film is now split between Mao and two male co-stars, Carter Wong and Sammo Hung. While it is Mao who survives these both to take revenge for their deaths, when she does so, it is accompanied by a senior colleague sent from Korea, who 'is drafted into the climax as though simply to ensure that a woman does not triumph where male heroes have failed'.[21] In *Opium Trail*, too, Mao's heroic role is split once again with Carter Wong.

THE OBJECTIFICATION AND FETISHIZATION OF ACTION WOMEN

In any case, to whatever extent female kung fu stars assert themselves through violence, the films also inevitably insist on their sexual attractiveness in addition to any heroism or power they express. This serves to limit and manage whatever threat the strong woman may pose by presenting her as an image that can be mastered by men's objectifying desire.[22] For example, the fan literature around kung fu films examined by Leon Hunt often clearly displays a fixation on female martial arts stars as sexual objects. He cites British popular film critic Jonathan Ross, who writes, 'The whole idea of sexy Chinese girls wearing tight superhero-type costumes, fighting and then having sex, is possibly the finest development in the hundred years of cinema history a man could possibly hope for.'[23] Another journalist descends further into S&M fantasy when writing about action actress Moon Lee, whom he lauds for 'kickass moves and kewpie-doll looks', going on to comment, 'If only Moon would wind

The American release poster for *Lady Whirlwind* (aka *Deep Thrust*).

up bound and gagged, my column would be complete.'[24] Even fan literature that has sought to be more knowing with regard to gender politics often remains packed with 'glamour' images of the actresses it discusses, inadvertently reinforcing the objectification of fighting women film stars at the same time as it seeks to challenge this.[25]

The reception and marketing of stars such as Angela Mao in the West developed this process of objectification further. For American release, *Lady Whirlwind* was retitled *Deep Thrust*, a name not only inherently loaded with sexual innuendo but one, as mentioned, that at the time would also clearly have evoked the film *Deep Throat* (1972), which had created a furore the previous year by bringing pornography into the mainstream. Brimming with further double entrendres, its poster promises 'the deadly stroke of bare-hand combat' and shows a bare-legged Chinese woman, who seems to bear no particular resemblance to Mao, in a skimpy, low-cut mini-dress that displays the cleavage of ample breasts as she punches and kicks a male opponent. In the film itself, the always demure Mao wears a simple peasant trouser suit throughout and with pigtailed hair makes a striking contrast to the vamp on the U.S. poster. Mao's *Opium Trail* was similarly rebranded as *Deadly China Doll*, with its poster once again promising a scantily clad heroine who is 'Dangerous! Devastating! Wicked! Deadly! Delicious!'

A similar process of reinterpretation of the figure of the female kung fu performer for the Western audience can be seen at work in the altered and marginal role Mao plays in *Enter the Dragon*. As Lee's sister, she gets to showcase her prodigious martial arts abilities early on in the film, when she is chased by Han's henchman O'Hara and a group of flunkies. Eventually backed into a corner and facing rape, she decides to commit suicide, stabbing herself with a shard of glass. Her vulnerability to male violence – and explicitly sexual violence – seems incongruous with the persona of her previous

Hong Kong films.[26] As reimagined within Hollywood, the female Asian kung fu star is figured now as an object – whether she wills it or not – of male sexual attention, and however proficient she may be, she is also imagined as ultimately weaker than men. Moreover, as the occasion for *Enter the Dragon*'s revenge narrative, Mao's role becomes simply to supply the motivation of the film's male hero.

FEMINIST APPROPRIATIONS

In spite of the extent to which these films and their images of fighting females are compromised by a set of male fantasies, some have stressed that there is nonetheless material in them that has been ripe for appropriation by women as images of empowerment. They associate women with an iconography of power and freedom and undermine 'the conventional notion that women are, or should be, represented exclusively through the codes of femininity'.[27] In doing so, they deal something of a blow to the symbolic order, striking at 'the all-important divide between women and men' – defined as this so often is around the capacity for power and violence.[28] Already in 1976, Blondie's eponymous debut album included a song, 'Kung Fu Girls', which presented a martial arts heroine, engaged in a narrative of self-assertion against men, as an object not of male but female desire, with Debbie Harry repeatedly calling out, over the closing bars of the song, her need to 'get close' to her 'kung fu girl'.

It was in relation to debates on women's self-defence within feminism in particular that these images were taken up. For example, Martha McCaughey and Neal King discuss their work in the 1980s and '90s within the student anti-rape movement where they used images of action heroines within their activism. These enabled them to 'celebrate women who knocked the stuffing out of men who bothered them . . . It seemed not only easy but also productive to identify with, enjoy, and share images of women who could express

Arthur Wallis Mills, 'The Suffragette that Knew Jiu-Jitsu', published in *Punch*, 6 June 1910. A diminutive suffragette resists arrest as a crowd of policemen cower in fear. The cartoon was inspired by Edith Garrud, who trained the 'bodyguard' of the WSPU.

their rage, defend their bodies, and usurp some of manhood's most vital turf.'[29]

This was determined by a longer history of the Asian martial arts in the West and the ways that these were gendered. With the idea circulating in the early twentieth century that practices such as jujitsu allowed the weak to overpower the strong and with feminizing stereotypes of the Orient which associated the Asian male with a kind of symbolic femininity, women during the first wave of feminism were rapidly drawn into the landscape of martial arts instruction.[30] Recall the five-foot-one Yukio Tani, discussed earlier as one of Barton-Wright's instructors, who toured Edwardian Britain giving jujitsu demonstrations under the name 'Pocket Hercules'. If Tani and his like could defeat much larger European wrestlers through the mysterious techniques of Oriental self-defence, so the logic ran, might not this work for women, too? For example, studying at Raku Uyenishi's jujitsu school in London's Soho from the turn of the century was Edith Garrud, who went on, along with her husband, to be one of the institution's senior instructors. Garrud was famously recruited in 1909 by the Women's Social and Political Union (WSPU), Britain's leading militant suffragist organization, to train a 'bodyguard' for its leaders, including the Pankhursts. Beyond these duties, Garrud ran specialist classes for women, which she advertised in suffrage newspapers as 'ju-jutsu for suffragettes'.[31] As a fascinated media gathered around the figures of the female jujitsu practitioner and the suffragist martial artist, newspaper cartoons abounded, testifying to the anxiety that surrounded them. In August 1910, the *Daily Mail* recorded a demonstration which set the four-foot-eleven Garrud against a burly policeman, whom the article records as confident of his ability to subdue the 'little dot of a woman'. His confidence was rather upset when she threw him violently to the floor.[32] Even before the kung fu craze, ideas of the martial arts as a leveller for women found their way into the mainstream in a positive light, with, for example, Diana Rigg's Emma Peel in *The Avengers* (1965–8) even pre-dating Bruce Lee's Kato as an exponent of kung fu on the television screen.

As Angela Neustatter's article on the Chinese *wushu* team's tour of the UK in 1974 suggests, with its evocation of 'liberated women' in Australia taking up kung fu to protect themselves against rape, these histories were reactivated in one set of feminist responses to the boom in Hong Kong movies. This once more raised into public consciousness the potential for women to take up martial arts as a means of self-empowerment and defence against male violence. The seminal British feminist magazine *Spare Rib*, for example, ran a feature in its October 1973 issue by karate instructor Maggie Lomax.

'Goodbye to the Creeps': Michael Ann Mullen's cover image for a 'Self Defence Six Page Special' in the influential British feminist magazine *Spare Rib*, February 1977.

This outlined the history of the art and emphasized, to encourage women worried by the ideas they might have taken from the movies, that karate does not involve 'aggression'. Lomax also stressed the collective and nurturing aspects of training, the 'spiritual' aspects of the art and the ways it allows women to become comfortable with their bodies.[33] Alongside this was an article citing stark statistics and examples regarding women's vulnerability to sexual assault, discussing the need for women's self-defence and offering advice on finding classes. Central within its argument is that women's reluctance to embark on violence empowers male attackers. Its author bemoans the lack of specialist short courses for women in the UK but notes that in America, where 'the situation is so much worse than here in England . . . women are beginning to overcome their deeply ingrained female passive conditioning that denies them personal action against this violence'.[34] *Spare Rib* returned to the theme at even greater length in their issue of February 1977, the cover of which featured a woman in a T-shirt and karate trousers executing a high kick and promised, under the title 'Goodbye to the Creeps', a 'Self Defence Six Page Special'. By this time, *Spare Rib* could present a series of photos showing women-only karate and kung fu classes to illustrate the article. Alongside these, it ran interviews with a range of different women who had taken up these arts in order to feel fitter, more in touch with their physicality, less vulnerable, more self-confident and better able to fight back.[35]

RACE AND GENDER: WARRIOR WOMEN AND DEADLY CHINA DOLLS

The depictions of fighting women that arrived in kung fu cinema were images of race as well as gender. Part of the reason for the prominence of Angela Mao's films within the very earliest stages of the kung fu craze may well have been the way they resonated with the idea of the 'oriental obscene' discussed in the last chapter. Mao herself, in her pigtail and peasant suit, may have evoked for Western viewers familiar newsreels of 'liberated' female Cultural Revolution-era students or even the Vietcong. The coincidence between Angela Mao's surname and that of the chairman of the Chinese Communist Party no doubt reinforced this.

For women of East Asian descent in the West, kung fu cinema's fighting women constitute particularly complex, problematic images. On the one hand, they broke the mould of the twin stereotypes through which East Asian women had been most usually depicted in Western culture: either the delicate, submissive and eroticized 'lotus blossom', or the powerful but dangerous and sexually predatory 'dragon lady'.[36] But these films arguably only created a new and just as damaging stereotype: that of the phallic and fetishized 'kung fu babe'. The martial arts heroine might well remain an object of the 'racist love' involved in what Leon Hunt terms the 'Deadly China Doll syndrome'. This insists on the star as both 'deadly' fighter and yet also erotically delicate 'china doll'. The sexual fascination at the heart of the 'fanboy' responses to the genre mentioned above also involve a certain racial fixation.[37] This stereotype still adheres to Asian actresses, to the extent that when Jessica Henwick was offered the role of martial artist Colleen Wing in the Marvel Television/ABC drama *Iron Fist*, she was initially reluctant to take the part, fearing becoming typecast as a female performer of East Asian descent.[38]

However, certainly for some authors and artists, kung fu's images of female warriors clearly also had the potential to challenge expectations of Asian women as submissive, quiet and passive in both Western and Confucian culture. Without doubt, the most famous expression of this has been in Chinese American author Maxine Hong Kingston's quasi-autobiographical fantasy novel, *The Woman Warrior: A Childhood among Ghosts*, published in the shadow of the kung fu craze in 1976. In its second chapter, Kingston contrasts her own experience within the Chinese immigrant community of being unvalued as a girl and of powerlessness in the face of American racism with the stories and films of warrior women who made up the fantasy life of her childhood. To reimagine her real life, Kingston constructs, from a range of literary and pop-cultural sources, a mythical alternative version of her girlhood. In this, she is taken to the mountains by an elderly couple to train in the mystical martial arts of the dragon and the tiger, dresses as a man to join the military in her father's place and returns home to take revenge on the powerful and corrupt local tyrants who have been preying on her family and the people in her village. Kingston writes:

> When we Chinese girls listened to the adults talk-story, we learned that we failed if we grew up to be but wives or slaves. We could be heroines, swordswomen. Even if she had to rage across all China, a swordswoman got even with anybody who hurt her family. Perhaps women were once so dangerous that they had to have their feet bound . . . My mother told [stories] that followed swordswomen through woods and palaces for years. Night after night my mother would talk-story until we fell asleep. I couldn't tell where the stories left off and the dreams began, her voice the voice of the heroines in my sleep. And on Sundays, from noon to midnight, we went to the movies at the Confucius Church. We saw swordswomen jump over houses from a standstill; they didn't even need a running start.[39]

In Kingston's account of her own life – which her elders suggest is fated to be that of 'a wife and a slave' – she draws strength from such fantasies of swordswomen.[40] It is in part the dream of the warrior woman's power that leads her in her American life into an education, fosters a growing sense of independence and a concern for social justice, and ultimately brings her to take on the role of a writer. In this role, she assumes a 'great power' – though that of the pen rather than the sword – which she discovered in her mother's 'talk-story' itself.[41] Despite her inability to change either the circumstances of Chinese American immigrants or the nightmare of the Cultural Revolution back in China, Kingston concludes, 'The swordswoman and I are not so dissimilar.'[42]

The iconography surrounding the martial arts also had a resonance with women from minority ethnic groups beyond the

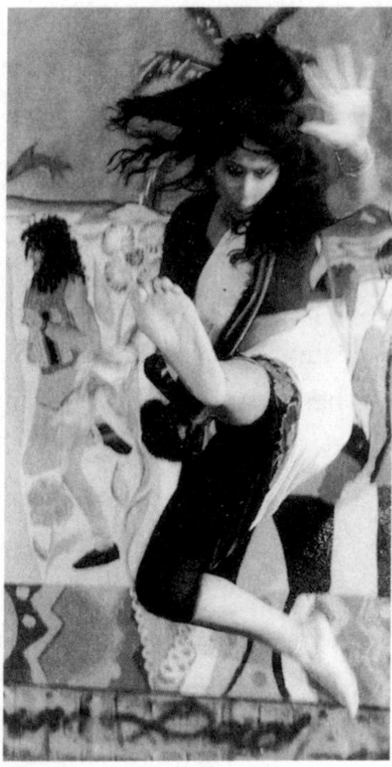

Chila Kumari Singh Burman, *Shotokan*, 1993, four black-and-white photographs.

Chinese community. One prominent example of this is in the work of the South Asian British artist Chila Kumari Singh Burman. In the 1970s, Burman took up karate as a means to challenge the gendered and racial expectations that surrounded her, just as they did Kingston, though in relation to British Indian rather than Chinese American identity. In Burman's work, which spans printmaking, photography, video, installation and performance, images of herself performing martial arts are presented alongside representations of women warriors from Indian history and mythology, such as the goddess Kali, the teenage warrior queen Jhansi Ki Rani, who took up arms against the British as a freedom fighter in the 1857 rebellion, and the bandit leader Phoolan Devi. Through these

conjunctions, Burman presents a version of South Asian femininity that is assertive and powerful. In her works, the martial arts also entail an enjoyment of and confidence with the physicality of exercise, which (as the *Spare Rib* articles mentioned above also argued) is itself an important aspect of women's empowerment. *Shotokan* (1993), for example, is a four-panel photographic work depicting Burman, dressed in a sari, performing a series of karate movements in front of a community mural she was instrumental in organizing and painting, her punches and flying kicks aimed towards the viewer as a gesture of defiance.[43]

7

A SECOND KUNG FU CRAZE?

As I have been exploring it so far, the legacy of the kung fu craze – up to the end of the twentieth century at least – presents us with a paradox. On the one hand, we have seen the images and ideas that it introduced permeating culture further and further. These images and ideas spawned new cinematic genres and influenced a range of media. They continue to articulate changing identities and social relationships in America and across the world. Paul Bowman's work on the British experience of the 'invention of martial arts' shows that rather than petering out with the waning of the brief film fad of the 1970s, there was in fact a mounting tide of representations of the Asian fighting arts in advertisements, music videos, instructional publications, television programmes, children's cartoons, comic books and much else besides.[1] On the other hand, in terms of cinema, during this time kung fu seems to have been a peripheral phenomenon, marked by its association with socially marginal audiences and by anxieties about a violence that threatened to overspill the boundaries of the cinema screen. Kung fu films were increasingly relegated to cult viewing at exploitation houses and Saturday afternoon or late-night cable TV slots. They were largely treated as cheap, exotic productions destined for niche shelves in video stores rather than wide theatrical release, and during this time Hong Kong martial arts movies made little or no impact whatsoever at the box office in America or other Western countries. In his essay on America's first reception of kung fu cinema, written at the end of the 1990s – just before all this was to change – David Desser bemoans the fact that the events he documents remained unrepeated. Even Jackie Chan at that point seemed to have failed to achieve significant and lasting success beyond East Asia. For Desser, the kung fu craze was like a 'brief . . . summer storm' because it not only arrived apparently without warning, but rapidly passed, too.[2]

However, the same year as Desser's essay was published, *Crouching Tiger, Hidden Dragon* (2000) was released. Upsetting the belief that multiplex audiences would not accept subtitled pictures, *Crouching Tiger* brought in a startling $128 million at the U.S. box office, breaking all records for a non-English-language film. In spite of a poor showing in China and a lukewarm reception in Hong Kong, it took over $200 million worldwide, not including the $112 million it went on to take in video and DVD rentals and sales in the United States alone. Its economic success was paralleled by a critical acclaim in stark contrast to the films of the original kung fu craze. It received no fewer than ten Oscar nominations and won four of these, including Best Foreign Language Film and Best Cinematography. At Cannes, the notoriously blasé audience of industry insiders gave it a standing ovation.[3] Critics raved, with Peter Rainer of *New York* magazine writing about it as 'a film that satisfies our craving for pop while giving us the transcendence of poetry', and the BBC proposing that 'you may never see a more beautiful movie – and certainly no more majestic film has yet been made.'[4] Suggesting that the genre had finally come of age (but in doing so displaying a lingering disdain for the classic era of kung fu cinema), the *Seattle Times* hailed it as, at last, 'a martial arts movie for adults'.[5] The *Washington Post* went as far as to suggest that its director, Ang Lee, had 'liberated conventional moviemaking'.[6]

A range of aspects made *Crouching Tiger* seem fresh and surprising to critics and audiences in the English-speaking world: the prominence of female characters and stars; its evocation of gravity-defying, weightless movement in its rooftop chases and bamboo-forest confrontations; its emphasis on the fantastical, rather than corporeal realism in fighting; its setting in the distant past; its lavish costumes and grand landscapes; and its incorporation of aspects of drama and even romance. All this appeared a revolutionary break from the low-brow machismo expected from 'kung fu'. Critics praised Lee for his daring transformation of the genre and his interest in giving it a novel feminist spin. However, Lee was in fact reaching back for all this to the *wuxia* tradition, as explored here earlier, with its roots in Shanghai's silent era and the Cantonese cinema of 1950s Hong Kong. In particular, *Crouching Tiger* seemed to draw on the works of King Hu, such as *A Touch of Zen* (1971), which it appears explicitly to reference at multiple points. The significance of *Crouching Tiger*'s success is perhaps the belated arrival of this older genre in the West.[7]

Crouching Tiger paved the way for a new wave of internationally produced and released *wuxia* blockbusters that combined high-art aesthetics with big budgets and spectacular action. *Hero* (2002) soon found wide distribution in the West and its director, Zhang Yimou, followed this with *House of Flying Daggers* (2004), *Curse of the Golden Flower* (2006), *The Great Wall* (2016) and *Shadow* (2018). As a range of pan-Chinese auteurs sought to explore the new possibilities of international-scale martial arts epics, these films were joined by Chen Kaige's *The Promise* (2005), Feng Xiaogang's *The Banquet* (2006), Ronny Yu's *Fearless* (2006) and John Woo's *Red Cliff* (2008–9). In 2008, Wong Kar-wai's beautiful and enigmatic deconstruction of the *wuxia* genre *Ashes of Time* (1994) was re-released as a director's cut for global DVD distribution, and his long-awaited picture *The Grandmaster* hit screens in 2013. The Taiwanese auteur Hou Hsiao-hsien's award of Best Director at Cannes for *The Assassin* (2015) propelled this to a release in both Europe and the USA that was surprisingly broad when we consider its exceptional narrative ambiguity and difficulty.

These 'martial-art-house' productions (as they soon came to be dubbed) were paralleled by interest in films that, though aimed at an international market and with upscale budgets to match, remained much more popular in address and generic in nature. In the comic register, Jackie Chan had made his Hollywood breakthrough with the *Rush Hour* series (starting in 1998) and continued to churn out international hits. Alongside him, Stephen Chow, already one of Hong Kong's most successful stars but one whose comedy had long been considered 'untranslatable' beyond this locale, made inroads into the international market with *Shaolin Soccer* (2001). He followed this up with *Kung Fu Hustle*, which became 2005's highest-grossing foreign-language film in America.[8] In a more 'heroic' vein, Wilson Yip's *Ip Man* series (2008–19) has spanned four episodes (and a spin-off about a subsidiary character), each garnering swelling box-office returns globally.

This new influx of martial arts films from greater China was echoed in an increasing interest in the martial arts in Hollywood. *The Matrix* (1999) and *Charlie's Angels* (2000) had both foregrounded kung fu performance and paved the way for *Crouching Tiger*. Jet Li appeared in *Romeo Must Die* (2000), *Kiss of the Dragon* (2001) and *Cradle 2 the Grave* (2003). Quentin Tarantino's *Kill Bill* (2003–4) paid homage to Asian popular cinema, with classic kung fu references abounding, and it included among its cast the iconic figures of Gordon Liu and David Carradine.

Does this add up to a 'second kung fu craze'? In many ways (and in spite of the title of this chapter), the term would be a misnomer. First of all, twenty-first-century *wuxia* pictures made up a sustained stream more than an intense but brief fad. With their 'highbrow' aesthetic, they also seemed to sever the associations of martial arts cinema with the low and the marginal and escaped much of the moral panic that the notion of the craze suggests. To my knowledge, the term was never employed within the media to any significant extent to describe them. The difference between the images of martial artistry involved between the kung fu genre and the twenty-first century's sophisticated, elegant take on *wuxia* also suggests a disconnection between the two moments, if not a downright reversal. As the film theorist Man-Fung Yip has argued, these new pictures mark a shift from the aesthetic of 'solid' and 'embodied' corporeality to one characterized by 'lightness, fluidity, and disembodiment'.[9]

However, there are reasons to see the new *wuxia* films as marking a similar kind of cultural event – a new or renewed 'encounter' between China and the West. Google Books' 'ngram' graphs recording the appearance of the term *kung fu* in its library points us to this. As the twenty-first century approaches, the graph turns rapidly more vertical, suggesting an amplification of interest. And in just the same way that the term *kung fu* suddenly appeared at the start of the 1970s, *wuxia* rose rapidly from obscurity in the early 2000s to make its mark on the English language.

How should we interpret this resurgence (or transformation) of cinematic representations of the martial arts in anglophone culture, and what does this tell us about the longer legacy and continued meaning of the kung fu craze?

KUNG FU AND 'TRANSNATIONAL' CULTURE

The first kung fu films to arrive on American and European screens were initially produced with regional East and Southeast Asian circuits in mind but, through the increasing mobility of culture, made their way beyond this context. Building on their impact, *Enter the Dragon* in many ways presaged the international financing and production of more recent films. As a joint venture between American and Hong Kong studios, it was soon followed, for example, though less successfully, by Hong Kong co-productions with Britain (*Legend of the Seven Golden Vampires*, 1974), Australia (*The Man from Hong Kong*, 1975) and Spain/Italy (*The Stranger and the Gunfighter*, 1974). Although they were relatively small-scale in terms of budgets, even the financing of martial arts films for grindhouse circuits or video distribution often involved pre-selling rights across a range of different territories and entailed collaboration between international cast and crew.

Indeed, the time when the kung fu craze erupted in the early 1970s is often identified as a significant one in the economic and cultural integration dubbed 'globalization', and we can trace the increasing pluralization of identities we have seen in the book so far to the increased presence of non-Western culture that this globalization produced.[10] Such globalization has indubitably accelerated in subsequent decades, forming new circumstances within which films are made and identities negotiated. A part of this has been China's increasing presence within the global realm. Its meteoric economic growth under Deng Xiaoping's leadership made China an object of renewed fascination in the West and also opened it up as a significant film market in itself, which American as well as East Asian film-makers could reach by embarking on co-productions.

Recent studies have considered these conditions through the concept of 'transnational cinema'. This term not only serves to recognize the increasing production and distribution of films beyond national boundaries, but it encompasses cinema's representation of contemporary life as transcending the boundaries of the nation state (as with the 'postnational' identities discussed earlier). It is as examples of such transnational cinema that we can understand the three films I will be examining here, helping us to further comprehend the map of the kung fu craze's complex legacy in the twenty-first century. Each of these films, in fact, is produced within a slightly different location within this map and offers us a different vantage on it: *Crouching Tiger* is a film by a Taiwanese American director; *Hero* by one from mainland China; and *The Grandmaster* by one working in Hong Kong.

HONG KONG ACTION AFTER THE KUNG FU CRAZE

Before going on to discuss these films, it seems helpful to briefly look back at some of the intervening changes in the Hong Kong film industry and its relation to Hollywood. Even as the kung fu craze was taking off in America, the dominance of the martial arts genre was fading locally (though it nonetheless remained a significant presence). In 1973, in spite of the posthumous release of Bruce Lee's *Enter the Dragon*, it was a comedy that topped the annual charts, Chor Yuen's *House of 72 Tenants*, and comedies continued to do so throughout the remainder of the decade. These comedies spoke to Hong Kong's contemporary life and local identity in a way that martial arts films, set in a fantastical and often generically Chinese past, perhaps did not.[11] Their success also motivated the development of the hybrid kung fu comedy genre towards the end of the decade and the rise of Jackie Chan's stardom.

The 1980s saw the ascent of gangster films, in particular with the work of John Woo, who extended the balletic choreography of bodies in violent motion from kung fu and *wuxia* into gunplay scenarios. (Woo's films, of course, often starred Chow Yun-fat, who would go on to play swordsman Li Mu Bai in *Crouching Tiger*.) Woo's transposition of themes and visual sensibilities developed through his work as an assistant for martial arts director Chang Cheh into the new genre was especially significant because of its influence on Hollywood. Woo's *A Better Tomorrow* (1986) was the most profitable Hong Kong film up to its own moment, and the film journalist and historian Barna Donovan claims it 'changed the way the world would see Hong Kong cinema and crime films'.[12] With the rise of video and DVD formats, cinema from across the world had become increasingly available, and (alongside an awareness of auteurs such as Wong Kar-wai) a cult 'extreme Asia' audience developed in the West, incorporating not only martial arts but violent crime films, anime, horror and even softcore films from Japan, Hong Kong and Korea.[13]

Processed through these video-shop fan sensibilities, the Hong Kong gangster film became highly influential on American action. Tarantino, who famously worked in a video store in his youth, is a case in point: he has spoken of John Woo as a key stylistic influence, and his debut *Reservoir Dogs* (1992) drew heavily on Ringo Lam's *City on Fire* (1987). Woo's gracefully flying bodies, shot in super-slow motion while bullets, shattering glass and explosions wrack the space around them, 'impressed Hollywood so much that the whole American genre was overhauled after Woo made the move to Hollywood in 1992'.[14] Woo was nonetheless just one pioneer of a swelling presence of Hong Kong stars, directors and action choreographers in American cinema during the 1990s. These enabled the incorporation of stylistic and technical aspects from the local industry into the norms of U.S. production, a process that the film theorist Leon Hunt has discussed as Hollywood's 'Hongkongification'.[15]

Kung fu Orientalism in cyberspace: Neo (Keanu Reeves) takes a martial arts lesson in a virtual dojo, decorated in traditional Japanese style and adorned with katanas, in *The Matrix*.

This Hongkongification created a familiarity with visual tropes and stylistic features that must have made the characteristics of *wuxia* more familiar to audiences when they finally arrived and even introduced the names of a range of directors and choreographers to Western audiences. Yuen Woo-ping, in particular, came to prominence in 1999 with his work on *The Matrix*, which blended elements of Woo-esque slow-motion gunplay with martial arts choreography and innovative computer-generated effects in a plot that brought together Orientalist kung fu mysticism with the more mainstream genre of sci-fi. Borrowing training-montage conventions from the kung fu genre and giving them a high-tech spin, its hero Neo (Keanu Reeves) uploads kung fu skills directly into his brain and enters a virtual dojo to learn lessons in the nature of reality from the cyber-guru Morpheus (Laurence Fishburne).

Meanwhile, the 1990s had also seen renewed interest in martial arts pictures in Hong Kong. Producer/director Tsui Hark, in particular, pioneered a new take on the swordplay genre, making use of the increased access of local film-makers to special effects and even digital technologies to re-engage with the fantastical dimensions of *wuxia*.[16] Tsui's films and the imitations he inspired are characterized by dramatic chiaroscuro lighting, dizzyingly tilted camera angles, bombastic soundtracks, rapid cutting and the bending of gender and genre alike. The critic Bhaskar Sarkar has described the ensuing style as 'hysterical', and we can understand this hysteria as motivated by both the anxieties of the looming handover of Hong Kong from British to Chinese rule and a broader pan-Asian condition of postmodern uncertainty about identity and about a future trapped within the intercontinental flows of an increasingly precarious and unstable economic reality.[17] These films paved the way for the globally produced *wuxia* of the following decade in their development of soaring 'wire-fu' choreography. Perhaps, in this respect, their 'hysteria' relates to a condition with global rather than just regional significance.

CROUCHING TIGER, HIDDEN DRAGON

When it arrived, *Crouching Tiger* was hailed in much of the popular media, on both sides of the Pacific, as a fundamentally Chinese success. Several factors contributed to its 'conspicuous Chineseness': its choice of the seemingly quintessential national genre of *wuxia*, its lavish use of historical costumes and interiors, its release in the Mandarin language and of course its display of iconic locations and landscapes, which included the Gobi Desert, the bamboo forests of Anhui, the temple complex at Mount Wudang and the palaces at Chengde (once the summer resort of the imperial family).[18] American critics viewed its success as evidence of a new cosmopolitanism in Hollywood's marketplace, while enthusiasts in greater China and the Chinese diaspora swelled with pride at a local film that had made the crossover to the West.[19]

As many have since argued, though, the film is not nearly as unambiguously a 'Chinese' cultural expression as it may have seemed. Rather, like *Enter the Dragon* so many years before, it was a complex production spanning nations and even continents. This is evident, to begin with, in the biography of its director, Ang Lee. Lee was born in Taiwan to parents who had fled mainland China when the Communists came to power, but he moved to the USA for his university education and by the time *Crouching Tiger* was in production had lived there for nearly as long as he had in his country of birth. His first films, a trilogy of modern-day domestic dramas, found funding and critical acclaim in Taiwan, but his career increasingly shifted to Hollywood. By the time he embarked on *Crouching Tiger*, Lee had won renown for his production of Jane Austen's *Sense and Sensibility* (1995) and followed this up with *The Ice Storm* (1997), set in suburban America, and *Ride with the Devil* (1999), a Civil War drama.

Lee's relation to the 'Chinese' subject-matter of the film is not best understood in straightforward terms of national cinema or subjectivity; rather, it is better understood as a 'work of diasporic cinema'.[20] The film's fantasy of the Chinese past – lovingly and lavishly constructed as this is through costume, location and sets, as well as determined by the choice of the *wuxia* genre – is marked by the nostalgia for an absent homeland so broadly characteristic of diasporic culture. Indeed, it is set in a country Lee had only visited for a single five-day trip before making *Crouching Tiger*.[21] Lee has written of the film as 'a kind of dream of China, a China that probably never existed except in my boyhood fantasies in Taiwan'. This dream, he suggests, was inspired by 'the martial arts movies I grew up with and by the novels of romance and derring-do I read instead of doing my homework'.[22] Elsewhere, he located its 'classic Chinese textures' as emerging 'from history, from my parents, movies'.[23]

The nostalgia here helps make sense of the very different relationship to authority and tradition Lee's film expresses compared to the rebellious kung fu movies of the 1970s. *Crouching Tiger* is set in the middle of the Qing dynasty (1644–1911), so at a similar historical moment to many classic kung fu outings. But whereas kung fu's protagonists typically find themselves fighting its authorities as a despotic, foreign regime (for example in the Shaw Brothers' Shaolin cycle), the Qing social order appears in *Crouching Tiger* as a generally benign, prosperous and stable one. Far from being its opponents, Li Mu Bai and Yu Xiulian act as its agents, while Jen is a member of its ruling elite. They are, in fact, just the types who are likely to have been the villains of a 1970s movie. With this kind of revisionist spin, the film also lacks the monstrous patriarchal tyrants whom kung fu's young heroes so often have to defeat. If there are intergenerational tensions in the film, one might suggest that it is Jen's youthful rebelliousness, which Mu Bai and Xiulian must bring into check and integrate back into the social fold, that is the 'problem'.

Despite all this, the film's relation to tradition is not without ambivalence. Lee has discussed his early work as revolving around the unease of modern Chinese people with their 'betrayal' of their ethnic patrimony (and by extension their parents and ancestors) in the adoption of 'modern' and 'Western' ways of life.[24] As a fantasy of the past, *Crouching Tiger* may involve an uneasy reconciliation with such a heritage. The moment chosen for the film's setting seems highly symbolic in this regard. The date on Xiulian's travel permit when she enters Beijing towards the start of the film allows us to locate the story in the year 1778. This was almost exactly the high point of the Qing dynasty – one of the pinnacles of Chinese power, wealth and stability across the whole of its long imperial history. It is also, however, the moment just before the Qing empire's traumatic encounter with growing Western imperial ambitions during the nineteenth century and the last time that China might be represented (in the contemporary imagination, at least, if not in fact) in some kind of 'pristine' state before its fall into modern history.

Indeed, we can ask whether the society depicted in the film has not already passed its zenith, with intimations of decadence seeming to creep in. For example, Jade Fox's sexual abuse at the hands of the former master of the Wudang monastery, a sacred space in which both the spiritual and martial traditions of the nation are preserved and handed down, seems to locate corruption within its heart. Her revenge on him before the action of the film begins leaves Wudang symbolically fatherless, and her resentment has spread poison into the ruling elite, among whom she is hiding, acting as governess to Jen, the daughter of an aristocratic family. Stirred up by Jade Fox's stories and made cynical about authority, Jen rejects both an arranged marriage and Wudang discipleship to wander the martial world, causing chaos everywhere she goes. Similarly, the spiritual vacuum created by the death (and corruption) of the Wudang patriarch leaves his disciple Li Mu Bai's spiritual training unfinished, despite his masterly skill with a sword. At the start of the film, he discusses reaching a state of meditation for which his master's teachings had not prepared him, and his inability to resolve the difficulties that this posed him determines much of the film's unfolding narrative and the indecisions that typify his role within it.

Crouching Tiger is at once nostalgic and critical of tradition, and it remains anxious about the nature of heritage even as it desires this. This ambivalence makes it typical of much diasporic art, stemming as this does from a social experience in which multiple and shifting positions concerning both homeland and host country are inherent and in which forms of 'double consciousness' abound.[25]

This perspective also places Lee in an advantageous position to produce a mobile, border-crossing film, capable of what the film theorist Felicia Chan calls 'migrancy', in terms of both its production and its address to different audiences.[26] This migrancy is seen first in the access that Lee had to contacts and collaborators across the globe. Though shot on location and in studios in China, the project was produced by some five companies, spanning Taiwan, Hong Kong, the PRC and the USA, with backing from the Japanese media giant Sony and its subsidiaries in both Asia and America.[27] Its stars, chosen to give the film appeal across a broad geography, were pan-Chinese. Michelle Yeoh was born in Malaysia. Chow Yun-fat and Cheng Pei-pei are both Hongkongers, though the latter has been resident in California since the 1970s. Zhang Ziyi is from mainland China, and Chang Chen from Taiwan. Yeoh and Chow, furthermore, had already made their mark in Hollywood productions (*Tomorrow Never Dies*, 1997, and *The Replacement Killers*, 1998, respectively). Choreography was provided by Hong Kong veteran Yuen Woo-ping, who had also made the jump to Hollywood, winning acclaim for his work on *The Matrix*, a fact used to sell *Crouching Tiger* in the West. Its iconic soundtrack was composed by Chinese-born Tan Dun, now resident in the USA, and features Chinese American cellist Yo-Yo Ma.

Lee himself has talked of the resulting film as having 'a story with a global sense', and his co-producer and long-term collaborator James Schamus has described it as 'an eastern movie for western audiences and in some ways a more western movie for eastern audiences'.[28] This ambition towards international cross-address is borne out in the development of the script, which was produced by shuttling drafts back and forth between Schamus in New York and his co-author Wang Hui-ling in Taipei, a process that entailed repeated translation from Chinese to English and back. Indeed, Lee's foremost achievement is perhaps the extent to which he was able to mould the early twentieth-century novel that he was adapting, and the *wuxia* genre overall, into a format familiar to a Hollywood audience. Narratively, the story is cast in the mould of a European psychological novel – Lee was, after all, best known up to this point for his Jane Austen adaptation, and he himself has called it '*Sense and Sensibility* with martial arts'.[29]

Crouching Tiger's cinematic style, too, drew on Hollywood conventions rather than Hong Kong's *wuxia* tradition. As many commentators have observed, it takes some fifteen minutes before the first action scene. This time allows Lee to set up the unfamiliar elements of a fictional universe that Chinese-language viewers and genre fans alike might be able to take for granted. When the action does arrive in the rooftop chase and combat initiated by Jen's theft of the sword Green Destiny, Lee draws on conventions developed in 1930s Hollywood musicals to slowly ease the viewer from the narrative mode of psychological realism to the spectacle of the set piece. Lee shifts the setting from indoors to outdoors, and we first have a tantalizing glimpse of Jen as she flits across a roof before seeing her wirework-enhanced movements more clearly. The pace of editing accelerates and the soundtrack builds. The ringing of the alarm within the film blends into the accelerating drum beats of the score. The chase brings us to a separate arena in which the fight finally takes place.[30] All this reduces the jolting effect that might be caused for a Western audience by the leap from storytelling to set piece. For viewers already attuned to the genre, however, this leap would be quite expected and untroubling. For these audiences, the film often lacked pace, and one Hong Kong viewer interviewed in *The Guardian* found it 'so slow it's a bit like listening to grandma telling stories'.[31] This, perhaps, helps us understand the relatively lukewarm reception it had there.

Due to this adaptation to Hollywood norms, one set of complaints emerging from greater China and the Chinese diaspora was that the film broke too many conventions of the genre and was 'inauthentic'.[32] With actors rather than trained martial artists in the lead, the action lacked vitality, and its wirework looked 'artificial'. Furthermore, Mandarin speakers, especially in mainland China, found the faltering pronunciation and foreign accents of its Hong Kong, Malaysian and even Taiwanese stars comically jarring when projected back into the distant national past. In addition, the collaborative process of its writing introduced many anachronous Anglicisms into the script.[33]

The nostalgia of Lee's vision of China also elicited different responses in its different audiences. Sinophone criticism often reacted to the nationalism involved in Lee's return to the past, with some finding this a cause for patriotic enthusiasm and others responding more anxiously in the light of the conservatism and cultural essentialism suggested by looking back to myth and history.[34] Critics have also noted the extent to which the film, with its 'panoramic sweeps of exotic landscape and the fetishization of sexual repression and Oriental sensuality', elicited 'suspicion of stereotyping . . . and pandering to a Western gaze'.[35] Wu Chia-chi, for example, accused the film of 'self-Orientalizing' and noted that popular discussions of it 'constantly fall prey to Orientalist clichés'.[36] For other critics, especially those in the West, it was the film's innovations with regard to just these traditional genres and the seemingly conservative 'Chinese' ideologies they supported that lent it a cast of cosmopolitan liberalism and made it acceptable.[37]

At the core of the debates on the film's negotiation of the national/traditional and the cosmopolitan/modern are the interlinked issues of the tension between desire and repression and its treatment of gender. Lee himself has placed the conflict between individual desire and duty towards the collective good at the heart of the film, and this same thematic core can be traced from his early Taiwanese films through to later Hollywood works such as *Brokeback Mountain* (2005).[38] (Of course, the conflict between 'sense' and 'sensibility' is also at stake here.) *Crouching Tiger* contrasts the long-repressed love between Mu Bai and Xiulian with the wildness of Jen's affair with Lo and her quest for absolute freedom and personal authenticity. This contrast has often been interpreted as reflecting that between China and the West or tradition and modernity.[39] However, undermining this, Lee himself has tended to emphasize that the clash between lovers' forbidden desires and the forces of social propriety has in fact been the 'great Chinese theme', expressed throughout its history in poetry, drama, literature and visual art.[40]

The interpretation of this theme in *Crouching Tiger* has often revolved around Lee's decision to place female protagonists at the centre of its narrative. This has led many – especially those less familiar with the tradition of women warriors in *wuxia* or the films of King Hu, which are one of his clearest points of reference – to interpret the film as offering a genre-busting critique of Confucian patriarchy. The suggestion of a 'feminist' narrative and the presence of strong women in the film was even a deliberate part of its marketing to female viewers in America.[41] Indeed, Lee's interest in gender as a theme does, perhaps, serve to destabilize any traditionalist ideology emerging from the choice of genre.[42] But the film's treatment of repression and gender – marked both by Lee's double consciousness and by the need to address very different audiences – cannot simply be understood as a novel Western (and hence progressive) spin on a familiar Chinese (and hence regressive) genre. As

Wu Chia-chi argues, its 'sexual politics are ambivalent at best, with Shu Lien remaining a sexually repressed advocate of the Confucian order, Jade Fox punished for her refusal to submit, and Jen finally acquiescing'. The possession of the Green Destiny, a classic symbol of phallic power, remains forbidden to all three.[43] The film is neither as radical as it seemed to many in its inclusion of women warriors within the martial arts genre, nor as unambiguously feminist in its treatment of them.[44]

HERO

At first sight, *Hero*, released in China in 2002 and the USA in 2004, seems to share a lot with *Crouching Tiger*. It was a big-budget, multi-award-winning Chinese-language *wuxia* with international backing and sales and acclaim from critics in Europe and America as well as in Asia. It featured prominent women warrior characters, breathtaking airborne action, sweeping landscapes and a high-art sensibility that orchestrated the narrative as a symphony of colour. Though slightly less exceptional in its internationalism, the film was produced through the collaboration of mainland Chinese and Hong Kong studios and bankrolled in part by licensing rights in North America and Europe to the Disney subsidiary Miramax. Its main star, Jet Li, first came to prominence in the PRC as a *wushu* performer before establishing his superstardom in Hong Kong and then making the move to Hollywood. Appearing alongside him, Maggie Cheung and Tony Leung were Hong Kong stars, while Zhang Ziyi and Chen Daoming were both from the mainland. Donnie Yen grew up in Hong Kong and America before returning to Asia to train as a martial artist, make his name in Hong Kong cinema and finally win acclaim in Hollywood as a choreographer on *Highlander: Endgame* (2000) and then *Blade II* (2002). Behind the camera was Australian-born cinematographer Chris Doyle, and the score, composed again by *Crouching Tiger*'s Tan Dun, prominently featured the Japanese drumming ensemble Kodo.

Indeed, *Hero* can easily be seen as falling foul of some of the same criticisms levelled at *Crouching Tiger*. In terms of a domestic audience, its romantic vision of the deep Chinese past seems to locate it immediately within a backwards-looking reconstruction of national identity. Abroad, its sensory overload, its eroticism, the familiar tropes of 'kung fu' and the use of iconic landscapes might all smack of playing to exoticism and Orientalism. But the film also emerges from a very different, specific place within transnational Chinese cinema, and this marks it in very different ways.

The film's director, Zhang Yimou, first came to notice in the 1980s as part of a group of film-makers from the PRC usually dubbed the 'fifth generation'. These were known for their deconstruction of the orthodoxies of 'people's cinema', formal experimentation, emphasis on subjectivity and – even with the memory of the Cultural Revolution still fresh – 'willingness to test the boundaries of ideological control'.[45] From his directorial debut *Red Sorghum* (1987) onwards, Zhang became known for his highly imagistic style. As the Chinese film industry became increasingly commercialized in the 1990s, he turned more and more to foreign backing and 'world cinema' circuits to produce his films, though this also came with criticisms that his works played to Western stereotypes. As political tides turned later in the decade, resulting in foreign backing becoming less viable, Zhang returned to the domestic market, making increasingly commercial and conventional films. *Hero* marked another twist in his career: it is both his first foray into the martial arts or action genres and also new in the sheer scale of budget and distribution, which located him for the first time in the field of a popular cinema with global reach.

Making films within an authoritarian state, Zhang's career has been moulded by a 'complex dance with the official censors' that sets his experience apart from Ang Lee's.[46] His films (often the same ones!) are sometimes understood as offering 'penetrating critiques of power' and sometimes as too obediently toeing the party line.[47] Either way, his work involves a close awareness of its relation to the authorities and the market forces that allow it to be made. *Hero* resembles *Crouching Tiger* in the ambiguous and open narrative it offered a global audience, but this emerges from very different pressures to Ang Lee's. The film was, in any case, subjected to a range of interpretations of its politics that varied radically across its markets.

Much of the anxiety of English-language critics has been that the film may act as an apologia for the mounting authoritarianism of the Communist Party. This criticism often revolves around the movie's revisionist take on the kung fu genre's attitude to rebellion. Most particularly, this is seen in its depiction of the first emperor, Qin Shi Huangdi, who ended the long and chaotic Warring States period to unite the nation in 221 BC, setting the start date for the two-millennia-long imperial era. Qin has come down in Chinese history as – at best – an ambivalent character. He is indeed remembered as a national unifier: he standardized the national writing system and started work on both the Great Wall that protected the nation from invaders and the canal system that linked north and south. However, he is most squarely known as a tyrant who set out to annihilate all opposition to his rule. His crimes include book burnings, the burial alive of Confucian scholars and the death in forced labour of countless conscripts on the Great Wall and his extravagant tomb. Qin died soon after his conquest of the nation, sent mad by the mercury pills he took in the search for immortality. In the hands of his incompetent son, his empire soon disintegrated.

Hero, however, represents him in a surprisingly positive light. Though the film seems in its opening section to follow a conventional kung fu narrative where heroic rebels attempt to unseat a villainous tyrant, by the end the film's protagonist, Nameless (Jet Li), under the influence of the wise Broken Sword (Tony Leung), has come to realize the historical importance of the emperor's unifying mission as a means to future peace and stability. As a result, he abandons his assassination attempt. This reversal of genre expectations (paralleling that of *Crouching Tiger*) is all the more startling when we consider the transformation *Hero* has made of its source material. The film seems to take as its inspiration a famous story by China's first historiographer, Sima Qian. In this, an assassin, Jing Ke, attempts but fails to kill the future first emperor, an act that Sima lauds as heroic in its aim to curb tyranny through individual sacrifice.[48] Sima, in fact, devoted two chapters of his historical work to the deeds of assassins and martial artists who had taken on such a role, romanticizing their independence of mind and heroism in cleaving to justice and righteousness in the face of political oppression. Sima's stories have undoubtedly influenced the literary treatment of the martial arts in China ever since.[49] Zhang's story, however, seems a deliberate reversal of the tale of Jing Ke, which Chinese viewers would be likely to know well. *Hero* makes a striking contrast to Chang Cheh's paean to rebellion and political revolt in *The Assassin* (1967), as discussed earlier, which adapts a neighbouring tale in Sima's history.

Zhang's representation of Qin Shi Huangdi would have carried significance because of parallels often made between him and Mao. In this, *Hero* may start to appear as an apologia for the Communist Party's draconian grip on power as necessary to ensure national unity, stability and prosperity. Like the first emperor, the film might suggest, Mao ended a century of poverty, weakness and civil war. To rebel against this (as the Tiananmen Square protesters in 1989 had done) was to court a return to chaos.

The critic and film director Evans Chan, for example, sees these allegorical aspects, combined with *Hero*'s evocation of a myth of national origins, as amounting to a dangerously 'fascist' vision, calling it a 'pernicious apology for a (post)totalitarian regime'.[50] Chan's revulsion is amplified by the film's staging of its narrative in high aesthetic form, which might remind us of the cultural critic Walter Benjamin's warning, written in the shadow of Hitler's rise to power, about fascism as operating through the seductive 'aestheticization of politics'.[51] As Chan points out, the martial arts film is 'the genre film *par excellence* to aestheticize combat and death', and Zhang's narrative is all the more disturbing because of the ethic of sacrifice for the state it implies.[52] Its spectacular choreography of bodies becomes a rehearsal for the opening and closing ceremonies of the 2008 Beijing Olympics, which Zhang also went on to direct. In these, hundreds of perfectly coordinated martial arts performers moved in unison to form a mass-media image of the relation between the individual and state power. This spectacular image asserted an essential and powerful 'Chineseness' through the image of 'kung fu', which the PRC had been using as a means of 'soft power' since at least the appearance of a youthful Jet Li as part of the touring *wushu* troupe on the White House lawn back in 1974. Similarly, the beautiful and highly technological display of Chinese martial arts on the big screen – produced at a level of industrial sophistication to match American cinema – can be interpreted as an assertion of global power and the ability to compete. This high-end 'production glamour' reverses the developing-world underdog look of 1970s kung fu movies.[53] With all this in mind, Chan sees Zhang as 'the closest thing to being the Leni Riefenstahl of China'.[54]

Despite these criticisms, it is striking that very different interpretations of its politics were often made in China itself. While Western critics equated the film's emperor with the Communist Party, many Chinese viewers saw him as an apologetic image of American global dominance under George W. Bush.[55] Commentators pointed out

The high-tech, massed and disciplined ranks of the Qin army in *Hero*.

the visual echoes between the attack on the calligraphy school within the film and still-recent newsreel footage of the destruction of the Chinese embassy in Belgrade in the 1998–9 Kosovo conflict. The high-tech might of the American military finds its analogue in the mechanistic ranks of the Qin army in the film, equipped as these are with point-and-shoot crossbows (the cutting edge of weapons technology in the Warring States period) rather than the romantic martial artistry of the *wuxia* heroes they are lined up against. The calligraphy school was also a highly symbolic location in terms of ethnic identity, with the written word a key symbol of Chineseness within the film itself. Broken Sword – a calligrapher as well as a martial artist – notes the chaos of the multiple ways in which the word 'sword' can be written across the different warring states of the time and (even amid the bombardment) produces a giant image of the character created as an amalgamation of these variations. When Nameless presents this to the emperor, he reads in it an echo of his own unifying ambitions, and we have in this an origin myth for Chinese identity itself.

But in the calligraphy school attack, we have an image of an assault precisely on the kind of ethnic identity that is enshrined in writing itself as a vehicle for culture. Is this an image of the unifying but homogenizing power of the global American order, which transcends the 'local' and national identity of China? And if the film embraces the emperor and Broken Sword's vision of unity, does it therefore embrace the continued power of the USA?[56] This is supported by the fact that Zhang himself, in the DVD commentary to the film, has talked of it as a response to the attack on the Twin Towers in New York.[57] This offers us a rather different image of the knights-errant of the film and their defence of ethnic uniqueness against the unification and homogenization to come. They can now be understood as analogous to the Middle Eastern terrorists who stood against America's global order, and forms of Chinese nationalism are perhaps cast in this light, too. Zhang's later film, *The Great Wall* (2016), again celebrates the cosmopolitanism of an East–West collaboration, defending against monstrous, alien hordes. If the film does include a cosmopolitan message, this has only become more striking in the light of mounting tensions between China and America since its production, with nationalism and xenophobia reasserting themselves on both sides.

Much of the tension between these two interpretations of the film as on the one hand nationalist and on the other cosmopolitan hinges on how we understand a key term in it, *tianxia*. This is the word Broken Sword writes in the sand for Nameless to persuade him that he should abandon his assassination attempt. It is the ideal that has brought him to give up opposition to the dominance of the Qin over his own state. The subtitles for *Hero*'s original American release translated *tianxia* as 'our land', suggesting a nationalist message.[58] But *tianxia* is an altogether more complex concept with a long history in China, entailing various political uses. Literally meaning 'all under heaven', *tianxia* refers to a realm beyond particular states, which they are often competing to control. It has also been translated as 'world' and is a complex concept, open to both nationalist and cosmopolitan standpoints.[59]

Whichever power we interpret *Hero* as an allegory of, however, the attitude of the film towards it is less than obvious. Drawing on the precedent of multiple, conflicting narratives in, for example, Kurosawa's *Rashomon* (1950), the film offers us not one but three different versions of its story, in a kind of intellectual duel between Nameless and the emperor, who seeks the truth behind his visitor's initially deceptive tale. Though perhaps this 'truth' is told in the final account, repeated and contradictory tellings mean that an audience may well leave the cinema unsure about what event was part of which story and hence which were true or false. The sense of the unreliability of even its final telling is only exacerbated by an audience's potential awareness of the ways it competes with the established historical canon regarding the first emperor and the attempts on his life.

This subversive refusal of the mythmaking power of cinema, even as it acquiesces to its necessity, might well be a part of Zhang's 'complex dance with the official censors' remarked above, and of what has been typified as Zhang's 'enormous talent in picking his subject, creating shades and shadows around his position, or simply covering his tracks'.[60] Nameless – a warrior stripped at the start of the film not only of weapons but even of his very clothes – has only the evasive power of fiction with which to joust with the emperor. In this sense, Nameless could be interpreted as a self-portrait of Zhang himself as a film-maker.[61] The emperor's hall, after all, is a dark space in which an all-powerful figure is enthroned while a series of colourful illusions are conjured within it to tell of the world outside. It is a clear allegory, I would argue, for cinema itself. This suggests that it is us, the global cinema audience (not just censors and party apparatchiks but also viewers), into whose court he has entered.

This view is supported by one of the most subtle analyses of *Hero* I have come across, Margaret Hillenbrand's account of colour in Zhang's *wuxia* pictures.[62] Hillenbrand observes that Zhang – like a range of very different contemporary East Asian auteurs – foregrounds colour in his work. In this, he appears to be engaged in a project whereby a regional rather than just national style is being asserted, in the face, perhaps, of a Western 'chromophobia', the distrust of colour as unreliably subjective and as inflaming the senses.[63] This denigration of colour has been expressed in the very tendency over much of the twentieth century to see the austerity of 'black and white' as the mark of a serious film rather than a superficial, populist one. Underlining this 'East Asian' identity implied in the embrace of colour, the key reference point in *Hero* seems not to be anything from Chinese cinematic history but Kurosawa's *Ran* (1985). (The Japanese reference is reinforced with the prominence of the Kodo drummers on the soundtrack.) For Hillenbrand, this makes transnational cinema itself, as imagined in *Hero*, a kind of *tianxia*, and it makes the pan-Asian embrace of colour a riposte to Hollywood's dominance.

But what Hillenbrand values in Zhang's interest in colour is – as with its storytelling – its 'troubling and unmanageable surfeit of meaning'.[64] Colour, she argues, plunges us into the sensory realm and into that of 'feeling', addressing us as embodied beings and through a kind of broad humanism. Colour in this regard is an 'esperanto of the senses'.[65] Far from being a trivial matter (as some critics, for example, of Zhang's *House of Flying Daggers* complained), it is 'all that makes us not just sentient but humane, too'.[66] This locates Zhang's bid to define cinematic *tianxia* as entailing a very different politics to the ones that some of his interpreters in both China and the West have proposed. For Hillenbrand, what typifies the communication of colour is its intense subjectivity, akin to the ambiguity of Nameless's storytelling, and the power at its heart. This plunge into the subjective and the plural would seem to undermine the standardization and homogenization at the heart of the emperor's project and of totalitarian order more broadly.

THE GRANDMASTER

Ang Lee's *Crouching Tiger* and Zhang Yimou's *Hero* give us different takes on the reality they operate within – both that of the cinema industry and the underlying processes and conditions of globalization. They each use the imagery of the Chinese martial arts, as established in global popular culture by the kung fu craze, in rather different ways to say something about this. Lee's film emerged from the experience of the Chinese diaspora. Zhang's belongs to the fraught politics of the PRC and the conditions of making films for global release within an authoritarian state, as well as the continued international dominance of Hollywood.

Wong Kar-wai's *The Grandmaster*, released in 2013, offers us another perspective again: that of a Hong Kong-based director. It also appeared at a slightly later moment in time, although this gulf is less than it first appears if we consider the extraordinarily long gestation of the project. It had already gone into production in 2008, but even before this, its script was registered in 2001, and Tony Leung was training for the fight scenes by 2004. Wong himself has discussed its creation as a decade-long task. This dates its inception to the same moment as the other two films I have just discussed, even if it also speaks to the particular conditions of Hong Kong in the 2010s.[67]

Like Lee's and Zhang's pictures, *The Grandmaster* brings an art-house sensibility to the popular martial arts genre. It exploits the high budgets and production values that the global appeal of such films allows and includes spectacular martial arts sequences choreographed with the aid of wirework and computer effects by

Crouching Tiger's Yuen Woo-ping. Indeed, the casting suggests that the film was very much calculated to appeal to fans of the other two movies: its lead, Tony Leung, had played the role of Broken Sword in *Hero*, while Zhang Ziyi, its female star, had appeared not only in that picture and *House of Flying Daggers*, but in *Crouching Tiger*, too. Chang Chen, who played her love interest in that story, also reappears with third billing in *The Grandmaster* as the character Razor, although much of his intended role seems to have fallen prey to Wong's cutting-room floor. In terms of their origins, the three map out the familiar triangle of Hong Kong, mainland China and Taiwan. *The Grandmaster* also shares with Lee and Zhang's films its international scale of production, with input from companies in Hong Kong, the USA and mainland China. It was the first of Wong's films to have a release in the PRC, and the Weinstein Company bought the distribution rights for much of the English-speaking world, with Wong producing radically different cuts for these different markets and another for the art-house circuit.[68]

The Grandmaster also, even in its broadest characteristics, departs significantly from *Crouching Tiger* and *Hero*. While these remain relatively conventional and clearly function within the parameters of their genre, Wong extends the stamp of his authorial vision further, making this essentially an 'art' film which plays on – and against – the expectations of martial arts cinema rather than remaining within its confines. Its non-linear narrative is presented in a highly impressionistic form, and its dialogue is often enigmatic and allusive, contributing to the film's thematic textures rather than driving the plot forwards. This all makes it 'difficult' viewing rather than an easy narrative pleasure. In addition, it took up the signature keynote of all of Wong's films – the evocation of romanticized, melancholy longing, elevated in itself into a ravishing sensuality, which struck many critics as a strange fit with the action genre.[69]

Furthermore, it eschews the distant past in which both *Hero* and *Crouching Tiger* occur, locating its story within the tumultuous politics of twentieth-century China instead. *The Grandmaster* takes the form of a biopic of real-life wing chun practitioner Ip Man, who was significant as the teacher of Bruce Lee. Through Lee's fame, the art he practised has been transformed from an obscure regional style to one of the most globally promulgated forms of kung fu today. But Ip's biography also allows Wong to reconstruct the bigger context of the Republican-era martial arts world. One of the reasons for the long gestation of the film was the lengthy research he and scriptwriter Xu Haofeng embarked on, interviewing numerous surviving 'grandmasters' from the time and creating events and characters in the film as composites from their accounts.

Ip is especially interesting to Wong as someone who migrated from China to Hong Kong in the 1950s, the decade in which Wong was born. When just five years old, Wong, too, would become a Hong Kong immigrant, and he has spoken of the cinema (with all its martial arts fantasies) as a childhood refuge from a world he was separated from by linguistic difference. The presence of expatriate martial arts teachers such as Ip was a feature of the urban landscape of Kowloon where he grew up and formed a precondition of the emergence of the kung fu movies he enjoyed as a child. As in Lee's film, then, the traditions of the martial arts become a marker of dislocation from an absent homeland. Wong's picture, however, locates them much closer to home, both geographically and temporally, than *Crouching Tiger*. Because of this closeness to the contemporary world, in *The Grandmaster* the martial arts become a means to meditate on our relation to Chinese tradition and its transmission into the present. Our awareness of Bruce Lee as Ip's future student should remind us that it is not only the martial arts but their cinematic representations that are at stake in these questions. Wong is surely concerned with the ways the globalizing power of cinema itself places 'tradition', as an expression of the local, in question. This is implicit in both *Hero* and *Crouching Tiger*, but *The Grandmaster* is certainly the most explicit of the three in thematizing the legacy of the kung fu craze as a moment of global contact.

Because of Ip's link to Lee, he had, in fact, in the years during which Wong was working on *The Grandmaster*, become an object of increased cinematic fascination, serving as a means to mythologize local and national identities and their place in the global landscape. The first instalment of Wilson Yip's highly successful *Ip Man* franchise, starring Donnie Yen, was released in 2008, with a second following in 2010 (and two more until the present date). Competing with these were Herman Yau's *The Legend Is Born: Ip Man* (2010) and *Ip Man: The Final Fight* (2013).

Wilson Yip's representations of Ip's life were much more straightforward genre stories than *The Grandmaster*. Yip's films looked back to the kung fu era rather than to *wuxia* and self-consciously drew on Bruce Lee movies, in particular, to underline the link between Ip and Lee's legend, often reimagining scenes from Lee's onscreen roles as events in his teacher's real life. The first film, for example, echoed the patriotic plot of *Fist of Fury*, setting Ip against Japanese invaders during the Second World War. It even included a scene where Donnie Yen defeats an entire dojo of Japanese karate practitioners, clearly in direct imitation of Lee. Its finale sets Ip against a Japanese officer on a public stage, evoking the tournament fights in *Enter the Dragon*. Similarly, the third instalment reiterated the iconic David-and-Goliath East–West battle between Lee and Norris in *The Way of the Dragon* by setting Yen up against Mike Tyson. The trope was repeated in the fourth instalment, which depicted Ip visiting America and defending the local Chinese community against the racist bullying of an officer from the U.S. marines. With

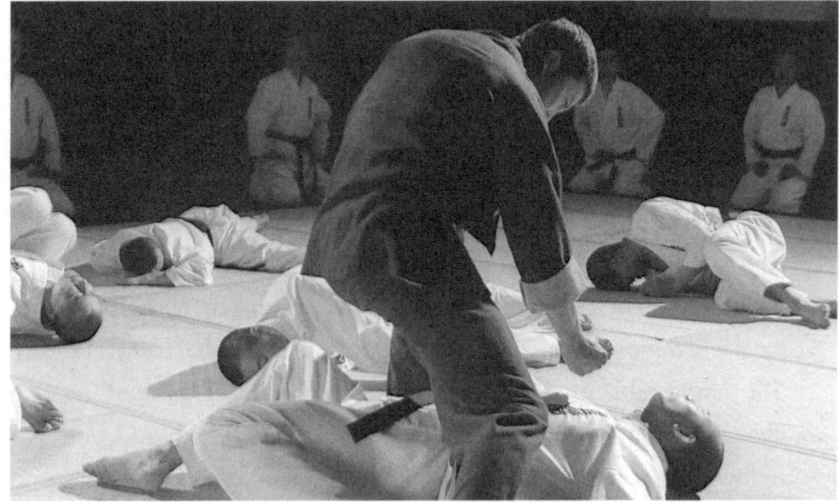

In *Ip Man*, Donnie Yen demolishes an entire dojo of Japanese karate practitioners, in clear imitation of Bruce Lee in *Fist of Fury*.

its nationalist themes, in any case, *Ip Man* seemed calculated to play to the PRC's censors and to the mainland Chinese market, which was its single largest source of revenue on theatrical release.

Despite the patriotic narrative of a number of his films, Lee, however, is not just understood as a nationalist figure. As Hongkongers increasingly defined their identity in opposition to rather than in terms of 'Chineseness', Lee also became a specifically local hero, embodying ideas that set Hong Kong apart from the mainland. Lee was, after all, of mixed race, and his association with Hollywood echoed the hybridity of Hong Kong identity, its close economic and cultural links to the West and its embrace of modernity rather than tradition. Lee was even adopted as an icon of the 2019 pro-democracy protesters, who took up his injunction to 'be like water' as a battle tactic. This phrase – emphasizing change, pragmatism and adaptation – might also offer a broader slogan for virtues often associated with Hong Kong itself.

How should we interpret *The Grandmaster*'s position on this? Its very appeal to the theme of the martial arts as a matter of tradition seemed to some critics to line it up with the ethnic nationalism of Yip's films.[70] In visual terms, its close attention to the detail of particular kung fu styles (with the camera lingering in close up on the ways that hands are held, or feet placed on the floor) amplifies this sense of tradition.[71]

But Wong's handling of this may be more complex. The questions of the local, the national and the global quickly assert themselves as explicit concerns. Our first clue to Wong's relationship with tradition (and with the role of the past as a source of identity in a globalizing world) is contained in Ip's voiceover at the start of the film: 'Kung fu: two words. One horizontal, one vertical. If you're wrong, you'll be left lying down. If you're right, you're left standing, and only the ones who stand have the right to talk.' As we first hear them, accompanying a brutal fight scene, the words seem to refer simply to combat, expressing the 'street reality' pragmatism with which Ip and his student Lee have often been associated. However, as the film develops, it becomes clear that this is a metaphor for life more generally, especially within the turbulent and testing times that the film depicts. While there are many in the film with the requisite skill to be counted the 'grandmaster' of the title, Ip is the exceptional figure who lives to pass on his art to posterity and so take up this mantle.

This question of survival and transmission – being left 'vertical' by history – seems determined by one's relation to the past and future. Ip's pragmatism entails not simply a rejection of the past and embrace of the modern but a balance between looking forwards and looking backwards, which other characters fail to achieve. This is true in particular of the two inheritors of the northern master of the Wudang arts, Gong Yutian: his top student Ma San and his daughter Gong Er. In a key scene, Master Gong attempts to dissuade the ambitious Ma from becoming a traitor to his country by collaborating with the Japanese. Speaking in metaphors, Gong tells him that he has failed to understand the key principle of his signature kung fu move, which is 'looking back in reflection'. Ma refuses his reprimand – 'A warrior moulds himself to the times. What if I can't look back?' – and he kills his teacher.[72] Ma, however, is then killed by Gong Er in revenge, precisely through the signature move that he would or could not understand. But if Ma is destroyed by his failure to integrate the past, Gong Er suffers from the opposite tendency. Vowing to never teach or marry in order to dedicate herself to revenge, she is unable to adjust to the world after this task is completed. She sticks to her vows after she has moved to Hong Kong despite suggestions from others around her that the world in which the vows were made no longer exists and that they are no longer relevant. Instead, she retreats into an opium-fuelled haze of memories of her happy childhood in the distant, snowy north. Only Ip, it seems, manages to look back to tradition while remaining pliable to the circumstances around him and so hand on something of that past to the future. Ip's triumph is also a melancholy one, admittedly, but this is entirely of a piece with the disconsolate Romanticism of Wong's overall artistic vision.

Wong's attitude to tradition and modernity, to Chinese or Hong Kong identity and globalization, and to his vision of kung fu cinema's historic role as a bridge between these, is demonstrated in another important scene. *The Grandmaster*'s action is instigated when Master Gong arrives in Ip's southern Chinese hometown, Foshan. Gong is the head of the Nationalist Party's official martial arts institute. He is about to retire, and his dream has been the unification of the Chinese martial arts. He is hoping with his visit to cement his organization's authority over the southern Chinese

Gong Yutian (Wang Qingxiang) and Ip Man (Tony Leung) cross hands in a battle of skill and philosophy, as Gong challenges Ip to break the biscuit in his hand in *The Grandmaster*.

martial arts community by holding a challenge match against their chosen representative. Ip, of course, is selected to face him. When the two meet, what they perform is a philosophical contest as much as a fight, with Gong challenging Ip to break a biscuit he holds in his hand. The biscuit, he intimates, is a metaphor for the integrity of the nation's martial arts and, through them, of the bigger political project of the GMD to hold together a nation constantly disintegrating into warring factions. Managing to defeat Gong, Ip admonishes him:

> The world is a big place. Why limit it to north and south? It holds you back. To you this cookie is the country. To me, it's much more . . . If the southern arts go far, what boundary is the north?

Anticipating the spread of wing chun and the southern Chinese martial arts through the Hong Kong community's close links to the broader Chinese diaspora, and through the influence of Hong

Kong's martial arts cinema, Ip reverses Gong's judgement that the local arts are parochial and so should be subsumed within a larger project of cultural nationalism. The horizon opened up by Ip and Lee – and by kung fu cinema – is a global one in which it is nationalism that starts to appear as the limited and parochial view.

This internationalist perspective was at odds with the prevailing view of the Communist Party in China. Like the GMD before them, the Party was not only promoting nationalism as a basis for its authority, but pursuing this agenda through a policy of homogenization. In opposition, Ip's martial arts (and, metaphorically, the Hong Kong martial arts movies he exemplifies) are cosmopolitan and pluralist, though no less rooted in 'tradition'.[73] Wong presents an alternative vision of identity and of the relation to the past to that being promoted by the Chinese state. It is one that places him far closer to the 'localist' concerns and values of the 'umbrella revolution' that burst out the year after *The Grandmaster*'s release, as well as the protesters of 2019.

CONCLUSION

The three films discussed in the previous chapter constitute part of the latest stage of kung fu cinema's 'journey to the West'. They were created at a moment of increasing global integration – of cinema in particular and the cultural and economic in general – that exceeds by far what was possible at the remarkable moment, back in the 1970s, when the kung fu craze exploded onto the screens of the English-speaking world. Through their analysis I sought to suggest that the ongoing legacy of the martial arts and of Chinese martial arts cinema has been, paradoxically, not just to preserve traditions rooted in the local but to transcend these in new, dizzyingly international forms.

Indeed, the global media landscape left by the kung fu craze's lasting impact includes a vertiginous array of phenomena. Mixed martial arts competitions such as the Ultimate Fighting Championship draw in huge crowds and rival more long-standing combat sports such as boxing in terms of pay-per-view revenue. By contrast, in 1993 the *Mighty Morphin' Power Rangers* made the martial arts a matter of children's entertainment, and since then, in the field of kids' cartoons, the *Jackie Chan Adventures* (2000–2005) have been joined by, for example, the movie *Kung Fu Panda* (2008) and the television series *Ninjago* (2011–).[1] In spite of the controversies around media violence that have surrounded kung fu, the increased creation of martial arts media targeted at children is less surprising when we consider the degree to which the multi-billion-dollar industry of martial arts classes is aimed at the young, with parents hoping to impart discipline, spirituality or just self-confidence in their offspring.[2] In the realm of family entertainment, the action scenes of the Marvel and DC Comics superhero franchises – which pack the list of the highest-grossing films to date – are unimaginable without the martial arts, while the *Star Wars* franchise draws on martial arts performance for its dazzling lightsaber fights and also plays on martial arts mythology in its vision of the monk-like Jedi knights and their spiritual beliefs. (Jediism has now even been adopted as a real-world religion, and one can also take classes and join competitions in lightsaber combat.[3])

Kung fu cinema has been joined by a range of martial arts films from around the world, such as Thailand's *Ong Bak* (2003) and *The Raid* (2011), which was filmed in Indonesia and starred the Jakarta-born performer Iko Uwais but was written and directed by a Welshman, Gareth Evans. In the slums of Kampala, Isaac Godfrey Geoffrey Nabwana pioneered the creation of the ultra-low-budget 'Wakaliwood' action movies, which are often filmed for less than $200, relying on the skills of local martial artists, and have become the object of cult Internet viewing. At the time of writing, Nabwana's first feature, *Who Killed Captain Alex?* (2010), has 5.8 million views on its official YouTube channel alone.

But was this always what kung fu's journey to the West meant? Certainly, as I've pursued it in this book, Hong Kong's martial arts cinema has been a contributing force within the cultural changes brought on by globalization, and indeed the very appearance of East Asian popular culture in the West bears testimony to this. The rise of interest in martial arts was involved in both the avant-garde and countercultural opposition to establishment values and materialist culture and to the insularity of conservatism. Being non-Western, kung fu movies were also associated with the twentieth-century movements of decolonization across Asia and Africa and were taken up by Asian and Black Americans and Europeans as a means to imagine their own opposition to ongoing racism and marginalization at home. The images they offered also, perhaps, contributed to the increased fluidity and plurality of gender identities.

Nonetheless, Chinese martial arts cinema has its roots in specifically nationalist and ethnic identities, often articulating an insular jingoism. It has been taken up as a means to shore up and reassert Western masculinities in a more reactionary manner, and the link to violence makes it problematic to laud kung fu cinema as only a liberalizing and pluralizing force. With its emphasis on violence and sacrifice, martial arts cinema may be the perfect form for the fascist aestheticization of death. If *Hero* seemed to some to embark on nationalist myth-making, the pursuit of cultural essentialism through the martial arts has certainly been one of the projects of Chinese cinema since the 2010s. Meanwhile, in the West, kung fu can still function as an Orientalizing stereotype through which the line between 'us' and 'them' can be demarcated, representing Asians in terms of an obscene and threatening violence that belongs elsewhere and far away.

Nonetheless, Bruce Lee himself was already expressing his hope for the cosmopolitan potential of kung fu in his interview with Pierre Berton, conducted for Canadian television in 1971, so it may be of use, in concluding this book, to hold what Lee says there alongside the achievements of contemporary directors such as Ang Lee, Zhang Yimou and Wong Kar-wai.[4] Though the kung fu craze itself – and Lee's rise to become a household name across the world – was still tantalizingly over the horizon, he had at this point just become the new 'superstar' of Hong Kong cinema with the runaway success of *The Big Boss*. He had also made an impact on the American public with *The Green Hornet* and *Longstreet* and was faced with the dilemma of which industry to seek fame and fortune in. Berton, in fact, directly posed this question – Hong Kong or Hollywood? – to Lee in the interview. Lee, of course, emphatically expressed his determination to conquer both, refusing to be limited by one or the other.

During the interview, Berton repeatedly comes back to the question of what is 'Oriental' and what is 'Western', and Lee, it seems to me, though sometimes answering in these terms, seeks to evade being captured by them or identified by one or the other alone. In some respects, it is a little like watching Nameless's interview with the emperor in *Hero*, as Lee weaves and reweaves stories around himself to resist the definitions that Berton attempts to impose on him. (The comparison is, perhaps, a little unfair to the sympathetic questioning of the famously liberal Berton, who in any case stands in for his wider North American audience. But it is, in many ways, a real-life example of the 'fighting without fighting' that Lee's character in *Enter the Dragon* utilizes to defeat the bullying Parsons on the boat to Han's island, where words and wit substitute for actual fisticuffs. In trying to pin Lee down as belonging to either Hong Kong or Hollywood, Berton is asking something very like Parsons's question, 'What's your style?')

As the interview comes towards its end, Berton asks Lee whether he thinks that Nixon's changing policies with regard to China will have an impact on his prospects of American success, and Lee – though he denies an interest in politics as such – says, prophetically:

> I do think that things Chinese will be quite interesting in the next few years . . . It will bring more understanding, more

> things that are – hey! – different, you know? And maybe in the contrast of comparison, some new thing might grow.

Lee's response intimates that East and West, like Master Gong's North and South in *The Grandmaster*, are limiting concepts, which we must shake ourselves free of in order to see broader horizons.

To bring the interview to a close, Berton attempts one final time to pin Lee down: 'Do you ever think of yourself as Chinese, or as North American?' Lee's answer eludes either position: 'You know what I want to think of myself? As a human being.' Then, Lee clarifies this by the traditional Chinese four-character proverb *tianxia yi jia*, which he translates into the Californian vernacular, 'Under the sky and the heaven, man, there is but one family.' In doing so, Lee scrambles any easy equation of the West with the sole source of progressive ideas and even undermines the simple opposition of the embrace of tradition to the modern. The concept of *tianxia* that Lee uses is, of course, the same as the one invoked in Zhang Yimou's *Hero*. Echoing the pluralism that *The Grandmaster*, too, espouses, Lee adds: 'It just so happens, man, people are different.'

REFERENCES

Introduction

1 Many Hong Kong pictures from the 1970s have been released under a range of different titles for different markets, with the initial U.S. releases often differing significantly from the titles in the international or Hong Kong markets. Since Hong Kong was a British colony, they were usually released there with both a Chinese and an English title. In this book, I will primarily refer to the films by their original Hong Kong title, as over time these have become the most common way that the films are known, noting American titles on first mention or where this is significant to the discussion.

2 David Desser, 'The Kung Fu Craze: Hong Kong Cinema's First Reception', in *The Cinema of Hong Kong: History, Arts, Identity*, ed. Poshek Fu and David Desser (Cambridge, 2000), p. 24.

3 Ibid., p. 34.

4 Ibid., p. 35.

5 Ibid.

6 See the testimony of series writers Ed Spielman and Howard Friedlander, and producer Tom Kuhn, in 'From Grasshopper to Caine: Creating Kung Fu', special feature in *Kung Fu: The Complete First Season*, DVD box set, disc 1, 2004.

7 B. P. Flanigan, 'Kung Fu Krazy, or the Invasion of the "Chop Suey Easterns"', *Cineaste*, VI/3 (1974), p. 10.

8 Grady Hendrix, 'Old School Kung Fu Wants You!', www.screenanarchy.com, 19 April 2019.

9 See Leon Hunt, *Kung Fu Cult Masters: From Bruce Lee to Crouching Tiger* (London, 2003), pp. 184–200; Andreas Rauscher, 'In Search of the 36th Virtual Chamber: Martial Arts in Video Games from Screen Fighting to *Wuxia* Worldbuilding', in *Chinese Martial Arts and Media Culture: Global Perspectives*, ed. Tim Trausch (London, 2018), pp. 161–74.

10 Paul Bowman, *The Invention of Martial Arts: Popular Culture between Asia and America* (Oxford, 2021).

11 See for example Davis Miller's account of his first encounter with Bruce Lee (pp. 3–6) and the desire for self-transformation through the martial arts that this unleashed in him (pp. 71–9) in *The Tao of Bruce Lee: A Martial Arts Memoir* (London, 2000).

12 Michael Molasky, 'The Phone Book Project: Tracing the Diffusion of Asian Martial Arts in America through the Yellow Pages', in *The Martial Arts Studies Reader*, ed. Paul Bowman (London, 2018), pp. 57–72.

13 Ibid., p. 58. In 1969, Molasky finds advertisements for only two schools offering Chinese martial arts in the four cities he studied, and both of these in were in San Francisco, with its significant Chinese population. By 1974, there were over fifty listings. Molasky concludes that it is only after Bruce Lee that kung fu instruction 'extended to the public sphere' from its base in the Chinese communities.

14 Miller, *Tao of Bruce Lee*, p. 148. Miller does not cite a source for his figures.

15 Matthew Polly, *Bruce Lee: A Life* (London, 2018), p. 492.

16 Miller, *Tao of Bruce Lee*, p. 149.

17 Ibid.

18 Paul Bowman, 'Bruce Lee: Cult (Film) Icon', in *The Routledge Companion to Cult Cinema*, ed. Jamie Sexton and Ernest Mathijs (London, 2019), pp. 460–67.

19 Barna William Donovan, *The Asian Influence on Hollywood Action Films* (Jefferson, NC, 2008), pp. 174–91.

20 Christina Klein, '*Crouching Tiger, Hidden Dragon*: A Diasporic Reading', *Cinema Journal*, XLIII/4 (2004), p. 18.

21 Among these publications are, to list just a few, John Little, ed., *Bruce Lee: Artist of Life* (Boston, MA, 1999); Bruce Lee and M. Uyehara, *Bruce Lee's Fighting Method: The Complete Edition* (Valencia, 2008); Tommy Gong, *Bruce Lee: Evolution of a Martial Artist* (Valencia, 2014); and John R. Little, *Bruce Lee: Words from a Master* (Lincolnwood, IL, 1999). The British Library catalogue lists some 612 books on Lee.

22 Miller, *Tao of Bruce Lee*, p. 149.

23 Billy Blanks, speaking in the documentary *Iron Fists and Kung Fu Kicks* (dir. Serge Ou, 2019).

24 Miller, *Tao of Bruce Lee*, p. 93.

25 Ibid., pp. 26, 94.

26 Ibid., p. 96.
27 May Joseph, 'Kung Fu Cinema and Frugality', in *The Visual Culture Reader*, ed. Nicholas Mirzoeff, 2nd edn (London, 2002), pp. 433–50; Ivo Ritzer, 'Imagining Transcultural Mediascapes: Martial Arts, African Appropriation, and the Deterritorializing Flows of Globalization', in *Chinese Martial Arts and Media Culture*, ed. Trausch, pp. 81–99.
28 Vijay Prashad, *Everybody Was Kung Fu Fighting: Afro-Asian Connections and the Myth of Cultural Purity* (Boston, MA, 2001), pp. 126–9.
29 Polly, *Bruce Lee*, p. 493.
30 Jeffie Lam, Naomi Ng and Su Xinqi, 'Be Water, My Friend: Hong Kong Protesters Take Bruce Lee's Wise Saying to Heart and Go with the Flow', www.scmp.com, 22 June 2019.
31 Rudyard Kipling, 'The Ballad of East and West' (1889), available online at www.kiplingsociety.co.uk.
32 Polly, *Bruce Lee*, pp. 321–6.
33 Meaghan Morris, 'Transnational Imagination in Action Cinema: Hong Kong and the Making of a Global Popular Culture', *Inter-Asia Cultural Studies*, v/2 (2004), p. 185.
34 Ibid., p. 184.
35 Edward Said, *Orientalism* (London, 1995), esp. pp. 1–28.
36 Ibid., p. 2.
37 David Massarella, 'Some Reflections on Identity Formation in East Asia in the Sixteenth and Seventeenth Centuries', in *Multicultural Japan: Paleolithic to Postmodern*, ed. D. Denoon, M. Hudson, G. McCormack and T. Morris Suzuki (Cambridge, 1996), p. 139.
38 Michael Gold, 'New Yorkers Have a Constitutional Right to Nunchucks, Judge Rules', www.nytimes.com, 19 December 2018.
39 Review of *The Big Boss* (*Fists of Fury*), in *Variety*, 27 June 1973, cited in Desser, 'Kung Fu Craze', p. 23.
40 Sylvia Shin Huey Chong, *The Oriental Obscene: Violence and Racial Fantasies in the Vietnam Era* (Durham, NC, 2011).
41 Bawlife, review of *Birth of the Dragon* (2016) on www.imdb.com, quoted in Catherine Shoard, '*Birth of the Dragon*: Anger over Whitewashing of Bruce Lee Biopic', www.theguardian.com, 5 October 2016.
42 Kuan-Hsing Chen, *Asia as Method: Toward Deimperialization* (Durham, NC, 2010), pp. vii, 3–4.
43 See for example Morris, 'Transnational Imagination'; Ritzer, 'Imagining Transcultural Mediascapes'.

1 Hong Kong's Martial Arts Cinema

1 David Desser, 'The Kung Fu Craze: Hong Kong Cinema's First Reception', in *The Cinema of Hong Kong: History, Arts, Identity*, ed. Poshek Fu and David Desser (Cambridge, 2000), p. 20.
2 Man-Fung Yip, *Martial Arts Cinema and Hong Kong Modernity: Aesthetics, Representation, Circulation* (Hong Kong, 2017), p. 4.
3 Ibid.; Desser, 'Kung Fu Craze', p. 31.
4 Stephen Teo, *Chinese Martial Arts Cinema: The Wuxia Tradition* (Edinburgh, 2009), pp. 8–10.
5 Congmin Ge, 'Photography, Shadow Play, Beijing Opera and the First Chinese Film', *Eras*, 3 (2002); Hu Jubin, *Projecting a Nation: Chinese National Cinema before 1949* (Hong Kong, 2003), p. 39.
6 This is certainly the claim of Chen Mo, in *Daoguang xiaying mengtaiqi: Zhongguo wuxia dianying lun* (Montage of Swordplays and Swordfighters: A Treatise on Chinese Martial Arts Cinema) (Beijing, 1996), pp. 78–9, cited in Teo, *Chinese Martial Arts Cinema*, p. 24.
7 Ge, 'Photography'.
8 Matthew Polly, *Bruce Lee: A Life* (London, 2018), pp. 11–47.
9 John Christopher Hamm, *Paper Swordsmen: Jin Yong and the Modern Chinese Martial Arts Novel* (Honolulu, HI, 2005), p. 20. Teo, in *Chinese Martial Arts Cinema*, p. 3, dates the serialization to 1922 rather than 1923.
10 Victor Fan, 'From the Shadow Play to Electric Shadows', in *Electric Shadows: A Century of Chinese Cinema* (London, 2014), p. 12.
11 Immanuel Chung-yueh Hsü, *The Rise of Modern China*, 4th edn (Oxford, 1999), p. 123.
12 Ibid., pp. 124–6.
13 Stephen R. Platt, *Autumn in the Heavenly Kingdom: China, the West, and the Epic Story of the Taiping Civil War* (London, 2012), p. xxii.
14 Andrew D. Morris, *Marrow of the Nation: A History of Sport and Physical Culture in Republican China* (Berkeley, CA, 2004), pp. 185–229.
15 Yip, *Martial Arts Cinema*, pp. 4–5.
16 Teo, *Chinese Martial Arts Cinema*, pp. 27–31, 38.
17 Joseph Esherick, *The Origins of the Boxer Uprising* (Berkeley, CA, 1987).
18 Morris, *Marrow of the Nation*, p. 194.

19 In April 1927, the Nationalist Guomindang (GMD) party unleashed the Shanghai Massacre on its Communist allies, initiating a struggle between the two groups that would last decades. Warlordism still split the country into a range of factions, each with its power base, and in 1926, Chiang Kai-shek, the GMD leader, had begun the Northern Expedition to quell warlords who resisted the GMD's authority. Japan at the time was also gearing up her imperial ambitions, and in 1931 would invade Manchuria, in the north of China's territories.

20 Teo, *Chinese Martial Arts Cinema*, p. 33, citing Robert Kung, *Gong jianong congying huiyi lu* (Hong Kong, 1968), pp. 158–9.

21 Mao Dun, 'Fengjian de xiao shimin wenyi', *Dongfang zazhi*, XXX/3 (1933), as translated in Teo, *Chinese Martial Arts Cinema*, pp. 38–9.

22 Teo, *Chinese Martial Arts Cinema*, p. 30.

23 Christine Harris, '"The Romance of the Western Chamber" and the Classical Subject in 1920s Shanghai', in *Cinema and Urban Culture in Shanghai, 1922–1943*, ed. Zhang Yinjin (Stanford, CA, 1999), p. 56, cited in Teo, *Chinese Martial Arts Cinema*, p. 41. Harris's italics.

24 Hamm, *Paper Swordsmen*, p. 18.

25 Lau Yam, 'Wong Fei-hung Films and Related Works', in *Mastering Virtue: The Cinematic Legend of a Martial Artist*, ed. Po Fung and Lau Yam (Hong Kong, 2012), pp. 125–39.

26 Leon Hunt, *Kung Fu Cult Masters: From Bruce Lee to Crouching Tiger* (London, 2003), p. 29.

27 Ibid., p. 31.

28 Stephen Teo, *Hong Kong Cinema: The Extra Dimensions* (London, 1997), p. 7.

29 See Poshek Fu, 'Introduction: The Shaw Brothers Diasporic Cinema', in *China Forever: The Shaw Brothers and Diasporic Cinema*, ed. Poshek Fu (Urbana, IL, 2008), pp. 2–6.

30 According to Desser, at their height Shaws were turning out films at the rate of one per week. Desser, 'Kung Fu Craze', p. 33.

31 Fu, 'Introduction', pp. 6–7.

32 Peter Gravestock, 'The Real and the Fantastic in the *Wuxia Pian*', *Metro Magazine*, 148 (2006), p. 106.

33 In interview with Lau Shing-hon in *A Study of the Hong Kong Swordplay Film, 1945–1980*, ed. Lau Shing-hon and Leong Mo-ling (Hong Kong, 1981), p. 204.

34 Quoted in Teo, *Chinese Martial Arts Cinema*, p. 91.

35 Yip, *Martial Arts Cinema*, pp. 56–7.
36 See Chang's own account in Zhang Che, 'Creating the Martial Arts Film and the Hong Kong Cinematic Style', in *The Making of Martial Arts Films: As Told by Filmmakers and Stars*, exh. cat., Hong Kong Film Archive (1999), p. 21. See also Teo, *Chinese Martial Arts Cinema*, pp. 94–5.
37 An official census showed that half the colony's population in 1961 was under 21. Poshek Fu, 'The 1960s: Modernity, Youth Culture, and Hong Kong Cantonese Cinema', in *The Cinema of Hong Kong: History, Arts, Identity*, ed. Poshek Fu and David Desser (Cambridge, 2000), p. 73.
38 Ibid., pp. 72–4.
39 Ibid., p. 73.
40 Gary Ka-wai Cheung, *Hong Kong's Watershed: The 1967 Riots* (Hong Kong, 2009).
41 Yip, *Martial Arts Cinema*, pp. 56–66.
42 Zhang, 'Creating the Martial Arts Film', p. 21.
43 *Southern Screen* (cited in Hunt, *Kung Fu Cult Masters*, p. 9) called him a 'handsome he-man' and a 'flashy, rip-roaring type'.
44 See Zhang, 'Creating the Martial Arts Film', pp. 21–2.
45 See Luke White, 'A "Narrow World, Strewn with Prohibitions": Chang Cheh's *The Assassin* and the 1967 Hong Kong Riots', *Asian Cinema*, XXVI/1 (2015), pp. 79–98.
46 In the following years, Cheng would go on to star in three films by Ho Meng-hua (*Jade Raksha*, 1968; *Lady of Steel*, 1970; *Lady Hermit*, 1971) and five films by Lo Wei (*Raw Courage*, 1969; *The Golden Sword*, 1969; *Dragon Swamp*, 1969; *Brothers Five*, 1970; *Shadow Whip*, 1971).
47 For example, Lisa Chiao Chiao (*Black Butterfly*, 1968), Shih Szu (*Lady of the Law*, 1971), Li Ching (*Vengeance of a Snowgirl*, 1971) and Shu Pei-pei (*The Devil's Mirror*, 1972).
48 Teo, *Chinese Martial Arts Cinema*, pp. 119–20.
49 Ibid., p. 120.
50 Ibid.
51 Ibid., p. 121.
52 Ibid., p. 143.
53 Ibid., p. 75.
54 Olivier Assayas and Charles Tesson, 'Interview with Lau Kar-leung: The Last Shaolin', trans. Yves Gendron and Steve Feldman, at www.stickgrappler.net, 14 July 2013. First published in French in *Cahiers du cinéma*, 362–3 (1984), pp. 26–30.

55 Polly, *Bruce Lee*, p. 297.
56 Ibid., pp. 291–4.
57 Desser, 'Kung Fu Craze', p. 33.
58 Polly, *Bruce Lee*, p. 304.
59 Ibid., p. 330.
60 Ibid., p. 331.
61 Robert Clouse, *The Making of Enter the Dragon* (Burbank, CA, 1987), p. 17, cited in M. T. Kato, *From Kung Fu to Hip Hop: Globalization, Revolution, and Popular Culture* (Albany, NY, 2007), p. 12.
62 Vijay Prashad, *Everybody Was Kung Fu Fighting: Afro-Asian Connections and the Myth of Cultural Purity* (Boston, MA, 2001), p. 140.
63 Polly, *Bruce Lee*, p. 374.
64 Desser, 'Kung Fu Craze', p. 30.
65 Ibid., p. 33.
66 Teo, *Hong Kong Cinema*, pp. 111–12.

2 The American Connection

1 Paul Bowman, *The Invention of Martial Arts: Popular Culture between Asia and America* (Oxford, 2021), pp. 12–14.
2 Pankaj Mishra, *From the Ruins of Empire: The Revolt against the West and the Remaking of Asia* (London, 2013), p. 1.
3 Gary J. Krug, 'At the Feet of the Master: Three Stages in the Appropriation of Okinawan Karate into Anglo-American Culture', *Cultural Studies: Critical Methodologies*, 1/4 (2001), p. 398.
4 Wendy L. Rouse, *Her Own Hero: The Origins of the Women's Self-Defense Movement* (New York, 2017), p. 39.
5 John Christopher Hamm, 'From the Boxers to *Kung Fu Panda*: The Chinese Martial Arts in Global Entertainment', in *Chinese Martial Arts and Media Culture: Global Perspectives*, ed. Tim Trausch (London, 2018), p. 105.
6 Emelyne Godfrey, *Masculinity, Crime and Self-Defence in Victorian Literature: Duelling with Danger* (Basingstoke, 2010), pp. 25–6.
7 Conan-Doyle, however, misspelt the art as 'baritsu', probably after a similar error in a 1901 article in *The Times*. See Godfrey, *Masculinity*, pp. 131–9.
8 Bowman, *Invention*, p. 50.
9 For Roosevelt and judo, see Rouse, *Her Own Hero*, pp. 39–47.

10 Krug, 'Feet of the Master', pp. 401–2.
11 Chuck Norris, *The Secret of Inner Strength: My Life Story* (Boston, MA, 1988) and *Against All Odds: My Story* (Nashville, TN, 2004), cited in Barna William Donovan, *The Asian Influence on Hollywood Action Films* (Jefferson, NC, 2008), p. 109.
12 Michael Molasky, 'The Phone Book Project: Tracing the Diffusion of Asian Martial Arts in America through the Yellow Pages', in *The Martial Arts Studies Reader*, ed. Paul Bowman (London, 2018), pp. 58, 61.
13 Ibid.
14 For more on Presley's karate career see Wayne Carman, *Elvis's Karate Legacy: The Untold Story of Elvis's Faith, Spirit, and Discipline* (Branson, MO, 1998).
15 For a further analysis of these advertisements, see Bowman, *Invention*, pp. 63–5.
16 Krug, 'At the Feet of the Master', pp. 399–402.
17 See J. J. Clarke, *Oriental Enlightenment: The Encounter between Asian and Western Thought* (Abingdon, 1997).
18 Harry Harootunian, 'Postwar America and the Aura of Asia', in *The Third Mind: American Artists Contemplate Asia, 1860–1989*, ed. Alexandra Munroe, exh. cat., Guggenheim, New York (2009), pp. 49–51.
19 In psychoanalysis, Jung drew strongly on therapeutic ideas from Buddhism and also wrote a foreword to Richard Wilhelm's translation of the *I Ching*. Campbell set out to develop a comparative mythology that took in the East and West. Huxley proposed a universalizing history of mystical experience drawing together Daoism with often heterodox Judaeo-Christian traditions.
20 Cited in Alexandra Munroe, 'Buddhism and the Neo-Avant-Garde: Cage Zen, Beat Zen and Zen', in *The Third Mind*, ed. Munroe, p. 210.
21 Alan Watts, 'Zen in Fencing and Judo', episode 17 of *Eastern Wisdom and Modern Life*, KQED, first broadcast 31 December 1960.
22 Gary Snyder, 'Buddhist Anarchism', *Journal for the Protection of All Beings*, 1 (1961), pp. 10–12.
23 Wolfe Lowenthal, *There Are No Secrets: Professor Cheng Man-ch'ing and His Tai Chi Chuan* (Berkeley, CA, 1991), p. 45.
24 Ginsberg's poem 'In My Kitchen in New York' (1984), a humorous account of the difficulties of practising tai chi at home, is dedicated to Faigao.

25 Charles Russo, *Striking Distance: Bruce Lee and the Dawn of Martial Arts in America* (Lincoln, NE, 2016), pp. 146–8.
26 Bruce Lee, 'Liberate Yourself from Classical Karate', *Black Belt* (September 1971), pp. 25–7.
27 Matthew Polly, *Bruce Lee: A Life* (London, 2018), pp. 181–95.
28 Ibid., pp. 217–39.
29 Ibid., p. 222.
30 Cynthia Lucia, Roy Grundmann and Art Simon, eds, *American Film History: Selected Readings, 1960 to the Present* (Chichester, 2016), pp. 3–4.
31 Ibid., p. 17.
32 Ibid.
33 Controversies around violence were ignited, for example, by films such as Arthur Penn's *Bonnie and Clyde* (1967), Sam Peckinpah's *The Wild Bunch* (1969) and Francis Ford Coppola's *The Godfather* (1972). As well as setting the tone for America's reception of martial arts cinema, these films were also, of course, an influence on the growing 'realism' in Hong Kong cinema's depictions of violence. Perhaps the most iconic controversy around sex was ignited by *Deep Throat* (1972), which constituted 'a moment of middle-class transgression for a population renegotiating a shift in local mores'. Ibid., p. 12.
34 '*Billy Jack*', *Variety*, 5 May 1971, p. 22.
35 Howard Thompson, 'A Misguided Billy Jack', *New York Times*, 29 July 1971, p. 42.
36 Sharon Waxman, 'Billy Jack Is Ready to Fight the Good Fight Again', www.newyorktimes.com, 20 June 2005.
37 Spielman, interviewed in 'From Grasshopper to Caine: Creating *Kung Fu*', special feature in *Kung Fu: The Complete First Season*, DVD box set, disc 1, 2004.
38 Friedman, interviewed in 'From Grasshopper to Caine'.
39 Advertisement, *New York Times*, 18 January 1973, p. 83.
40 David Carradine, interviewed in Tom Burke, 'David Carradine, King of Kung Fu: Hot Water Again?', *New York Times*, 29 April 1973, p. 141. Original emphasis.
41 Both authors are cited in an advertisement for the show in the *New York Times*, 15 March 1973, p. 87.
42 Matthew Polly, interviewed in the documentary *Iron Fists and Kung Fu Kicks* (dir. Serge Ou, 2019).
43 Dan Menaker, 'Don't Look Now, but TV Is Growing Up', *New York Times*, 20 May 1973, p. 21.

44 The show's producers did in fact audition several Asian American actors for the part – including Bruce Lee – but in the end felt that 'none of them measured up'. See Jerry Thorpe and Tom Kuhn in interview, in 'From Grasshopper to Caine'; Polly, *Bruce Lee*, pp. 322–6.

45 Frank Chin '*Kung Fu* Is Unfair to Chinese', *New York Times*, 24 March 1974, sect. D, p. 19. Spielman wrote a response to Chin's criticism, 'I'm Proud to Have Created *Kung Fu*', printed on the same page, in which he argued that the show's portrayal of Caine 'changed the negative Oriental stereotype to an image of sensitivity and dignity' and that by far the most mail he received in response to the series from Asian American viewers were letters of thanks. Spielman foregrounds the importance of the martial arts as providing the means to transform this stereotype, enabling images of their practitioners as 'intelligent, brave, disciplined and humane'.

46 '*Kung Fu*: A Sweet Poison', *Getting Together*, 22 October–4 November 1972, p. 5. *Getting Together* was a nationally distributed bilingual, biweekly newspaper published by the Chinese American leftist organization I Wor Kuen.

47 Polly, *Bruce Lee*, pp. 278–9.

48 See George Dent, '*My Three Sons* Dropped by CBS', *New York Times*, 4 April 1972, p. 86.

49 *New York Times*, 15 November 1972, p. 94.

50 Burke, 'David Carradine', p. 141.

51 See for example *The Guardian*'s listings of 14 October 1972.

3 The Craze Unfolds

1 Ted Ashley, interviewed in Tom Buckley, 'Hollywood's New Leaders Worship Old God – Profits', *New York Times*, 18 July 1974, p. 37.

2 Vincent Canby, '"Have You Seen Shu Lately?" "Shu Who?"' *New York Times*, 13 May 1973, p. 14; David Desser, 'The Kung Fu Craze: Hong Kong Cinema's First American Reception', in *The Cinema of Hong Kong: History, Arts, Identity*, ed. Poshek Fu and David Desser (Cambridge, 2000), p. 24; Verina Glaessner, *Kung Fu: Cinema of Vengeance* (London, 1974), pp. 9–10.

3 See for example 'Trivia' in *Lone Wolf McQuade* (1983)', www.imdb.com, accessed 30 December 2019.

4 Glaessner, *Kung Fu*, p. 7.

5 '*Five Fingers of Death*', *Variety*, 21 March 1973, p. 18.

6 John Gillett, '*King Boxer*', *Monthly Film Bulletin* (December 1972), p. 251.
7 The reviewers were Patrick Gibbs (*Daily Telegraph*), Margaret Hinxman (*Sunday Telegraph*) and Derek Malcolm (*The Guardian*).
8 Gene Siskel, 'Mortal Combat, East and West', *Chicago Tribune*, 20 April 1973, sect. 2, p. 3.
9 Roger Greenspun, '*5 Fingers of Death*', *New York Times*, 22 March 1973, p. 54.
10 See, for example, Glaessner, *Kung Fu*, pp. 73–82.
11 Quoted in Desser, 'Kung Fu Craze', p. 22.
12 Desser, 'Kung Fu Craze', p. 22.
13 Matthew Polly, *Bruce Lee: A Life* (London, 2018), pp. 1–5.
14 Desser, 'Kung Fu Craze', p. 23.
15 Polly, *Bruce Lee*, pp. 278–81.
16 Ibid., pp. 403–5.
17 Further support was given in the martial arts scenes by the American karate practitioner Bob Wall, by Mr Hong Kong bodybuilding champion Bolo Yeung, by *Lady Whirlwind* star Angela Mao, who plays Lee's sister in an early scene, and by veteran martial arts actor and choreographer Sammo Hung, who plays Lee's opponent in the film's opening combat. The villain of the film, Shih Kien, was chosen because he had played the iconic villain in the Wong Fei-hung films, and would have been instantly recognizable as such to a Hong Kong audience.
18 Polly, *Bruce Lee*, p. 407.
19 M. T. Kato, *From Kung Fu to Hip Hop: Globalization, Revolution, and Popular Culture* (Albany, NY, 2007), pp. 141–2.
20 For box-office figures, see Polly, *Bruce Lee*, p. 480.
21 Kato, *From Kung Fu*, p. 135.
22 Ibid., pp. 71–170.
23 Ibid., p. 106.
24 Ibid., p. 152.
25 By contrast, imdb.com estimates the budget of Lee's preceding, and next most expensive, film, *The Way of the Dragon*, at $130,000 and the budget of *The Exorcist*, Warner's other great hit of 1973, at $11 million.
26 According to B. P. Flanigan, Warner gave *Enter the Dragon* 'a promotional campaign that hadn't been seen by the American film industry in over 25 years'. This included 'free karate classes, illustrated flip books, comic books, posters, photographs, news releases, radio and TV spots, interviews and personal appearances'. It's not clear

from Flanigan's account to what extent this campaign pre-dated the film, or was a reaction to its success. Flanigan, 'Kung Fu Krazy, or the Invasion of the "Chop Suey Easterns"', *Cineaste*, VI/3 (1974), p. 9.

27 Polly, *Bruce Lee*, p. 477.

28 Desser, 'Kung Fu Craze', p. 34.

29 Polly, *Bruce Lee*, p. 478.

30 Polly notes that with regular re-releases, each of which also shot up the charts, the film grossed an astonishing $350 million over the next 45 years. Ibid.

31 Ibid.

32 Kenneth Turan, 'The Apotheosis of Bruce Lee: An Actor Dies; a Posthumous Industry Is Born', *American Film*, I/1 (1975), p. 67.

33 Polly, *Bruce Lee*, p. 483.

34 Turan, 'Apotheosis', p. 67.

35 Weintraub, quoted in Polly, *Bruce Lee*, p. 492.

36 Desser, 'Kung Fu Craze', p. 34.

37 Ibid., p. 35.

38 Ibid.

39 Polly, *Bruce Lee*, p. 478.

40 Cynthia Lucia, Roy Grundmann and Art Simon, eds, *American Film History: Selected Readings, 1960 to the Present* (Chichester, 2016), p. 12.

41 Desser, 'Kung Fu Craze', p. 35.

42 Paul Bowman, *The Invention of Martial Arts: Popular Culture between Asia and America* (Oxford, 2021), p. 70.

43 James Robert Parish, *Jet Li: A Biography* (Studio City, CA, 2016), pp. 26–7. The story goes that when meeting the troupe after the performance, an impressed Nixon suggested that when he grew up, Li might become his bodyguard. The young, patriotic performer responded that he would prefer to remain a defender of the entire Chinese people, rather than just one man.

44 Al Harvin, '"Martial Artists" Hold Exhibition Today', *New York Times*, 1 June 1974, sect. D, p. 3.

45 Desser, 'Kung Fu Craze', p. 23.

46 Review of *Deep Thrust* in *Variety*, 23 May 1973, quoted in Desser, 'Kung Fu Craze', p. 23.

47 Canby, '"Have You Seen Shu Lately?"', p. 14.

48 Howard Thompson, 'Enter Dragon, Hollywood Style', *New York Times*, 18 August 1973, p. 26.

49 'School for Scoundrels and Hard Knocks', *New York Times*, 27 September 1973, p. 45.

50 See for example his review of *The Magnificent Chivalry* in *Monthly Film Bulletin*, 468 (1 January 1973), p. 229.
51 Marya Mannes, 'The Killing Has to Stop', *New York Times*, 14 April 1974, sect. D, p. 19.
52 George Vecsey, 'Precarious Truce Remains after Rampage in St. Albans', *New York Times*, 21 February 1974, p. 37.
53 Joseph B. Treaser, 'Youthful Violence Grows and Accused Are Younger', *New York Times*, 4 November 1974, p. 1.
54 Stuart Kaminsky, 'Italian Westerns and Kung Fu Films: Genres of Violence', in *Graphic Violence on the Screen*, ed. Thomas R. Atkins (New York, 1976), pp. 47–68. Kaminsky's argument was earlier published in 'Kung Fu Film as Ghetto Myth', *Journal of Popular Film and Television*, III/2 (1974), pp. 129–38.
55 Ibid., p. 60.
56 Desser, 'Kung Fu Craze', p. 25.
57 Ibid.
58 Ibid.
59 '*Five Fingers of Death*', p. 8.
60 '*Legend of the Seven Golden Vampires*', *The Guardian*, 22 August 1974, p. 10.
61 Susan Sontag, 'Notes on Camp', in *Against Interpretation and Other Essays* (New York, 2001), pp. 275–92.
62 Andrew Ross, *No Respect: Intellectuals and Popular Culture* (London, 1989), pp. 135–70.

4 Enter Black Dragons

1 See Anna Paul, 'Afro Supa Heroes: Posters by Jon Daniel, in Pictures', www.theguardian.com, 6 October 2018.
2 Paul Bowman, *The Invention of Martial Arts: Popular Culture between Asia and America* (Oxford, 2021), pp. 70–71.
3 Gina Marchetti, 'Jackie Chan and the Black Connection', in *Keyframes: Popular Cinema and Cultural Studies*, ed. Matthew Tinkcom and Amy Villarejo (London, 2003), pp. 137–58.
4 Frances Gateward, 'Wong Fei-hung in Da House: Hong Kong Martial Arts Films and Hip-Hop Culture', in *Chinese Connections: Critical Perspectives in Film, Identity, and Diaspora*, ed. Tan See-kam, Peter X. Feng and Gina Marchetti (Philadelphia, PA, 2009), p. 59.
5 Ibid., p. 61.
6 Bowman, *Invention*, pp. 145–76.
7 Gateward, 'Wong Fei-hung', p. 55.

8 Vijay Prashad, *Everybody Was Kung Fu Fighting: Afro-Asian Connections and the Myth of Cultural Purity* (Boston, MA, 2001), p. 130. Sanders would later join the Nation of Islam, and changed his name to Sijo Saabir Quwi Muhammad.
9 Maryam Aziz, 'Our Fist Is Black: Martial Arts, Black Arts, and Black Power in the 1960s and 1970s', www.chinesemartialstudies.com, 21 January 2016.
10 Prashad, *Everybody*, p. 134.
11 Ibid., p. 133.
12 Aziz, 'Our Fist Is Black'.
13 Prashad, *Everybody*, p. 136. See also Gateward, 'Wong Fei-hung', pp. 64–5; Bill Brown, 'Global Bodies/Postnationalities: Charles Johnson's Consumer Culture', *Representations*, 58 (1997), p. 35.
14 Prashad, *Everybody*, p. 141.
15 Ibid., p. 131.
16 See M. T. Kato, *From Kung Fu to Hip Hop: Globalization, Revolution, and Popular Culture* (Albany, NY, 2007), p. 127.
17 Ibid., pp. 17, 41–5.
18 Warrington Hudlin, speaking in the documentary *Iron Fists and Kung Fu Kicks* (dir. Serge Ou, 2019).
19 Kato, *From Kung Fu*, pp. 140, 60.
20 Verina Glaessner, *Kung Fu: Cinema of Vengeance* (London, 1974), p. 15.
21 Prashad, *Everybody*, p. 141.
22 Ibid., p. 140.
23 Kato, *From Kung Fu*, p. 13.
24 Brown, 'Global Bodies', p. 31.
25 May Joseph, 'Kung Fu Cinema and Frugality', in *The Visual Culture Reader*, ed. Nicholas Mirzoeff, 2nd edn (London, 2002), pp. 433–50.
26 Ivo Ritzer, 'Imagining Transcultural Mediascapes: Martial Arts, African Appropriation, and the Deterritorializing Flows of Globalization', in *Chinese Martial Arts and Media Culture: Global Perspectives*, ed. Tim Trausch (London, 2018), pp. 81–99.
27 See Carey Dunne, 'Ghana's Golden Age of Hand-Painted Kung Fu Movie Posters', www.hyperallergic.com, 30 March 2016.
28 Hsiung-ping Chiao, 'Bruce Lee: His Influence on the Evolution of the Kung Fu Genre', *Journal of Popular Film and Television*, IX/1 (1981), p. 31.
29 See for example Bruce Lee collector Perry Lee's experience, as recounted in Tyrone Beason, 'Local Collector Pays Tribute to

Martial-Arts Legend Bruce Lee', https://archive.seattletimes.com, 27 May 2003.
30 Brown, 'Global Bodies', p. 33.
31 Desser, 'Kung Fu Craze', p. 38.
32 RZA and Andy Klein, feature commentary track, *The 36th Chamber of Shaolin*, Shaw Brothers Classic Collection, DVD, Momentum Pictures, 2009.
33 Brown, 'Global Bodies', p. 33. Original emphasis.
34 Ibid., p. 40.
35 A contemporary equivalent – taken to the extreme – might be the Ugandan 'Wakaliwood' productions of Isaac Nabwana in the slums of Kampala. His action/kung fu features are often produced for less than $200 with jerry-built equipment, but are made with what seems an irrepressible creative urgency and vitality, the final films being enormously enjoyable and exciting precisely in terms of what can be achieved against the odds by those with very few resources available. Few of Nabwana's fans will fail to notice the aesthetic limitations of the works (amateur acting, poor continuity, shoddy special effects and so on), but these are experienced as a joy, rather than a lack.
36 Jeff Chang, *Can't Stop, Won't Stop: A History of the Hip-Hop Generation* (London, 2007), p. 9.
37 Brown, 'Global Bodies', p. 36.
38 Kyle Barrowman, 'Bruce Lee and the Perfection of Martial Arts (Studies): An Exercise in Alterdisciplinarity', *Martial Arts Studies*, 8 (2019), pp. 5–28.
39 Brown, 'Global Bodies', pp. 25–6. The story appears in Johnson's collection, *The Sorcerer's Apprentice: Tales and Conjurations* (New York, 1987).
40 Ibid., p. 24.
41 Ibid., p. 36.
42 Ibid., p. 37; Stuart Hall, 'Notes on Deconstructing the Popular', in *People's History and Socialist Theory*, ed. Raphael Samuel (London, 1981), p. 235, cited in Brown, 'Global Bodies', p. 37.
43 Davis Miller, *The Tao of Bruce Lee: A Martial Arts Memoir* (London, 2000); Matthew Polly, *American Shaolin: One Man's Quest to Become a Kung Fu Master* (London, 2007).
44 According to *Variety*, it was 'the first U.S.-lensed martial arts actioner'. See 'U.S. Rage of Chop-Socky Films: Karate Breaks Out of Chinatown', *Variety*, 9 January 1974, p. 72.
45 See, for example, the account offered in Chang, *Can't Stop*, pp. 7–85.

46 Tricia Rose, *Black Noise: Rap Music and Black Culture in Contemporary America* (Middletown, CT, 1994), pp. 27–34.
47 Chang, *Can't Stop*, p. 115.
48 Ibid., p. 116.
49 Jorge Pabon, cited in Chang, *Can't Stop*, p. 115.
50 Chang, *Can't Stop*, p. 137.
51 See for example Rose, *Black Noise*.
52 Alvin Blanco, *The Wu-Tang Clan and RZA: A Trip through Hip Hop's 36 Chambers* (Santa Barbara, CA, 2011).
53 Greg Tate, 'In Praise of Shadow Boxers', *Souls*, V/1 (2003), pp. 128–36; Ken McLeod, 'Afro-Samurai Techno-Orientalism and Contemporary Hip Hop', *Popular Music*, XXXII/2 (2013), pp. 259–75.
54 Rose, *Black Noise*, p. 4.

5 White Men, Asian Arts

1 Lee's posthumously released *Game of Death* also involves a similar trope. Lee fights his way up a pagoda, at each level meeting a more formidable opponent. At the top is American basketball star Kareem Abdul-Jabbar, another of Lee's martial arts students. Abdul-Jabbar's place is complex here. On the one hand, he can be taken, within the pattern of Lee's other Hong Kong films, as another figure representing 'America' (as one of its most famous athletes of the time) and the West more generally. As a racial other to the Chinese audience, his unusual height afforded a parallel to the monstrosity that, as we have seen, was attributed to Norris's hairy and bulky torso in *The Way of the Dragon*. However, Abdul-Jabbar is also, of course, Black. (If Black American culture embraced a cross-ethnic identification with Asian others, this was not always mirrored in films made for a Hong Kong market. Where Black martial artists appear in these, it is often as a particularly threatening and exotic form of the Western other.) Abdul-Jabbar's depiction in *Game of Death* is further complicated by the overall narrative of Lee's progress up the pagoda, which involves a rejection of 'traditional' martial arts and an embrace of an eclectic, cosmopolitan and 'modernized' – perhaps Westernized – version of the martial arts, which Abdul-Jabbar also seems to embody alongside Lee himself.
2 Stephen Teo, *Hong Kong Cinema: The Extra Dimensions* (London, 1997), pp. 110–21, citing Tony Rayns, 'Bruce Lee: Narcissism and Nationalism', in *A Study of the Hong Kong Martial Arts Film*, exh. cat., Hong Kong International Film Festival (1980).

3 David Desser, 'The Kung Fu Craze: Hong Kong Cinema's First Reception', in *The Cinema of Hong Kong: History, Arts, Identity*, ed. Poshek Fu and David Desser (Cambridge, 2000), p. 38.
4 See for example Dick Hebdige, *Subculture: The Meaning of Style* (London, 1979). As Hebdige notes, the reliance of white subcultures on Black music and style is far from something that inoculates them against racism.
5 Barna William Donovan, *The Asian Influence on Hollywood Action Films* (Jefferson, NC, 2008), p. 108.
6 See Yvonne Tasker, *Spectacular Bodies: Gender, Genre and the Action Cinema* (London, 1993).
7 Donovan, *Asian Influence*, p. 122.
8 Sylvia Shin Huey Chong, *The Oriental Obscene: Violence and Racial Fantasies in the Vietnam Era* (Durham, NC, 2011), p. 252.
9 Ibid., p. 253.
10 Ibid., p. 254.
11 Sean Tierney, 'Themes of Whiteness in *Bulletproof Monk*, *Kill Bill*, and *The Last Samurai*', *Journal of Communication*, LVI/3 (2006), pp. 607–24.
12 Ibid., p. 609.
13 Among films that closely follow this pattern are, for example, *Blood Sport* (1988) and *Kickboxer* (1989) with Jean-Claude Van Damme, *Enter the Ninja* (1981), *Karate Kid Part II* (1986) and *Blind Fury* (1989). Donovan goes as far as to describe Norris's own *Missing in Action* films, in particular, in terms of the 'image of a Caucasian martial artist rampaging over hordes of Asian villains'. Donovan, *Asian Influence*, p. 118.
14 Tierney, 'Themes', pp. 608–9.
15 Chong, *Oriental Obscene*, pp. 2–4.
16 Ibid., pp. 9–10.
17 Ibid., pp. 33–5.
18 Ibid., pp. 25–6.
19 David Freeman, 'Karate Flicks: What It All Means', *Village Voice*, 17 May 1973, cited in Chong, *Oriental Obscene*, p. 177.
20 Chong, *Oriental Obscene*, p. 207.
21 Ibid., pp. 213–15. Chong draws on arguments from Aaron Anderson, 'Action in Motion: Kinesthesia in Martial Arts Films', *Jump Cut*, 42 (1998), pp. 1–11, 83.
22 Ibid., pp. 141–3, 176–7, 189, 206–7.

23 Davis Miller, *The Tao of Bruce Lee: A Martial Arts Memoir* (London, 2000); Matthew Polly, *American Shaolin: One Man's Quest to Become a Kungfu Master* (London, 2007).
24 Walter Benjamin, 'On the Mimetic Faculty', in *Reflections*, ed. Peter Demetz, trans. E. Jephcott (New York, 1979), p. 333, cited in Michael Taussig, *Mimesis and Alterity: A Particular History of the Senses* (London, 1993), p. 33.
25 Taussig, *Mimesis*, p. xviii.
26 Ibid., p. 33.
27 Luke White, *Legacies of the Drunken Master: Politics of the Body in Hong Kong Kung Fu Comedy Films* (Honolulu, HI, 2000), p. 51.
28 Douglas Wile, *Lost T'ai-chi Classics from the Late Ch'ing Dynasty* (New York, 1996), p. xv.
29 Chong, *Oriental Obscene*, p. 243.
30 Ibid.
31 Ibid.
32 Tasker, *Spectacular Bodies*, p. 73.
33 Donovan, *Asian Influence*, p. 114.
34 Ibid., pp. 114–15.
35 Mark Gallagher, 'Masculinity in Translation: Jackie Chan's Transcultural Star Text', *Velvet Light Trap*, 39 (1997), p. 38.
36 Paul Smith, *Clint Eastwood: A Cultural Production* (Minneapolis, MN, 1993), p. 173, cited in Gallagher, 'Masculinity', p. 37.
37 Kyle Barrowman, 'Book Review: *Legacies of the Drunken Master*', *Martial Arts Studies*, 10 (2020), p. 147.
38 See for example Olivier Assayas, 'Chang Cheh, l'ogre de Hong Kong', *Cahiers du cinéma*, 362–3 (1984), pp. 50–55.
39 David Anthony Kraft and Jim Salicup, 'Frank Miller's Ronin', *Comics Interview*, 2 (1983), pp. 7–21. The Hand was introduced in *Daredevil* no. 174, and Stick first appears in no. 176.
40 Man-Fung Yip, *Martial Arts Cinema and Hong Kong Modernity: Aesthetics, Representation, Circulation* (Hong Kong, 2017), p. 161.
41 Ibid., p. 172.
42 For the relation between mimesis and paranoia, see Roger Caillois, 'Mimicry and Legendary Pyschesthenia', *October*, XXXI (1984), pp. 17–31.
43 Laura Mulvey, 'Visual Pleasure and Narrative Cinema', *Screen*, XVI/3 (1975), pp. 6–18.
44 Donovan, *Asian Influence*, p. 149.

45 Meaghan Morris, 'Transnational Imagination in Action Cinema: Hong Kong and the Making of a Global Popular Culture', *Inter-Asia Cultural Studies*, v/2 (2004), p. 191.
46 Jeffrey A. Brown, '"They can imagine anything they want . . .": Identification, Desire, and the Celebrity Text', *Discourse*, XIX/3 (1997), p. 122. Original emphasis.
47 Tasker, *Spectacular Bodies*, pp. 40–42.
48 Morris, 'Transnational Imagination', p. 186.
49 Ibid., p. 184.
50 Chong, *Oriental Obscene*, p. 278.
51 Black Belt Theater started syndicating across cable channels in the spring of 1981. See Chris Poggiali, 'Drive in Movie on WNEW Metromedia Channel 5 (1981–1988)', www.dvddrive-in.com, 2007.
52 Chong, *Oriental Obscene*, p. 205.
53 Alex Channon, 'Western Men and Eastern Arts: The Significance of Eastern Martial Arts Disciplines in British Men's Narratives of Masculinity', *Asia Pacific Journal of Sport and Social Science*, I/1–2 (2012), pp. 111–27.
54 See for example Chong, *Oriental Obscene*, pp. 276–80.

6 Women Warriors

1 David Desser, 'The Kung Fu Craze: Hong Kong Cinema's First Reception', in *The Cinema of Hong Kong: History, Arts, Identity*, ed. Poshek Fu and David Desser (Cambridge, 2000), pp. 20–21.
2 'Deadly China Doll', www.imdb.com, accessed 25 August 2020.
3 Verina Glaessner, *Kung Fu: Cinema of Vengeance* (London, 1974), pp. 73–82.
4 Stephen Teo, 'The "Missing" Female Knight-Errant in Hong Kong Action Cinema, 1965–1971: Back in Critical Action', *Journal of Chinese Cinemas*, IV/2 (2010), pp. 143–54.
5 Meaghan Morris, 'What Can a *Gwei Por* Do? Cynthia Rothrock's Hong Kong Career', *Inter-Asia Cultural Studies*, XII/4 (2012), pp. 559–75.
6 Neal King and Martha McCaughey, 'What's a Mean Woman Like You Doing in a Movie Like This?', in *Reel Knockouts: Violent Women in the Movies*, ed. Martha McCaughey and Neal King (Austin, TX, 2001), p. 4. See also Kwai-Cheung Lo, *Excess and Masculinity in Asian Cultural Productions* (Albany, NY, 2010), pp. 109–10.
7 Wendy Arons, '"If Her Stunning Beauty Doesn't Bring You to Your Knees, Her Deadly Drop Kick Will": Violent Women in the

Kung Fu Film', in *Reel Knockouts: Violent Women in the Movies*, ed. McCaughey and King, p. 30.

8 See Bey Logan, *Hong Kong Action Cinema* (London, 1995), p. 170.

9 For the centrality of this premise see for example Patricia Pender, *I'm Buffy and You're History: Buffy the Vampire Slayer and Contemporary Feminism* (London, 2016), p. 10. Interestingly, Crawford's labour in creating the character through action often seems under-examined in 'Buffy studies' in favour of an analysis of dramatic content. (Pender's book, for example, does not even include an index entry for her.) As a martial arts fan, I find myself wondering if, given the series' premise, Gellar and Crawford aren't equal authors of the character, and whether we might not equally understand Gellar as the 'acting double' for Crawford.

10 See Lauren Steimer, 'From *Wuxia* to *Xena*: Translation and the Body Spectacle of Zoë Bell', *Discourse*, XXXI/3 (2009), pp. 359–90.

11 Lo, *Excess and Masculinity*, p. 114.

12 Angela Neustatter, 'Kung and Chop Phooey', *The Guardian*, 8 June 1974, p. 13.

13 See for example Benjamin N. Judkins and Jon Nielson, *The Creation of Wing Chun: A Social History of the Southern Chinese Martial Arts* (Albany, NY, 2015), pp. 112, 132, 137–8, 141.

14 Sasha Vojković, *Yuen Woo Ping's Wing Chun* (Hong Kong, 2009), p. 4. Vojković speculates that the Buddhist and Daoist traditions, which 'acknowledge, at least theoretically, women's equality with men', are one enabling factor within these surprisingly empowering representations (p. 7).

15 See Siu Leung Li, *Cross-Dressing in Chinese Opera* (Hong Kong, 2003), pp. 83–107. The story of the women of the Yang family going to war has been given movie treatment in *The 14 Amazons* (1972) and *Legendary Amazons* (2011).

16 Ibid., p. 89.

17 Kam Louie and Louise Edwards, 'Chinese Masculinity: Theorising "*Wen*" and "*Wu*"', *East Asian History*, 8 (1994), p. 140.

18 See for example Yvonne Tasker, *Spectacular Bodies: Gender, Genre and the Action Cinema* (London, 1993); Sherrie Inness, *Tough Girls: Women Warriors and Wonder Women in Popular Culture* (Philadelphia, PA, 1999); McCaughey and King, eds, *Reel Knockouts*; Sherrie Inness, ed., *Action Chicks: New Images of Tough Women in Popular Culture* (New York, 2004); Pender, *I'm Buffy*; Lo, *Excess and Masculinity*, pp. 107–40.

19 Lo, *Excess and Masculinity*, p. 115.

20 Glaessner, *Kung Fu*, p. 77.
21 Leon Hunt, *Kung Fu Cult Masters: From Bruce Lee to Crouching Tiger* (London, 2003), p. 128.
22 Tasker, *Spectacular Bodies*, p. 19.
23 Jonathan Ross, foreword to Rick Baker and Toby Russell, *The Essential Guide to Deadly China Dolls* (London, 1996), p. 7, cited in Hunt, *Kung Fu Cult Masters*, p. 117.
24 Ric Meyers, 'Ric and Infamous', *Asian Cult Cinema*, 20 (1998), p. 59, cited in Hunt, *Kung Fu Cult Masters*, p. 120.
25 Hunt, *Kung Fu Cult Masters*, p. 120.
26 Tasker, *Spectacular Bodies*, p. 24.
27 Ibid., p. 132.
28 King and McCaughey, 'A Mean Woman Like You', p. 6.
29 Ibid., p. 5.
30 See Wendy L. Rouse, *Her Own Hero: The Origins of the Women's Self-Defense Movement* (New York, 2017), esp. pp. 54–60.
31 Ibid., p. 130. For more on the suffrage movement and the martial arts, see also the graphic novel by Tony Wolf and Joao Vieira, *Suffrajitsu* (Seattle, WA, 2015).
32 'Suffragettes and Policemen: Amazons in the Making', *Daily Mail*, 25 August 1910. This echoes a set of photographs in the *Illustrated London News*, 6 July 1910, also showing Garrud demonstrating a range of techniques on a policeman.
33 Maggie Lomax, 'Self Defence without Aggression', *Spare Rib* (October 1973), pp. 30–31.
34 Stephanie Gilbert, 'Self Defence', *Spare Rib* (October 1973), p. 32.
35 Victoria Green and Rozsika Parker, 'Defending Ourselves', *Spare Rib* (February 1977), pp. 6–11.
36 Lisa Funnell, *Warrior Women*, pp. 8–10.
37 Hunt, *Kung Fu Cult Masters*, pp. 120–21.
38 Henwick, interviewed in the documentary *Iron Fists and Kung Fu Kicks* (dir. Serge Ou, 2019).
39 Maxine Hong Kingston, *The Woman Warrior: Memories of a Girlhood among Ghosts* (New York, 1989), p. 19.
40 Ibid., pp. 45–53.
41 Ibid., p. 20.
42 Ibid., p. 53.
43 Lynda Nead, *Chila Kumari Burman: Beyond Two Cultures* (London, 1995).

7 A Second Kung Fu Craze?

1 Paul Bowman, *The Invention of Martial Arts: Popular Culture between Asia and America* (Oxford, 2021).

2 David Desser, 'The Kung Fu Craze: Hong Kong Cinema's First American Reception', in *The Cinema of Hong Kong: History, Arts, Identity*, ed. Poshek Fu and David Desser (Cambridge, 2000), pp. 19–20.

3 Christina Klein, '*Crouching Tiger, Hidden Dragon*: A Diasporic Reading', *Cinema Journal*, XLIII/4 (2004), p. 18.

4 Peter Rainer, 'Martial Bliss', https://nymag.com, 11 December 2000; William Gallagher, 'Crouching Tiger Hidden Dragon', www.bbc.co.uk, 18 December 2000.

5 Quoted on '*Crouching Tiger Hidden Dragon* Reviews', www.rottentomatoes.com, 10 January 2021.

6 Desson Howe, 'Keep Your Eye on the "Tiger"', www.washingtonpost.com, 22 December 2000.

7 See Stephen Teo, *Chinese Martial Arts Cinema: The Wuxia Tradition* (Edinburgh, 2009), p. 176.

8 See Shelly Kraicer, 'Stephen Chow: A Guide for the Perplexed', *Cinema Scope*, 10 (2002).

9 Man-Fung Yip, 'The Effortless Lightness of Action: Hong Kong Martial Arts Films in the Age of Immediacy', in *Chinese Martial Arts and Media Culture: Global Perspectives* (London, 2018), pp. 61–2.

10 See for example Fredric Jameson, *Postmodernism; or, The Cultural Logic of Late Capitalism* (New York, 1991); David Harvey, *The Condition of Postmodernity: An Inquiry into the Origins of Cultural Change* (Malden, MA, 1990).

11 Luke White, *Legacies of the Drunken Master: Politics of the Body in Hong Kong Kung Fu Comedy Films* (Honolulu, HI, 2020), pp. 33–5.

12 Barna William Donovan, *The Asian Influence on Hollywood Action Films* (Jefferson, NC, 2008), p. 180.

13 Daniel Martin, *Extreme Asia: The Rise of Cult Cinema from the Far East* (Edinburgh, 2015).

14 Donovan, *Asian Influence*, p. 182.

15 Leon Hunt, *Kung Fu Cult Masters: From Bruce Lee to Crouching Tiger* (London, 2003), p. 160. Hunt asks how we should interpret this: is it Hollywood's neocolonial 'incorporation' of Hong Kong, or does it open a 'third space' where identities blur and interchange becomes possible?

16 He pioneered the use of digital effects in his film *Zu: Warriors of the Magic Mountain* (1983), and with Ching Siu-tung further reinvigorated the fantastical martial arts genre with *A Chinese Ghost Story* (1987), but it is the success of his film *The Swordsman* (1990) that is commonly credited with sparking Hong Kong's return to *wuxia* in the 1990s.
17 Bhaskar Sarkar, 'Hong Kong Hysteria: Martial Arts Tales in a Mutating World', in *At Full Speed: Hong Kong Cinema in a Borderless World*, ed. Esther C. M. Yau (Minneapolis, MN, 2001), pp. 159–76.
18 Klein, '*Crouching Tiger*', p. 19.
19 Felicia Chan, '*Crouching Tiger, Hidden Dragon*: Cultural Migrancy and Translatability', in *Chinese Films in Focus II*, ed. Chris Berry (London, 2008), pp. 73–4.
20 Klein, '*Crouching Tiger*', p. 18.
21 Ibid., p. 23.
22 Ang Lee, 'Foreword', in *Crouching Tiger, Hidden Dragon: A Portrait of the Ang Lee Film, Including the Complete Screenplay*, ed. Linda Sunshine (London, 2001), p. 7.
23 'Ang Lee and James Schamus' (interview), www.theguardian.com, 7 November 2000.
24 Kenneth Chan, 'The Global Return of the *Wu Xia Pian* (Chinese Sword-Fighting Movie): Ang Lee's *Crouching Tiger, Hidden Dragon*', *Cinema Journal*, XLIII/4 (2004), p. 8.
25 Sieglinde Lemke, 'Diaspora Aesthetics: Exploring the African Diaspora in the Works of Aaron Douglas, Jacob Lawrence and Jean-Michel Basquiat', in *Exiles, Diasporas and Strangers*, ed. Kobena Mercer (Cambridge, MA, 2008), pp. 122–44.
26 Chan, '*Crouching Tiger*', pp. 73–81.
27 Klein, '*Crouching Tiger*', p. 19.
28 'Ang Lee and James Schamus' (interview).
29 Ibid.
30 Klein, '*Crouching Tiger*', pp. 32–3.
31 Steve Rose, 'The Film Is So Slow – It's Like Listening to Grandma Telling Stories', www.theguardian.com, 13 February 2001.
32 Chan, 'Global Return', p. 4.
33 See for example Klein, '*Crouching Tiger*', p. 37; Wu Chia-chi, '*Crouching Tiger* Is Not a Chinese Film', *Spectator*, XXII/1 (2002), pp. 69–70; Chan, '*Crouching Tiger*', p. 79.
34 Chan, 'Global Return,', p. 4; Wu, '*Crouching Tiger*', p. 68.
35 Chan, 'Global Return', pp. 6, 3–4.

36 Wu, '*Crouching Tiger*', p. 66.
37 Chan, 'Global Return', p. 7.
38 Lee, cited in William Leung, 'Crouching Sensibility, Hidden Sense', *Film Criticism*, XXVI/1 (2001), p. 46.
39 Chan, 'Global Return', pp. 7–8.
40 Lee, cited in Klein, '*Crouching Tiger*', pp. 21–2.
41 Chan, '*Crouching Tiger*', p. 74.
42 Chan, 'Global Return', p. 7.
43 Wu, '*Crouching Tiger*', p. 72.
44 See also the conclusions of Stephen Teo, *Chinese Martial Arts Cinema*, p. 175. Teo cites Tze-lan D. Sang, 'The Transgender Body in Wang Dulu's *Crouching Tiger, Hidden Dragon*', in *Embodied Modernities: Corporeality, Representation and Chinese Cultures*, ed. Fran Martin and Larissa Heinrich (Honolulu, HI, 2006), pp. 98–112, which argues that in fact Jen's character in the original novel is far more subversively transgender than she is in the film.
45 Zhang Xiaoling. 'The Death of Heroes in China', *China Information*, XXII/1 (2008), p. 120.
46 Evans Chan, 'Zhang Yimou's *Hero*: The Temptations of Fascism', in *Chinese Connections: Critical Perspectives on Film, Identity, and Diaspora*, ed. Tan See-Kam, Peter X. Feng and Gina Marchetti (Philadelphia, PA, 2009), p. 263.
47 Ibid.
48 James Liu, *The Chinese Knight-Errant* (London, 1967), pp. 25–34.
49 Ibid., pp. 3–7.
50 Chan, 'Zhang Yimou's *Hero*', pp. 263–4.
51 Walter Benjamin, *Illuminations* (London, 1992), pp. 234–5.
52 Chan, 'Zhang Yimou's *Hero*', p. 269.
53 Ibid., p. 274.
54 Ibid., p. 275.
55 See Maurizio Marinelli, 'Heroism/Terrorism: Empire Building in Contemporary Chinese Films', *Asian Cinema*, XVI/2 (2005), p. 191.
56 Ibid., p. 193.
57 Cited in Marinelli, 'Heroism/Terrorism', p. 199.
58 Jason Anderson, 'Getting Lost in Translation', www.eye.net, 30 September 2004.
59 Margaret Hillenbrand, '*Hero*, Kurosawa and a Cinema of the Senses', *Screen*, LIV/2 (2013), pp. 127–8.
60 Chan, 'Zhang Yimou's *Hero*', p. 266.

61 Marinelli, 'Heroism/Terrorism', p. 189.
62 Hillenbrand, '*Hero*', pp. 127–51.
63 For this concept, see David Batchelor, *Chromophobia* (London, 2001).
64 Hillenbrand, '*Hero*', p. 143.
65 Ibid., p. 149.
66 Ibid., p. 151.
67 Silver Wai-ming Lee and Micky Lee, eds, *Wong Kar-wai: Interviews* (Jackson, MI, 2017), pp. 103, 142–3.
68 Compared with the more linear Weinstein edit, the cut released in the Chinese-language markets was slightly longer, and it organizes the film through a more convoluted structure, as is more familiar within the *wuxia* tradition.
69 See for example Clarence Tsui, '*The Grandmaster*', *Hollywood Reporter*, CDXIX/3 (2013), p. 83.
70 See for example Paul Bowman, 'Return of the Dragon: Handover, Hong Kong Cinema, and Chinese Ethno-nationalism', in *A Companion to Hong Kong Cinema*, ed. Esther M. K. Cheung, Gina Marchetti and Esther C. M. Yau (Oxford, 2015), p. 307.
71 Overseen by Yuen Woo-ping, the film brought on board a number of specialists in the particular kung fu styles represented to ensure its 'authenticity'. Its concern with tradition and the past might also be seen as extending to cinema, with different fight scenes acting as homages to the past of martial arts movies.
72 For more on this scene see Wayne Wong, 'Action in Tranquillity: Sketching Martial Ideation in *The Grandmaster*', *Asian Cinema*, XXIX/2 (2018), pp. 212–14.
73 Tom Cunliffe, '*The Grandmaster*: Socio-Political Plurality in Contemporary Hong Kong', *Framework: The Journal of Cinema and Media*, LIX/2 (2018), pp. 101–20.

Conclusion

1 See for example John Christopher Hamm, 'From the Boxers to *Kung Fu Panda*: The Chinese Martial Arts in Global Entertainment', in *Chinese Martial Arts and Media Culture: Global Perspectives*, ed. Tim Trausch (London, 2018), pp. 101–18.
2 R. Anthony Cort of the Martial Arts Channel has claimed that the American industry alone amounts to $40 billion. 'Top Martial Artists Join Cable TV Advisory Board', *Black Belt* (September 2003), p. 19.

3 Benjamin N. Judkins, 'The Seven Forms of Lightsaber Combat: Hyper-Reality and the Invention of the Martial Arts', *Martial Arts Studies*, 2 (2016), pp. 6–22.
4 *The Pierre Berton Show*, 9 December 1971.

SELECT BIBLIOGRAPHY

Bordwell, David, *Planet Hong Kong: Popular Cinema and the Art of Entertainment*, 2nd edn (Madison, WI, 2010)

Bowman, Paul, 'Bruce Lee: Cult (Film) Icon', in *The Routledge Companion to Cult Cinema*, ed. Jamie Sexton and Ernest Mathijs (London, 2019), pp. 460–67

—, *The Invention of Martial Arts: Popular Culture between Asia and America* (Oxford, 2021)

—, 'Return of the Dragon: Handover, Hong Kong Cinema, and Chinese Ethno-Nationalism', in *A Companion to Hong Kong Cinema*, ed. Esther M. K. Cheung, Gina Marchetti and Esther C. M. Yau (Oxford, 2015), pp. 307–21

Brown, Bill, 'Global Bodies/Postnationalities: Charles Johnson's Consumer Culture', *Representations*, 58 (1997), pp. 24–48

Chan, Evans, 'Zhang Yimou's *Hero*: The Temptations of Fascism', in *Chinese Connections: Critical Perspectives on Film, Identity, and Diaspora*, ed. Tan See-Kam, Peter X. Feng and Gina Marchetti (Philadelphia, PA, 2009), pp. 261–77

Chan, Felicia, '*Crouching Tiger, Hidden Dragon*: Cultural Migrancy and Translatability', in *Chinese Films in Focus II*, ed. Chris Berry (London, 2008), pp. 73–81

Chan, Jachinson, 'Bruce Lee's Fictional Models of Masculinity', *Men and Masculinities*, II/4 (2000), pp. 371–87

Chan, Kenneth, 'The Global Return of the *Wu Xia Pian* (Chinese Sword-Fighting Movie): Ang Lee's *Crouching Tiger, Hidden Dragon*', *Cinema Journal*, XLIII/4 (2004), pp. 3–17

Channon, Alex, 'Western Men and Eastern Arts: The Significance of Eastern Martial Arts Disciplines in British Men's Narratives of Masculinity', *Asia Pacific Journal of Sport and Social Science*, I/1–2 (2012), pp. 111–27

Chiao, Hsiung-ping, 'Bruce Lee: His Influence on the Evolution of the Kung Fu Genre', *Journal of Popular Film and Television*, IX/1 (1981), pp. 30–42

Chong, Sylvia Shin Huey, *The Oriental Obscene: Violence and Racial Fantasies in the Vietnam Era* (Durham, NC, 2011)

Clarke, J. J., *Oriental Enlightenment: The Encounter Between Asian and Western Thought* (Abington, 1997)

Cunliffe, Tom, '*The Grandmaster*: Socio-Political Plurality in Contemporary Hong Kong', *Framework: The Journal of Cinema and Media*, LIX/2 (2018), pp. 101–20

Desser, David, 'The Kung Fu Craze: Hong Kong Cinema's First Reception', in *The Cinema of Hong Kong: History, Arts, Identity*, ed. Poshek Fu and David Desser (Cambridge, 2000), pp. 19–43

Donovan, Barna William, *The Asian Influence on Hollywood Action Films* (Jefferson, NC, 2008)

Fan, Victor, 'From the Shadow Play to Electric Shadows', in *Electric Shadows: A Century of Chinese Cinema* (London, 2014), pp. 8–13

Flanigan, B. P., 'Kung Fu Krazy, or the Invasion of the "Chop Suey Easterns"', *Cineaste*, VI/3 (1974), pp. 8–11

Fu, Poshek, ed., *China Forever: The Shaw Brothers and Diasporic Cinema* (Urbana, IL, 2008)

—, and David Desser, eds, *The Cinema of Hong Kong: History, Arts, Identity* (Cambridge, 2000)

Funnell, Lisa, *Warrior Women: Gender, Race, and the Transnational Chinese Action Star* (Albany, NY, 2014)

Gallagher, Mark, 'Masculinity in Transition: Jackie Chan's Transcultural Star Text', *Velvet Light Trap*, 39 (1997), pp. 23–41

Glaessner, Verina, *Kung Fu: Cinema of Vengeance* (London, 1974)

Godfrey, Emelyne, *Masculinity, Crime and Self-Defence in Victorian Literature: Duelling with Danger* (Basingstoke, 2010)

Gravestock, Peter, 'The Real and the Fantastic in the Wuxia Pian', *Metro Magazine*, 148 (2006), pp. 106–10

Hillenbrand, Margaret, '*Hero*, Kurosawa and a Cinema of the Senses', *Screen*, LIV/2 (2013), pp. 127–51

Hunt, Leon, *Kung Fu Cult Masters: From Bruce Lee to Crouching Tiger* (London, 2003)

Inness, Sherrie, *Tough Girls: Women Warriors and Wonder Women in Popular Culture* (Philadelphia, PA, 1999)

—, ed., *Action Chicks: New Images of Tough Women in Popular Culture* (New York, 2004)

Joseph, May, 'Kung Fu Cinema and Frugality', in *The Visual Culture Reader*, ed. Nicholas Mirzoeff, 2nd edn (London, 2002), pp. 433–50

Kaminsky, Stuart, 'Italian Westerns and Kung Fu Films: Genres of Violence', in *Graphic Violence on the Screen*, ed. Thomas R. Atkins (New York, 1976), pp. 47–68

Kato, M. T., *From Kung Fu to Hip Hop: Globalization, Revolution, and Popular Culture* (Albany, NY, 2007)

Kingston, Maxine Hong, *The Woman Warrior: Memories of a Girlhood Among Ghosts* (New York, 1989)

Klein, Christina, '*Crouching Tiger, Hidden Dragon*: A Diasporic Reading', *Cinema Journal*, XLIII/4 (2004), pp. 18–42

Krug, Gary J., 'At the Feet of the Master: Three Stages in the Appropriation of Okinawan Karate into Anglo-American Culture', *Cultural Studies: Critical Methodologies*, I/4 (2001), pp. 395–410

Leung, William, 'Crouching Sensibility, Hidden Sense', *Film Criticism*, XXVI/1 (2001), pp. 42–55

Li, Siu Leung, *Cross-Dressing in Chinese Opera* (Hong Kong, 2003)

Lo, Kwai-Cheung, *Excess and Masculinity in Asian Cultural Productions* (Albany, NY, 2010)

Logan, Bey, *Hong Kong Action Cinema* (London, 1995)

Louie, Kam, and Louise Edwards, 'Chinese Masculinity: Theorising "*Wen*" and "*Wu*"', *East Asian History*, 8 (1994), pp. 135–48

Lucia, Cynthia, Roy Grundmann and Art Simon, eds, *American Film History: Selected Readings, 1960 to the Present* (Chichester, 2016)

McCaughey, Martha, *Real Knockouts: The Physical Feminism of Women's Self-Defense* (New York, 1997)

—, and Neal King, eds, *Reel Knockouts: Violent Women in the Movies* (Austin, TX, 2001), pp. 27–51

McLeod, Ken, 'Afro-Samurai Techno-Orientalism and Contemporary Hip Hop', *Popular Music*, XXXII/2 (2013), pp. 259–75

Marchetti, Gina, 'Jackie Chan and the Black Connection', in *Keyframes: Popular Cinema and Cultural Studies*, ed. Matthew Tinkcom and Amy Villarejo (London, 2003), pp. 137–58

Marinelli, Maurizio, 'Heroism/Terrorism: Empire Building in Contemporary Chinese Films', *Asian Cinema*, XVI/2 (2005), pp. 183–209

Miller, Davis, *The Tao of Bruce Lee: A Martial Arts Memoir* (London, 2000)

Molasky, Michael, 'The Phone Book Project: Tracing the Diffusion of Asian Martial Arts in America through the Yellow Pages', in *The Martial Arts Studies Reader*, ed. Paul Bowman (London, 2018), pp. 57–72

Morris, Andrew D., *Marrow of the Nation: A History of Sport and Physical Culture in Republican China* (Berkeley, CA, 2004)
Morris, Meaghan, 'Transnational Imagination in Action Cinema: Hong Kong and the Making of a Global Popular Culture', *Inter-Asia Cultural Studies*, v/2 (2004), pp. 181–99
—, Siu Leung Li and Stephen Chan Ching-kiu, eds, *Hong Kong Connections: Transnational Imagination in Action Cinema* (Durham, NC, 2005)
Munroe, Alexandra, ed., *The Third Mind: American Artists Contemplate Asia, 1860–1989*, exh. cat., Guggenheim, New York (2009)
Odham Stokes, Lisa, and Michael Hoover, *City on Fire: Hong Kong Cinema* (London, 1999)
Pender, Patricia, *I'm Buffy and You're History: Buffy the Vampire Slayer and Contemporary Feminism* (London, 2016)
Po Fung and Lau Yam, eds, *Mastering Virtue: The Cinematic Legend of a Martial Artist* (Hong Kong, 2012)
Polly, Matthew, *American Shaolin: One Man's Quest to Become a Kung Fu Master* (London, 2007)
—, *Bruce Lee: A Life* (London, 2018)
Prashad, Vijay, *Everybody Was Kung Fu Fighting: Afro-Asian Connections and the Myth of Cultural Purity* (Boston, MA, 2001)
Rouse, Wendy L., *Her Own Hero: The Origins of the Women's Self-Defense Movement* (New York, 2017)
Russo, Charles, *Striking Distance: Bruce Lee and the Dawn of Martial Arts in America* (Lincoln, NE, 2016)
Steimer, Lauren, 'From *Wuxia* to *Xena*: Translation and the Body Spectacle of Zoë Bell', *Discourse*, XXXI/3 (2009), pp. 359–90
Tan See-Kam, Peter X. Feng and Gina Marchetti, eds, *Chinese Connections: Critical Perspectives on Film, Identity, and Diaspora* (Philadelphia, PA, 2009)
Tasker, Yvonne, *Spectacular Bodies: Gender, Genre and the Action Cinema* (London, 1993)
Tate, Greg, 'In Praise of Shadow Boxers', *Souls*, v/1 (2003), pp. 128–36
Taussig, Michael, *Mimesis and Alterity: A Particular History of the Senses* (London, 1993)
Teo, Stephen, *Chinese Martial Arts Cinema: The Wuxia Tradition* (Edinburgh, 2009)
—, *Hong Kong Cinema: The Extra Dimensions* (London, 1997)
Tierney, Sean, 'Themes of Whiteness in *Bulletproof Monk*, *Kill Bill*, and *The Last Samurai*', *Journal of Communication*, LVI/3 (2006), pp. 607–24

Trausch, Tim, ed., *Chinese Martial Arts and Media Culture: Global Perspectives* (London, 2018)
Turan, Kenneth, 'The Apotheosis of Bruce Lee: An Actor Dies; a Posthumous Industry Is Born', *American Film*, I/1 (1975), pp. 67–70
Vojković, Sasha, *Yuen Woo Ping's Wing Chun* (Hong Kong, 2009)
White, Luke, *Legacies of the Drunken Master: Politics of the Body in Hong Kong Kung Fu Comedy Films* (Honolulu, HI, 2020)
—, 'A "Narrow World, Strewn with Prohibitions": Chang Cheh's *The Assassin* and the 1967 Hong Kong Riots', *Asian Cinema*, XXVI/1 (2015), pp. 79–98
Wolf, Tony, and Joao Vieira, *Suffrajitsu* (Seattle, WA, 2015)
Wong, Wayne, 'Action in Tranquillity: Sketching Martial Ideation in *The Grandmaster*', *Asian Cinema*, XXIX/2 (2018), pp. 201–23
Yau, Esther C. M., ed., *At Full Speed: Hong Kong Cinema in a Borderless World* (Minneapolis, MN, 2001)
Yip, Man-Fung, *Martial Arts Cinema and Hong Kong Modernity: Aesthetics, Representation, Circulation* (Hong Kong, 2017)
Zhang Che, 'Creating the Martial Arts Film and the Hong Kong Cinematic Style', in *The Making of Martial Arts Films: As Told by Filmmakers and Stars*, exh. cat., Hong Kong Film Archive, Hong Kong (1999), pp. 16–24

SELECT FILMOGRAPHY

The 36th Chamber of Shaolin (HK)/*Master Killer* (USA) (*Shaolin sanshiliu fang*), dir. Lau Kar-leung, Shaw Brothers, 1978

The Assassin (*Da cike*), dir. Chang Cheh, Shaw Brothers, 1967

The Assassin (*Nie Yinniang*), dir. Hou Hsiao-hsien, CMC Movie Corporation, 2015

Bad Day at Black Rock, dir. John Sturges, MGM, 1955

The Big Boss (HK)/*Fists of Fury* (USA) (*Tangshan daxiong*), dir. Lo Wei, Golden Harvest, 1971

Billy Jack, dir. Tom Laughlin, Eaves Movie Ranch/National Student Film Corporation/Warner Bros, 1971

Black Belt Jones, dir. Robert Clouse, Sequoia Productions/Warner Bros, 1974

Blood on the Sun, dir. Frank Lloyd, William Cagney Productions, 1945

The Boxer from Shantung (*Ma Yongzhen*), dir. Chang Cheh/Pao Hsueh-li, Shaw Brothers, 1972

The Burning of the Red Lotus Temple (*Huoshao Hongliansi*), dir. Zhang Shichuan, Mingxing Film Company, 1928–31

The Chinese Boxer (HK)/*Hammer of God* (USA) (*Longhu dou*), dir. Jimmy Wang Yu, Shaw Brothers, 1970

Cleopatra Jones and the Casino of Gold, dir. Charles Bail, Harbor Productions/Shaw Brothers/Warner Bros, 1975

Come Drink with Me (*Da zuixia*), dir. King Hu, Shaw Brothers, 1966

Crouching Tiger, Hidden Dragon (*Wohu canglong*), dir. Ang Lee, Asia Union/China Film Co-Production Corp./Columbia Pictures Film Production Asia/Edko/Good Machine/Sony Pictures Classics/United China Vision/Zoom Hunt, 2000

Dirty Ho (*Lantou He*), dir. Lau Kar-leung, Shaw Brothers, 1979

Dragon Inn (*Longmen kezhan*), dir. King Hu, Union Film, 1967

Drunken Master (*Zui quan*), dir. Yuen Woo-ping, Golden Harvest/Seasonal Film, 1978

The Eight Diagram Pole Fighter (HK)/*Invincible Pole Fighter* (USA) (*Wulang bagua gun*), dir. Lau Kar-leung, 1984

Enter the Dragon (*Longzheng hudao*), dir. Robert Clouse, Warner Bros/Concord, 1973

Fist of Fury (HK)/*The Chinese Connection* (USA) (*Jingwu men*), dir. Lo Wei, Golden Harvest, 1972

Five Deadly Venoms (*Wu du*), dir. Chang Cheh, Shaw Brothers, 1978

Good Guys Wear Black, dir. Ted Post, Action 1 Film/Mar Vista/Western Film Productions, 1978

The Grandmaster (*Yidai zongshi*), dir. Wong Kar-wai, Block 2/Jet Tone/Sil-Metropole/Bona Film, 2013

Hapkido (HK)/*Lady Kung Fu* (USA) (*Heqi dao*), dir. Huang Feng, Golden Harvest, 1972

Hero (*Yingxiong*), dir. Zhang Yimou, Edko/Zhang Yimou Studio/China Film Co-Production Corp./Sil-Metropole/Beijing New Picture, 2002

House of Flying Daggers (*Shimian maifu*), dir. Zhang Yimou, Beijing New Picture/China Film Co-Production Corp./Edko/Elite Group/Zhang Yimou Studio, 2004

Ip Man (*Ye Wen*), dir. Wilson Yip, Golden Harvest/Beijing Shengshi Huarei/China Film Co-Production Corp./Mandarin Films/New Film Studio of Beijing/Prosperity/Shanghai Film Group/Time Antaeus, 2008

The Karate Kid, dir. John G. Avildsen, Columbia/Delphi II/Jerry Weintraub Productions, 1984

Kickboxer, dir. Mark DiSalle/David Worth, Kings Road Entertainment, 1989

Kill Bill: Vol. I and II, dir. Quentin Tarantino, Miramax/A Band Apart/Super Cool ManChu, 2003–4

King Boxer (HK)/*Five Fingers of Death* (USA) (*Tianxia diyi quan*), dir. Jeong Chang-hwa, Shaw Brothers, 1972

Kung Fu Hustle (*Gongfu*), dir. Stephen Chow, Star Overseas/China Film Co-Production Corp./Columbia, 2004

Lady Whirlwind (HK)/*Deep Thrust: The Hand of Death* (USA) (*Tiezhang xuanfengtui*), dir. Huang Feng, Golden Harvest, 1972

The Last Dragon, dir. Michael Schultz, Delphi III/Motown Productions, 1985

The Legend of the 7 Golden Vampires (*Qi jinshi*), dir. Roy Ward Baker/Chang Cheh, Hammer/Shaw Brothers, 1974

Lone Wolf McQuade, dir. Steve Carver, 1818 Productions/Cinema 84/Topkick, 1983

My Young Auntie (*Zhangbei*), dir. Lau Kar-leung, Shaw Brothers, 1981

No Retreat, No Surrender, dir. Corey Yuen, Seasonal Film/New World Pictures, 1985

None but the Brave (HK)/*Attack of the Kung Fu Girls* (USA) (*Tie wa*), dir. Lo Wei, Golden Harvest, 1973

Once Upon a Time in China (*Huang Feihong*), dir. Tsui Hark, Golden Harvest/Film Workshop, 1991

One-Armed Swordsman (*Dubei dao*), dir. Chang Cheh, Shaw Brothers, 1967

The Opium Trail (HK)/*Deadly China Doll* (USA) (*Hei lu*), dir. Huang Feng, Panasia, 1973

The Prodigal Son (*Bai jia zai*), dir. Sammo Hung, Golden Harvest, 1981

The Red Heroine (*Hongxia*), dir. Wen Yimin, Youlian, 1929

Rumble in the Bronx (*Hongfan qu*), dir. Stanley Tong, Golden Harvest, 1995

Rush Hour, dir. Brett Ratner, New Line/Roger Birnbaum Productions, 1998

Shaolin Soccer (*Shaolin zuqiu*), dir. Stephen Chow, Star Overseas/Universe, 2001

Shaolin and Wu Tang (*Shaolin yu Wudang*), dir. Gordon Liu Chia-hui, Hing Fat Film Company, 1983

Sister Street Fighter (*Onna hissatsu ken*), dir. Kazuhiko Yamaguchi, Toei, 1974

Super Fly, dir. Gordon Parks Jr, Sig Shore Productions, 1972

A Touch of Zen (*Xianü*), dir. King Hu, Golden Harvest/International Film Co./Lia Bang/Union, 1971

Vengeance! (*Baochou*), dir. Chang Cheh, Shaw Brothers, 1970

The Way of the Dragon (HK)/*Return of the Dragon* (USA) (*Menglong guojiang*), dir. Bruce Lee, Golden Harvest/Concord, 1972

ACKNOWLEDGEMENTS

I would like to thank Middlesex University for their continued support of my research, and in particular for the leave that was arranged for me to complete this book during a period when resources were stretched. I'd also like to thank the colleagues who covered some of my other responsibilities during this period and took up the administrative headache of organizing this, in particular Alberto Duman, Paul Harper, Anne Burke, Alice Maude-Roxby and Bharain Mac an Bhreithiún. In many ways, this book is as much a product of your labour as mine; I hope it does you proud. Overall, I would like to thank all my colleagues and students at Middlesex, who make being an academic a pleasure and privilege. A big debt is due to the staff at Reaktion Books for their hard work, patience, expertise and efficiency, and in particular Dave Watkins, for his help in making this a much more readable book than it otherwise might have been. I'd also like to thank all those involved in the Martial Arts Studies Research Network: this book would have been much poorer without the many stimulating discussions with too many people to list – I think you know who you are. Some of the material in Chapter Five, in particular, was developed for a paper given at the MASRN conference Bruce Lee's Cultural Legacies in 2018. I'd like to thank Michael Ann Mullen, Chila Kumari Singh Burman, Tony Wolf of the Bartitsu Society and the Ernie Wolfe Gallery for their kindness in granting permissions to reproduce images in this book. I'd like to thank everyone at the Mei Quan Academy of Taiji for the richness of my own martial arts journey. Finally, and most importantly, I'd like to thank my family – my mum and dad, my sisters and my nieces: my gratitude for your love and support is beyond words.

ACKNOWLEDGEMENTS

[illegible]

PHOTO ACKNOWLEDGEMENTS

The author and publishers wish to express their thanks to the below sources of illustrative material and/or permission to reproduce it. Every effort has been made to contact copyright holders; should there be any we have been unable to reach or to whom inaccurate acknowledgements have been made, please contact the publishers, and full adjustments will be made to subsequent printings.

Chila Kumari Singh Burman: pp. 204–5; Ernie Wolfe Gallery, Los Angeles: p. 137; Everett Collection/Alamy Stock Photo: pp. 185, 195; photo Johnson Lau (CC BY-SA 2.5): p. 18; courtesy Michael Ann Mullen: p. 200; Pictorial Press/Alamy Stock Photo: p. 115; Tony Wolf/Bartitsu Society: p. 75.

PHOTO ACKNOWLEDGEMENTS

INDEX

Page numbers in *italics* refer to illustrations